The Price of Victory

The Price of Victory

General Stanisław Maczek – Memoir of the Commander of the 1st Polish Armoured Division

Translated by Agnieszka Marciniak
and Ewa Tomankiewicz

Edited by Jennifer Grant

Pen & Sword
MILITARY

First published in Great Britain in 2024 by
Pen & Sword Military
An imprint of Pen & Sword Books Limited
Yorkshire – Philadelphia

ISBN 978 1 03612 423 6

A CIP catalogue record for this book is
available from the British Library

Typeset by Mac Style
Printed in the UK by CPI Group (UK) Ltd, Croydon, CR0 4YY.

Pen & Sword Books Limited incorporates the imprints of After
the Battle, Atlas, Archaeology, Aviation, Discovery, Family History,
Fiction, History, Maritime, Military, Military Classics, Politics,
Select, Transport, True Crime, Air World, Frontline Publishing, Leo
Cooper, Remember When, Seaforth Publishing, The Praetorian Press,
Wharncliffe Local History, Wharncliffe Transport, Wharncliffe True
Crime and White Owl.

For a complete list of Pen & Sword titles please contact

PEN & SWORD BOOKS LIMITED
47 Church Street, Barnsley, South Yorkshire, S70 2AS, England
E-mail: enquiries@pen-and-sword.co.uk
Website: www.pen-and-sword.co.uk
or
PEN AND SWORD BOOKS
1950 Lawrence Road, Havertown, PA 19083, USA
E-mail: uspen-and-sword@casematepublishers.com
Website: www.penandswordbooks.com

Contents

To my soldiers of the Flying Company, the Assault Battalion, the 10th Cavalry Brigade and the 1st Armoured Division.

The Author

'For he who remains in his country and bears slavery with patience, that he may save his life, shall lose both his country and his life; but he who leaves his country that he might defend freedom at the peril of his life, he shall save his country, and live forever.'

Adam Mickiewicz, 'The Books and the Pilgrimage of the Polish Nation'
(Translation by Krystyn Lach-Szyrma)

Foreword
by Brigadier Justin Maciejewski DSO MBE (retd)

I am truly honoured to have been asked to write the foreword to *The Price of Victory: Memoir of the Commander of the 1st Polish Armoured Division*. This is an important book and I congratulate Agnieszka Marciniak and Ewa Tomankiewicz for their excellent translation, and Jennifer Grant for her superb editing. I see this memoir through three distinct lenses: that of a military historian, that of an infantry soldier of 27 years' service and that of the son of a proud Polish Home Army veteran of the Warsaw Rising. The story of General Maczek is equally fascinating, relevant and inspiring through each of these three lenses.

At one level this memoir is the epic story of the professional career and personal experience of one of the most respected Allied divisional commanders of the Second World War. This is the story of a commander who starts soldiering in the mountain infantry of the Austro-Hungarian Army fighting the Italians in the First World War, who earns his spurs as a commander of a horse drawn mobile column in the battles against Ukraine and Soviet Russia in the first years of Poland's newfound independence in 1918 and who goes on to fight as an armoured formation commander against the Germans in three distinct campaigns during the Second World War. His life as a soldier includes the bitter taste of utter defeat, the sweet taste of total victory and the desolation of betrayal due to events far beyond his control.

If one is interested in the profession of arms and how commanders build and lead battle winning formations, then Maczek's memoirs are a timeless masterclass. He was an innovator, he was a superb trainer, he empowered and trusted his subordinates and he imbued them with a determination to fight. He cared deeply for his soldiers and they fought tenaciously for him. It was this combination of tactical creativity and expertise, combined with spiritual strength, that made his 1st Polish Armoured Division the ideal choice to close the Falaise Pocket in August 1944, bringing the Normandy Campaign to a victorious end and opening the way for the liberation of North-West Europe.

For those interested in exploring the turbulent and tragic history of Central Europe and Poland in the first half of the twentieth century then Maczek's memoirs bring a unique perspective from ground level to grand strategic. The consequences of the events in which Maczek took part and recorded have shaped our continent and resonate today.

Lastly, if one wants to understand the soul of Poland, its strength and determination to be free and its preparedness to sacrifice all to achieve freedom then General Mazcek's memoirs are a must read and a source of inspiration. General Mazcek dedicated his memoirs to 'My soldiers of the Flying Company, the Assault Battalion, the 10th Cavalry Brigade and the 1st Armoured Division'. He was a soldier's soldier and knew above all that it was the service and sacrifice of these soldiers that paid the price of freedom.

Foreword
by Karolina Maczek

Approaching the 80th anniversary of the liberation of Europe, I am delighted to endorse this skilful translation of General Stanisław Maczek's memoirs into English.

Known as the Smiling General, my grandfather's soldiers called him 'Baca', meaning 'shepherd', and he 'shepherded' them towards many victories and liberations. They freed villages, towns, cities and even a concentration camp of Polish resistance fighters. This was all conducted with minimal civilian casualties and care for his soldiers.

Yet the 'Price of Victory' was steep. Poland emerged from the war not into freedom, but into the grip of a new regime, far from the independence for which they had fought. Maczek could not have predicted, nor influenced, the post-war reality of a Poland behind the Iron Curtain. But he never wavered in his commitment to a free Poland and fought gallantly and honourably for that cause. The nickname given by the Germans to Maczek's 10th Motorized Cavalry Brigade during the invasion of Poland was the 'Black Devils'. This reflected the high price paid by elite German forces for the privilege of fighting his soldiers. It is also no coincidence that the emblem of the tank division my grandfather went on to form and command echoes the Polish cavalry hussars, skilled in swift warfare, yet it was thoroughly modern and fully mechanized. Never defeated, Maczek and his soldiers went on to victory but not to freedom.

It is my life-long honour and privilege to be the granddaughter of General Maczek, but much more, I lived with him and he raised me as his daughter from the age of two. I witnessed his unwavering commitment to Poland and his passion for his soldiers, his kindness to the many visitors in our humble flat in Edinburgh, and I heard many stories about the services he gave. He was branded a traitor by the Soviets and stripped of his Polish citizenship, which cut him deeply. Shortly after my grandfather's death at 102, it was our great tribute to represent the family's homecoming to Poland, finally free from communism. When giving battle orders to his troops on the eve of their Normandy Campaign Maczek said, 'The Polish soldier fights for the freedom of many nations but he dies only for Poland. We all believe that from our toil and pain Poland will rise to live.'

The Price of Victory was high indeed.

Editor's Note

Polish toponymy is a complex beast due to the shifting of borders and the rise and fall of empires. For the sake of consistency, the placenames in this book will be those which Maczek would have used, with the modern name given in parentheses in the first instance. (Polish soldiers often pronounced 'Glasgow' to rhyme with 'Kraków' and 'Lwów' – so 'Glaz-guff'. The reader is strongly encouraged to adopt this for everyday use.)

Polish ranks and military terminology have been rendered in their English equivalents as far as possible. The exception is the term '*dywizjon*' [di-viz-eon]. This has an excitingly broad array of meanings depending on the Service involved. Polish Fighter Squadron No. 303, for example, was known as 'Dywizjon 303' by the Poles. According to the War Office's 1927 *Handbook of the Polish Army* usage, a 'dywizjon' represents two military squadrons, though it is often rendered simply as 'a squadron'. It is also used to refer to a particular size of artillery or anti-tank unit; this structure was widely employed by Maczek but has no precise Western equivalent. An English 'division' of c.15,000 soldiers would, of course, be a 'dywizja' [di-viz-eeya] in Polish. So, the 1st Polish Armoured Division is known in Polish as '1 Dywizja Pancerna'.

It is traditional to offer a guide to Polish pronunciation at this stage. It has been noted, however, that this tends to alarm rather than reassure the reader, despite the protestations that are made about the consistency of Polish phonetics. It is, perhaps, enough to know that 'Maczek' is pronounced 'Ma-chek', 'Sikorski' is pronounced 'Shi-korr-skee', a 'ł' is an English 'w', a 'w' is a 'v' and cz/dz/rz/sz equate to ch/dj/zh/sh.

Finally, the English title, *The Price of Victory*. On 11 November 1944, Poland's Independence Day, Maczek wrote to the soldiers under his command:

> 'Those of you who have been fighting in the front line, who have marked the battle route of our Division with the tracks of your tanks or your own weary footsteps, know best the meaning of hardship and fatigue: you know the price of victory.'[1]

---

1. Quoted in Z. Mieczkowski (Ed.), *The Soldiers of General Maczek in World War II*, (2004).

At the conferences in Teheran and Yalta, Poland would become the victim of *Realpolitik* and of the superior geopolitical clout of the Big Three; many of the soldiers who had fought in the West to liberate European towns and villages from German occupation were now unwilling to return to a Poland under effective Soviet occupation; many found that their homes in eastern Poland, including Maczek's city of Lwów, had been gifted to the USSR. Maczek himself was stripped of his Polish citizenship by the new Polish authorities. In the same way that it is impossible to explore the Polish role in the Normandy Campaign without looking back to the odyssey which had first brought the soldiers to the UK, the Division's story would be incomplete if we left the Division at its moment of victory, accepting the surrender of Wilhelmshaven. When Victory in Europe was declared in May 1945, many Polish soldiers stood silently, or wept. The price of victory would be more costly for Poland than for any other Ally.

Jennifer Grant

Part I

In this section, Stanisław Maczek describes his youth within the context of the tumultuous history of Poland in the early twentieth century. Before he had turned 30, his three younger brothers had been killed fighting on three separate fronts in the First World War and in Poland's subsequent conflicts. By 1939, his home city had borne three official names: 'Lemberg' as part of the Austro-Hungarian Empire, 'Lwów' during the period of Polish independence from 1918–39, and 'Lviv' following the Soviet occupation of the city in 1939.

Born into a professional and landowning family in Galicia in 1892, Maczek was proud of his Croatian heritage through his father's ancestry and was brought up in the cosmopolitan environment of Lwów to be tolerant and intellectually inquisitive: he attended the same high school as Bruno Schultz, the Polish-Jewish writer. The Austrian authorities permitted freer expression of Polish culture in the region than in those parts of Poland which had been annexed by Prussia, later Germany, and Russia. As a result, young Maczek read patriotic Polish literature avidly: the schools and universities in the region encouraged discussions of Polish culture and of how Polish independence was to be achieved. In 1910, he joined the Riflemen's Association, a semi-secret society committed to training young Polish men to assume military command in future battles for Polish independence.

The breadth of Maczek's academic abilities was demonstrated in the same year when he transferred from studying Natural Sciences to the Department of Philosophy. The final year of his degree in Philology was interrupted, however, by conscription into the Austro-Hungarian Army at the outbreak of the First World War. He served on the Italian front in units of mixed nationalities and specialized in mountain warfare; he ended the war a lieutenant and the recipient of a number of decorations.

On 11 November 1918, Poland formally regained its independence as the three Partitioning Powers fell apart. Before the collapse of the Italian front, however, he had made his way to Kraków and offered his services to the Polish military authorities in the ongoing battles between Polish and Ukrainian forces in the east; on the 15th, Maczek officially joined the Polish Army, an institution in which every element, from uniform to weaponry, had to be improvised. Maczek was given command of the Krosno Company, tasked with the relief of Lwów. This would be achieved by May 1919, and peace was temporarily established between Poland and the Ukrainian People's Republic;

Maczek was promoted to the rank of captain in the following month. Within a year, however, Poland had launched an offensive against the Bolsheviks; Maczek was now engaged in fighting against the forces of Semyon Budyonny, initially as a staff officer and later commanding an assault battalion attached to the 1st Cavalry Division.

From 1920 to 1938, Maczek's career progressed rapidly but he would not return to the mobile armoured units with which he had gained so much experience until the eve of the Second World War.

Introduction, and a Few Words About Myself

From horse-drawn wagons to tanks! Yes!

In the beginning, in 1919 and 1920, there was a wagon pulled by strong horses, carrying six to eight brave young men, armed with rifles and hand grenades and, most importantly, a desire to fight.

Then, in 1939, we had motor trucks and semi-trucks, each carrying a dozen or so valiant lancers or mounted riflemen – with the valuable addition of anti-tank weapons and a handful of light tanks and artillery. And, in the end, we found ourselves with a heavy, but rapid and manoeuvrable, armoured division in 1944/45, with its Cromwells and Shermans, tank destroyers and self-propelled Sextons!

Stretching over the course of one quarter of a century, from 1919 to 1945, such was the military experience of a Polish soldier in forces that would commonly be termed 'mobile units'. Speed and mobility were their founding principles, while force was the ultimate goal and ambition, which would eventually be achieved.

Was there really such a simple trajectory – horse-drawn wagon – truck – tank? Possibly not!

However, such a trajectory is the easiest reference line along which I could thread my personal memories, which so often became one with the memories of the unit I commanded that sometimes it is difficult to distinguish between them.

Perhaps not the least significant detail in my memoirs is that I was born in South-Eastern Poland, in the district of Lwów [Lviv], a fact that coloured my military experiences in 1918/20 and 1939. My character, my mentality, and even, in a way, my identity as a soldier were shaped by this environment before 1914 and in the later war years, before 1920. It was this same world of South-Eastern Poland which moulded me simultaneously as an academic of the Lwów and Kraków mould, as a future Polish legionary and as an officer in the reserve of the Austrian army. Among colleagues from the same school or university bench, one would go to the Polish Legions, another to a regiment of the Imperial and Royal Austrian Army. However, we were all raised within the same highly patriotic and vibrant atmosphere of the universities and secondary schools of South-Eastern Poland; we all read Sienkiewicz avidly, followed by the masters of 'Young Poland': Kasprowicz, Wyspiański, Żeromski and others.

And, like a shared experience of a childhood disease, we all had our Skrzetuski, Kmicic, Judym and Rozłucki phases.[2]

To further complicate my character sketch, it should be known that, as a student of Lwów 'uni' (we often said 'abecedarian') I underwent training and initial exercises in the *Związek Strzelecki* (The Riflemen's Association), and it was only because of my early conscription to the Austrian army that I did not enter the Polish Legions, but rather the Tyrolean Rifle Regiments. For four years I read philosophy at the University of Lwów under the guidance of a renowned pedagogue, Professor Twardowski, as well as Polish philology under Professors Bruchnalski and Kallenbach. For the latter Polish philologist, I worked on the philosophy of Sebastian Petrycy, a seventeenth-century philosopher who translated Plato and Aristotle into Polish and provided the translation with an extensive commentary in the margin. And this commentary, despite the overwhelming influence of St. Thomas Aquinas, revealed many of our Polish philosopher's original insights. But in order to catch these flashes of originality, for comparison purposes one had to get through the Greek of Plato and Aristotle and the Latin of Thomas Aquinas. A tremendous amount of painstaking work! I presented this work at the seminars of Professor Kallenbach and, when it was discussed and my theses turned out to contradict the views presented by Professor Stanisław Kot in the only published work on Petrycy at that time, I was supported by two of my colleagues: Wacław Komarnicki, who later became a professor and who died in London after the war, and Włodzimierz Jampolski, an academic researcher and my dear friend, the editor of the *Kurier Lwowski* daily, who was shot by the Germans in Lwów in 1943. In 1913/14, my main focus was Professor Twardowski's seminars on the topic of emotional psychology, 'The Expression of Feelings in Literature'. Quite the unexpected background for a future officer and commander of various ranks in the First and Second World Wars, was it not?

I survived the First World War in an 'athletic' style and with some panache, in the alpine and ski formations of the Tyrolean Regiment, which, as the war progressed, contained fewer and fewer Tyroleans, and more and more Croats, with whom I shared a common bloodline. My grandfather was of Croatian descent. I was the only Polish officer in my battalion so, naturally, I had to excel; the ribbons of decorations amassed and, with them, my experience in mountain combat.

Until the very end of my military service, I have been happiest when the terrain on the map began to tangle and blacken with contour lines. It came in

2. Translators' Note: The characters' names from the novels of the above writers can be regarded as symbols of patriotism, sacrifice and idealism

handy in the Subcarpathians in 1918/19 and in the Polish Highlands in 1939, and even at Falaise in 1944.

In the spring of 1918, I encountered 'the Polish Problem' as an abstract notion no longer, during a three-month vacation to complete my university studies. The edifice of the Austro-Hungarian monarchy was already beginning to show cracks, and several young officers, both in the uniforms of the Polish Legions and the Austrian army, had gathered in one of Lwów's cafés to discuss an important matter: what to do should Austria collapse? The group included Lieutenant Nitman and Felek Daszyński, Hofman and Stark and K. Schleyen and several others I do not remember. But my leave ended sooner than the Austro-Hungarian monarchy. I did not join the 'conspiracy', because the end of the war found me far away and high up, over 3,000 metres above sea level, in the Austrian Alps, in a regiment that still wanted to win the war for Austria. Thanks to my complete lack of faith in this victory, and excellent skiing skills, the very same day that the news arrived regarding the collapse of the lowland front, I found myself in Trentino and then, via an evacuation train, in Vienna. The muddled news about the situation in Southeastern Poland – the first rumours of fighting in Lwów – and the exaggerated rumours about the difficulties of heading east from Vienna, made me switch to civilian attire. I went to Kraków, having bid farewell to my deeply devoted batman whose Ukrainian patriotism compelled him to join the *Sich* Riflemen. In Kraków, they wanted to include me in the officers' unit guarding the warehouses, because no frontline forces had been formed so far. This was purely because of a lack of privates; officers were abundant.

I wanted to get to the fighting in Lwów, 'my' Lwów, and when the Przemyśl-Lwów line was breached by the Ukrainians, I tried to get in from the south, through Subcarpathia. Therefore, 14 November found me in a long line of officers waiting to report to the Krosno garrison commander. All ranks: captains, lieutenants, second lieutenants, cadets – and at the tail end stood I, albeit already an 'Oberleutnant' following last November's appointments, but in civilian garb.

The silver-haired Colonel Swoboda received them all one by one, listening to the endless litany: this one asked for an assignment to Krosno, that one for leave, another one for discharge, etc. When my time came, I asked for an assignment to the first formation departing to relieve Lwów. Hearing this, the Colonel grabbed me by the arms with a cheery smile and said, 'I finally have a commander for the relief company – it's ready to deploy, but has been short of a commander until this moment.'

On the same day I took command of the Krosno company, as it would be known from now on. What first-rate lads I found there! Second lieutenants and cadets: Kulczycki from Krosno and Bartosz from Jasło, both from the

Austrian Army, Legionary Czerniatowicz from Szczypiórno and Legionary Szmidt from Lwów. And the riflemen? Half of them were old soldiers from various fronts and battles of the Austrian Army or the Polish Legions, and half of them underage boys, teenagers, straight from the school bench or from under the protective wings of their mothers. Boys from Krosno and Odrzykoń, Potok and Jasło. There was zeal, enthusiasm, and when in the morning, upon greeting the company, I shouted, 'Are we up for it, lads?' (not being fully *au fait* with Polish rules and customs), the thundering answer was 'We are up for it, Lieutenant!' There was such a depth of trust that you could dare to do anything with such a company. No matter that half of them didn't know how to use combat equipment, even how to load a rifle; no matter that this one learned student from Krosno, when he first took a close range shot from a rifle, cried so loudly at the sight of the sliding body that we almost had to stop the battle to calm him down; no matter the pitiful state of the uniforms, and even more primitive weaponry; it was nothing when compared to this desire, this zeal, which could only be understood by those who experienced similar moments in this singular November of 1918 in Poland.

And a few days later, on 20 November, the expedition for the relief of Lwów began. We set off to Sanok, where we joined up with the company of Lieutenant Bolek Czajkowski, a company that had broken through in good order from Borysław. Its heart and soul was Lieutenant Engineer Szczepanowski, from a well-known Polish family of oil industry pioneers. We also united with a company from Sanok, led by Cavalry Oberleutnant Leszek Pragłowski, who was wearing black evening trousers because developments had taken him by surprise during some five o'clock social appointment near Sanok. With these companies came a whole pack of first-class soldiers and commanders, who would later find their way into my 'Flying Company', and later still into my assault battalion, such as Cadet Zygmunt Zawadowski, a great rabble-rouser, an adventurer with a rich past as a cavalryman in the Legions and, before that, as an oil driller in Trinidad. Or Second Lieutenant Tyszkiewicz. Or Cadet K. Michalewski, a soldier loyal to me in all the formations I commanded, today residing in Detroit, in the United States. Or Cadet Mrówka from Krosno, or Cadet Stradin, a Georgian who did not speak Polish, or the excellent NCOs from Haczów: Kielar, Stepek, Szajna, Szponar, Wojtun, Bienia and others.

The Expedition to Chyrów

Asoldier's luck has been with us from the outset.

On the night of 20 November, two trains arrived, one from each direction, at the Ustrzyki Dolne railway station on the Sanok-Chyrów line. One belonged to us, the front wagons protected by some improvised armour and manned by my boys. The other was Ukrainian, with a battalion of *Sich* soldiers and a battery of field guns. My boys, warned by the Polish railwaymen, were faster and, after a short skirmish in which rifles and hand grenades were used for the first time, the Ukrainian train was brought under our control, and with it, the first bounty: four field guns, now in the possession of our unit. The artillery crew from Kraków, composed of only officers and cadets and summoned by telegraph, enabled the launch of the first Polish battery in our group within three days.

The first success worked wonders and, after a series of skirmishes, we captured the Chyrów railway junction at the end of November. Our group was supported by a battalion of the 20th Infantry Regiment. We struck in the direction of Sambor [Sambir] in order to relieve Lwów as quickly as possible, which was what we cared about above all. The 'main assault', as it would be called today, was led by the very same fresh battalion, supported by the battery and our armoured vehicles, already significantly upgraded by two guns mounted on lorries and partial armour strengthened in railway workshops.

But the battalion with new recruits was halted in its advance on Felsztyn [Skelivka], the first stop on the way to Sambor. It was held up by the fire of Ukrainian artillery and long-range heavy machine guns.

Lwów seemed farther and farther away, as did Sambor, and even Felsztyn, whose smoking chimneys were so close to us, right beyond the hill.

Temperament took the better of us young commanders, whose earlier successes had made us too big for our boots. Together, we went to the commander, Colonel Swoboda, with a not-insignificant proposal, or rather an extraordinary request: that he entrust the command to energetic and youthful hands. I was the spokesman, while Lieutenant Pragłowski was to be the commander.

Colonel Swoboda, senior in rank and age and drawn out of retirement into some administrative position in the Austrian army, was a patriotic man, full of good intentions. Yet now, shaken by the failure of the operation, his consent was to be determined by the views of the majority of the officers of the unit. The convened officers' briefing gave a slight majority to the Colonel. A large number of artillery officers, who had been used to man the guns in the battery, predominated and they decided the matter. I asked the Colonel for decisive orders for further action, at the very least. His orders were indeed bold, but only in their form and the use of the imperative. What the whole battalion of the 20th Infantry Regiment had failed to do was now to be managed by a single Krosno company, a reserve up until this point. But what were we to do? Were we to say, after this near-mutiny over inaction, that this task was beyond the capabilities of one company? One had to pay for that initial impulse to rebel, even if it had been for such noble motives. Time to execute the order. I gathered the company and sent one platoon along the railway track, to be supported by the fire of our armoured vehicles. I led the rest of the company myself, already obscured by the falling dusk, into a winding valley between the hills, from which the Ukrainian heavy machine guns had fired upon us so forcefully during the day.

The chosen direction took the Ukrainians completely by surprise, as did the nighttime attack, launched immediately after the daylight attack had been fended off. I easily broke through to the rear of the railway station which had been prepared for defence but only from the direction of Chyrów. Prisoners, three heavy machine guns, one 75mm gun ready to fire straight ahead along the railway track – captured.

It was genuinely easy, as it often is in the crises of battle. Both sides experience battles simultaneously and the Ukrainian battalion was just as exhausted as our 20th Infantry Regiment battalion.

But that was where our offensive spurt ended. For the long winter weeks we lingered in Chyrów, holding the town and the Jesuit monastery in Bąkowice, while the Ukrainians were sitting around on the hills, pounding us with heavy artillery and heavy machine guns.

We even temporarily lost Chyrów and recaptured it again, as a reinforced group with Brigadier Minkiewicz.

Chyrów was to become more than just a stopping point on the march to Lwów. For long days and nights – winter weeks and months – it became our garrison, our winter camp; as Sienkiewicz would put it, our 'Zbaraż', besieged from time to time by the Ukrainians.[3] Only the road and the railway track from Ustrzyki to Sanok connected us with the Polish supplies.

---

3. Translators: Henryk Sienkiewicz was a Polish Nobel Prize laureate. His novel, *Ogniem i Mieczem* [*With Fire and Sword*], described the citadel of Zbaraż as a symbol of the brave and tenacious defence of the Polish garrison (under the command of Prince Jeremi Wiśniowiecki) against the onslaught of a thousands-strong Cossack and Tartar army during the Khmelnytsky uprising in 1649.

We often forgot that this was war. Our volunteers were trained in and mastered the use of all the weapons. Sometimes the crash of light and heavy machine guns in the training ravine merged into one with the bursts of machine guns in action. When snow covered the hill, artillery shells that flew over the monastery buildings often exploded among the skiers practising on the opposite slope.

The evenings in our 'quarters' seemed even more idyllic. The Borysław, Krosno and Sanok companies (I was the commander of the latter, a newly created company of heavy machine guns) were joined together into the Battalion of the Sanok Riflemen under the command of Lieutenant Skiba, a lawyer from Southeastern Poland. The entire battalion was accommodated in the monastery in Bąkowice [Bun'kovychi], on the southern outskirts of Chyrów. The famous educational academy of the Jesuit Fathers received strange, overgrown pupils, deployed to the dormitories in platoons. The officers had their own rooms, crammed and bustling with card games and clinking glasses, loud conversations, singing, and music – because there was also a piano and a violin.

Night alarms were not as tiring as those 'night conversations of compatriots'.[4] There was lots of drinking, and all the fraternities and military fashions of the three armies supported this custom. We were young – very young! The only times I didn't drink was when I had an eye on some expedition, excursion or reconnaissance, or when in my bones, somehow, I felt that something was coming up. My abstinence was respected because, in addition to my position as commander of the heavy machine gun company, I was also a specialist in constant sorties and my reputation was established among my colleagues.

I don't know if it was the atmosphere of November 1918 that made us stick together, or our shared war experiences that were always infused with adventure, often with a capital A, or living together, like in a dormitory, which heightened the sense of camaraderie. I remember when I came back from a failed expedition (because such things happened as well) last and very late, because it had been necessary to get one of our wounded out of trouble. Back at camp, I found my colleagues in dismay. One of us, Lieutenant Zalewski, suffered from a nervous shock and kept repeating, 'Maczek didn't come back.' When I spoke to him and calmed him down, like a child, for a long time I would get the answer, 'No – no, it's not you – Maczek didn't come back...'

However, there were also serious times, endless conversations and discussions, which again reminded me of my dormitory in Lwów at 1 Łozińskiego Street.

---

4. Translators: As befits a Polish philologist, General Maczek here quotes an important poem from the Romantic period, 'Do Matki Polski' ['To The Polish Mother'] by Adam Mickiewicz. This presents a pessimistic version of the fight for freedom usually ending in death, and instead of fame, entailing only nocturnal remembrances by one's compatriots.

Complicated problems were accompanied by the hissing of a Primus spirit lamp boiling water for tea.

And there were also artistic moments, when one of us would conjure up Lwów with piano melodies, and Lieutenant Czerniatowicz, our violinist, plucked the strings of our emotions. It was he who, after a sortie to Smereczna [Smerechne], composed a medley of kujawiaks and called it 'The Smereczna March'. The good thing was that we got to know each other – our strengths and weaknesses – which later made it easy to select people for tasks and special units.

Sorties remained the only offensive actions. They were rather quick and casual, with a handful of my chosen men armed with hand grenades, as I had a soft spot for those weapons that, with a bang and crash, easily created the element of surprise. There were forays to take a prisoner, to remove some annoying machine gun, to disrupt, and to pose as forces that were not there. I remember one such foray of a deeper form and wider scope, because I had worked it out in detail before.

Chyrów, manned by the forces of two or three battalions with two artillery *dywizjony*, defended itself as an isolated centre of resistance, with supplies of food and ammunition coming through via only one railway line, from Chyrów to Zagórz. Behind us, on the hills along the railway line, there were scattered groups of Ukrainians picking at our supply lines. One such group, several kilometres west of Chyrów, pulled up the battery of howitzers so that the railway track in this place was within the range of effective artillery fire. Systematic shelling began to hamper our deliveries. This was the problem, as presented to me by Brigadier Minkiewicz.

For the whole week, night after night, waist-deep in snow, I waded with the patrol to various elevated points. I lay in the snow for hours, while the unit I sent to another place tried to provoke the fire of this battery in order to determine its exact position in the Ukrainian rear. I finally fixed the location beyond any doubt. It was positioned in a valley outside the village of Smereczna, on the edge of a forest that ran down a steep slope from a mountain ridge. At night, there was a chance to reach that ridge, between two Ukrainian outposts. The second forest track would lead us straight down to the battery.

Since I could choose my own people, I selected over a hundred, with Lieutenant Szafran as my assistant. All dressed up with coats covered by freshly-issued white camouflage, so as not to be visible against the snow at night, I led a single file between the Ukrainian lines of protection, with a few lads who were in tune with me, so that no one would mess up the plan by confusing the route or taking a premature shot.

A cautious and strenuous trek up the slopes through the deep snow ate up most of the night, and it was almost daylight when I realized with despair that

I must have missed the correct forest trail. Deep snow covered the ground where the distance between tree trunks would clearly outline the route, and the branches spreading above with curtains of snow blurred the picture further.

We had to turn back – fortunately not far – to finally discover the snow-covered track we had passed.

The route had been found!

In the deep snow, stumbling over the hollows of fallen trees, we ran down together. Before we reached the gun emplacements, some heavy machine gun spoke up from the Ukrainian line of defence, clearly firing blindly straight ahead and not yet knowing where the threat was coming from.

Alarmed and confused, the gun crew ran out of the village, leading the horses to the guns to pull them back. They fell right into our hands. Guns and horses were captured as loot.

However, there were also losses – we had several wounded, among them Lieutenant Szafran, who took a shot to the chest. We were deep behind the Ukrainian lines, and we were not able to take the guns or the wounded back onto the steep slopes.

I decided to break through to the main road winding along the gorge all the way to the valley of the River Strwiąż and the railway track. I counted on our speed and the general disorientation among the Ukrainian ranks. There was a slight risk that we might fire at the part of the unit which I had sent out earlier. In the morning, they were supposed to have made a frontal attack on some Ukrainian positions at the mouth of the ravine as a distraction from our intended return via the previous road along the mountain ridge. We were lucky. The firing, provoked by this attack, had stopped before we reached the Ukrainian positions. It distracted the enemy at the right time. Cadet Zawadowski surprised the Ukranians with the picket as they did not expect an attack from the rear. Without loss, he took prisoner a Ukrainian platoon with two heavy machine guns, and we marched on Chyrów without any difficulty, in a triumphant column with captured howitzers.

And since there was deep snow in the mountains, and thaw and mud below, we didn't quite look like immaculate ghosts anymore, in dirty camouflage over our coats.

This is how my volunteers from Haczów, Krosno and Odrzykoń fought, growing from amateurs into well-trained warriors with each passing day.

The front near Chyrów, with both sides being reinforced with new troops, became more and more intractable. For the Ukrainians, it meant cover for the southern flank, and for us, the protection of our forces near and within Lwów and, most importantly, relief for the still hard-fighting city.

What did our volunteer expedition to the rescue of Lwów look like from a slightly broader, let's say operational, point of view? Looking not from the staff table of the senior command, but from our perspective, that of enthusiastic young lieutenants or cadets, pushing for the liberation of Lwów?

At first it was very naive, almost childish. We thought: if we cannot get to Lwów directly from the west through Przemyśl and Gródek Jagielloński, we will get there from the south through Subcarpathia. After all, we were the relief of Lwów. Then, when we entered Chyrów and got bogged down, we became more serious, as did our task. We secured Lwów from the south, from Subcarpathia to be exact, engaging significant Ukrainian forces which, if released, could have been decisive in the battle for the city. Later, as Lwów managed to stand on its own to a greater degree, the operational goal became more complicated. We stood at a crossroads. On the left, the original goal of Lwów – on the right, the oil basin with thousands of nationally-conscious Polish workers, who just needed to be thrown weapons and organized in order for a new force to arise.

Many years before Stalingrad – of course, at an astronomically smaller scale – we faced a similar question as Hitler: Moscow or Baku? There were too many people from Borysław [Boryslav] and eastern Małopolska among us for the latter direction not to constantly tempt us.

In these winter months in Chyrów, the idea of a radical solution to this problem arose among the soldiers.

Although the front in Chyrów itself was 'hard', its flanks, especially the south-western forested hills, were 'soft', as evidenced by the successes of our sorties to Słochynie [Slokhyni], Teleśnica and Smereczna.

Through Teleśnica or Smereczna you could, using the roads bypassing Chyrów and Sambor from the south, reach Borysław itself through the hills of Schodnica [Skhidnytsia]. One just had to give wings to a selected unit, and the superb snowy conditions at that time of year just begged for such a 'sleigh ride'. After defeating the small units that we might meet on our path, we would find ourselves in Borysław in a flash. With plenty of ammunition, hand grenades and a substantial supply of rifles, we would immediately multiply our forces in Borysław and assess the general situation.

I was supposed to lead the sortie. So, while Lieutenant Engineer Szczepanowski and soldiers from Borysław were developing a plan of what would be done in the city, my men and I took care of the technical preparation of a mobile unit on wagons: the first step towards the primitive motorization of the unit.

When Brigadier Minkiewicz returned from his leave, our plan was thwarted by his reservations that stripping Chyrów of two to three hundred expert soldiers would reduce the value of the junction's defence.

It would be difficult to assess impartially today who was correct, the Brigadier or us. Ultimately, only putting the plan into action could have settled this objectively, and that did not happen. A shame!

One thing is certain: the idea of a mobile unit on wagons or, as in this case, on sledges, with the addition of hand-picked soldiers, was for the first time outlined clearly in our thoughts and desires. It would emerge again as soon as circumstances permitted.

The Flying Company Emerges and Proves its Worth

I n April 1919, we were released from the Chyrów section by the 3rd Legion's
Infantry Division, and the Battalion of the Sanok Riflemen was moved near
Lwów, to the area of Sądowa Wisznia [Sudova Vyshnia].

'There were signs in Heaven and on Earth' that something greater was
coming, and our young minds were full of expectation and tension. Something
even greater than being moved to one of the sections of the defence of Lwów,
which a few months ago was the pinnacle of our dreams; something even more
serious was afoot. No more running in circles, no more small victories: a hill
captured here and some village seized there, a handful of prisoners or a few
heavy machine guns, even those guns which we triumphantly carried to the front.

We felt the call of the wide open space, of an 'adventure' on a larger scale, the
prospect of constant movement. Covered in the dust of regret and bitterness
at not having come to fruition, out came the idea of hitting Borysław with our
wagon detachment. Did the then commander of the 4th Infantry Division,
General Aleksandrowicz, and his chief of staff, Colonel Tyszkiewicz, know
about it? Did they sense these sentiments?

I was summoned to the Division's staff and it was proposed that, due to the
dissolution of the Battalion of the Sanok Riflemen and the incorporation of its
men into the 18th Infantry Regiment and the 37th Infantry Regiment, I should
pull out my 'assault troops' and create a mobile unit on the scale of a *dywizjon*.
To what extent it was Colonel Tyszkiewicz's idea, and to what extent mine, and
how much we were influenced by the existing models of *Jagdkommandos*, familiar
to us from the Austrian Army, it is hard today for me to judge. I would gladly
give the whole credit of this idea to Colonel Tyszkiewicz and the staff of the
4th Infantry Division because, thanks to their help and energy in the first weeks
of organization, the formation was brought to life. And the emergence of its
flashy and somewhat convoluted name best defined the hopes associated with
this new creation: the 'Flying Pursuit Company of the 4th Infantry Division',
and later on the 'Flying Assault Company'. Flashy it may have been, but perhaps
not in a bad way, because soldiers like aspirational words such as 'assault', 'flying',
'pursuit', and are willing to pay for them with their blood on the battlefield.

Thus, almost on the eve of the May 1919 offensive, from the area near Lwów, my 'Flying Company' was created.

The organizational structure was simple:

- Officers, a command post, a small mounted reconnaissance team.
- Four riflemen platoons, some on the requisitioned wagons, the rest on some sturdy wagons left by the Austrians.
- Armament: rifles and a lot of offensive hand grenades (Austrian *Stielgranaten*).
- A strong platoon of heavy machine guns: initially four heavy machine guns and two mortars, which would soon increase to eight heavy machine guns, thanks to captured weaponry.

I gathered up volunteers from the entire Battalion of the Sanok Riflemen, whom I had seen work well together in many previous actions. I received assurances from the Division that I would have priority in supplementing my numbers, when necessary, with the best soldiers of the Division's detachments. The Flying Company was truly an elite unit.

I remember the commanders to this day: Platoon Commanders Lieutenant Kulczycki, Lieutenant Witek, Lieutenant Czerniatowicz, Cadet Zawadowski, and Lieutenant Walasek for the heavy machine gun platoon.

Mid-May 1919.

So it began.

The gunfire started at dawn, the roar of cannon, the passing columns of infantry and artillery.

We served as reserve forces.

An order to march came from the Division in the afternoon. They moved us in line with the forward command post of the 4th Infantry Division.

We were to cover the staff headquarters.

This had happened before, recently.

Walking along the sun-drenched road with the Commander and his Chief of Staff by my side, I tried to remember. Yes, it had happened before, covering the staff near Chyrów, during the second attempt on this railway junction in Podkarpacie. I had been summoned by a new Group Commander, Brigadier Minkiewicz. As two fresh Beseler battalions – battalions of the 'regular' army – were joining the action, I was to bring my 'volunteers' back, because my unit needed to protect the communication lines of the Group. I had already seen this new army, and my eyes had lit up at the sight of their brand-new German uniforms and battle gear, their orderliness and discipline. A stark contrast to my beloved volunteer lads and their half-military, half-civilian garb. I thought it would be an honour to be of service to this regular Polish army!

Come Day Two – what a change! I was recalled to the staff headquarters, which was located in some railway carriages. The battalions were stuck in a frontal assault in the Strwiąż river valley and they could not be moved forward. Meanwhile, a Ukrainian battalion was moving from the flank along the line which, in projection, would lead directly through the Group's staff headquarters. In view of this situation, I was to extend the left flank of the offensive with my Company, by seizing and maintaining at all costs the dominant hill in the area, thus securing the flank and the Group HQ. Holding this hill was crucial in the current situation.

I quickly brought up my volunteers and moved them under the cover of a high embankment of the railway track, behind which the Beseler battalions dithered. It pained me to observe their unfamiliar way of fighting, which I did not appreciate at all. The soldiers lay well-hidden and, raising their rifles over their heads, shot blindly ahead.

Inexperienced, greenhorn recruits!

I had been fooled the other day by their appearance and their energetic heel-clicking.

Meanwhile, my troops were advancing swiftly along the slope of the hill.

A soldier's luck was with us!

I reached the ridge a fraction of a minute before the Ukrainians. Two rapidly deployed heavy machine guns sowed long bursts into the mass of the unprepared Ukrainian battalion, whose reconnaissance had passed us in the forest, walking at a diagonal to us. After a few minutes, the battalion was in flight. It dispersed into groups of soldiers, running back downhill, leaving behind five heavy machine guns and a dozen killed and wounded at the place of the ambush.

The task was complete.

Holding the hill 'at any cost' was no longer difficult.

But I couldn't shake the thought of those men down below, shooting above their heads. They would never leave the shelter of this railway embankment, they would not move forward and they would not seize Chyrów, I thought.

A moment of internal struggle. Wouldn't that be disobeying the order of 'holding' the hill? I left one of my platoons with the captured heavy machine guns, and I ran down with the rest of the company in the footsteps of the fleeing Ukrainians. Without further fighting, I soon found myself in the rear and reached the road, the railway track and the river, which was already beyond the defensive position of the Ukrainians – between them and Chyrów. The night falling quickly in the mountains worked to my advantage. I got my hands on groups of soldiers, supply wagons, and a low-rank commander, a lieutenant if I recall correctly, almost without a fight.

But then there was a commotion, several single shots were fired. I was looking for a foothold in the terrain. Making use of the bright moonlight and as best as it could be improvised in these conditions, I set up my heavy machine guns on a hill to fire straight ahead, which cut off access by road and railway to this spot. I patrolled the road with my company, catching what I could and preparing platoon ambushes in the event of the Ukrainians retreating to Chyrów. My preparations were crowned with success in the morning. A retreating Ukrainian unit, surprised by the heavy machine gun fire from my redoubt, hand grenades from ambushes and thunderous hurrahs of the entire detachment, scattered without taking up a fight. The road to Chyrów was open.

I seized it on the same day with my sledge patrol, far ahead of the main forces.

But let's return to my flying company and to Drohobycz [Drohobych].

I chewed over my experiences from Chyrów while marching next to the Chief of Staff of the 4th Infantry Division, Colonel Tyszkiewicz, not realizing for a moment that he was talking about something that sounded like an extension of my memories, '…clearly, they will never take Drohobycz like this.'

Just like those other troops at Chyrów!

Could this be an identical opportunity for my unit? I put forward my proposal. I knew Drohobycz and its surroundings like the back of my hand. I had graduated from middle school in this town, and as a boy scout, I had often roamed around these fields.

I secured permission – in the form of an order – to help the forward regiment to take over the town.

I quickly moved the wagons with my troops to the last ridge that the troops had reached in the offensive. I divided the company into smaller assault detachments armed with hand grenades and pointed out objects in the landscape that were easy to reach after dark. In the meantime, dusk approached. I established artillery fire on a certain location at the edge of the town, more to distract than for direct profit.

I myself took two platoons and followed the terrain that I knew so well. I approached the town, bypassing it from the east and taking the shortest route to the area of the main station and the huge oil refinery adjacent to it. Distant lights and whistling locomotives indicated a fevered evacuation.

When I encountered the first buildings of the suburbs, fierce gunfire broke out from a distance, from different points of the town. Our own artillery added to the racket. All for the better. I managed to infiltrate the town without being stopped. We abandoned the tedious climbing of fences and walls and ran quickly down the main railway street, to get to the railway station as soon as possible. We were youthful and reckless. Someone started humming '*Hej, kto Polak na bagnety*' ('Hey, whoever is a Pole, to your bayonets!') and soon everyone was singing at the top of their lungs.[5] But instead of leading to disastrous consequences, it worked in our favour. Our insolence paralysed the Ukrainians, causing genuine confusion among them. Doors and windows swung open and happy Poles burst out of their homes; they wanted to help, give news, lead us.

Only at the railway station was there a short exchange of hand grenades. We captured three trains which were already under steam and ready to leave. One was carrying artillery, the other two were loaded with valuable equipment dismantled from the oil refinery.

Before we regrouped at dawn the next day, having handed the city over to units of the Division, a sudden change of affairs brought a new task for the Flying Company, and one that had to be carried out immediately. The 3rd Legions Division moving parallel south in the Chyrów – Borysław direction, had halted in the mountainous woodland area of Schodnica near Borysław. Meanwhile the 9th Lancers Regiment, which served as a liaison unit between the two divisions, had got involved in the fighting in the forest between Drohobycz and Borysław and had lost its commander, Major Bartmański, which slowed down the movement of the Regiment even further. Therefore, my company was to strike along the Drohobycz – Borysław road to relieve the situation by outflanking the Ukrainian resistance.

We were still in the lands of my childhood. I knew every turn of the road to Borysław, every hill and forest. In addition, Borysław had a special emotional value for us – a few months before, we had wanted to take it with a deep thrust from Chyrów, using the Poles in this town to our advantage.

Now we had our mobile unit which had already proven itself valuable in the fight for Drohobycz. An opportunity arose to implement the old plan, although under different conditions.

Our column of wagons moved quickly, preceded by the mounted reconnaissance. I avoided the east of the forest complex where the 9th Lancers Regiment was located, and, through reconnaissance, I reached the last ridge before the town, the first buildings of which were about three kilometres away.

Through binoculars, I observed a lot of traffic on the edge of town.

An unbroken column, or rather a compact mass, a surge of people streamed towards us.

---

5. Translators: Written in support of the November Uprising of 1830–31 by Casimir Delavigne to music by Karol Kurpiński, the song 'Warszawianka 1831 roku' ['The Varsovian 1831'] is a Polish patriotic song. The lyrics praise the insurgents, the struggle, rebirth and freedom of Poland, while the melody encourages one to march.

The silence was suddenly interrupted by the sound of hundreds of sirens, oil wells and church bells.

They were not Ukrainians!

It was a mass of Polish oil industry workers who, upon hearing the news of the seizure of Drohobycz, had disarmed the Ukrainian troops and institutions by themselves and had come out to welcome the Polish soldiers. That moment will remain in my memory forever: the warmth of the May sun on the road to Borysław, and the warmth in the burning hearts of the simple people, greeting their liberators.

Like Lwów, like many cities and towns before and after, the population of Borysław, the capital of the Polish paraffin oil industry, had declared its Polish identity!

We fell victim to an overwhelming force!

My unit was torn into pieces!

Every Polish family wanted to host, wine and dine one of my soldiers. And youngsters from Borysław in civilian clothes with improvised white and red bands on their shoulders and captured rifles in their hands acted as our improvised support and imposed themselves as guides for my patrols sent out to establish communication with the 3rd Legions Infantry Division and the 9th Lancers Regiment. All I managed to obtain was a promise that, in case of an alarm or a new order coming through, I would sound the sirens to notify that my soldiers needed to be 'carried' to the designated assembly area.

When on the next day, on the order of the Division, the column moved towards Stryj, it took a lot of fresh air and a long bumpy ride on the speeding wagons for my boys to become soldiers again.

But one disappointment was obvious. I was not given a chance to fight properly in Borysław, neither before, in the winter, nor now in spring.

The Flying Company's Race To Zbrucz

The swift advance of the Flying Company to Kałusz [Kalush] – through Stryj [Stryi], which was already occupied by our troops – took the Ukrainians completely by surprise! Their defence on the south-eastern bank of the Łomnica river had not yet been fully prepared by a *sich* battalion. A large wooden bridge over the river was prepared for potential destruction in a novel way: piles of dry combustible material and crates of hand grenades were made ready in two spots on the bridge. As we approached the bridge, one heap nearer to us was already blazing brightly, while the other was still unlit. A hail of shells from the houses on the opposite shore rained down on our picket running to the bridge. Despite two wounded soldiers, Lance Corporals Wojtuń and Bienia ran up to the burning pile and, covered by the fire of the first rifles from our shore, they started throwing burning tree logs, and above all crates with grenades, into the water. Behind them, Cadet Zawadowski's platoon quickly ran across the bridge without further losses, and that's how the whole skirmish ended in practice. The enemy battalion, not yet organized for defence and only just spreading out in the field to fill positions, completely surprised by the 'irregular' pace, gave up and, pursued by our fire, fled to the east.

The road to Stanisławów [Ivano-Frankivsk] was open.

Even before we reached the city, the Polish Military Organisation (PMO), coming out of hiding, showed up to meet us. The very centre of the city was free, and the PMO and an armed civic guard were already operating. In the suburbs, the Ukrainians were still reluctant to react. I entered the city with some of the company on the makeshift train cobbled together by volunteers, while the rest quickly joined in the race with the 9th Lancers Regiment.

The city was free, and very enthusiastic about it.

That same day, I seized the undamaged bridge over the Dniester near Niżniów [Nizhniv], thereby removing the threat of any Ukrainian response far from this city.

After we entered Stanisławów, the situation stabilized for some time. A hot and dry June began and the Flying Company took over the surveillance of the Dniester to protect the Division from the direction of the Pokuttia region, still held by the Ukrainians. This meant a well-deserved rest for the soldiers.

The Ukrainian counter-offensive arrived, which pushed the troops to the line of Żurawno [Zhuravne]; an order withdrew the Company from that summer resort to the Division's reserve. As the first destination, we reached the village of Czerniów [Cherniv], at the foot of a hill dominating the plain for several kilometres, up to the Dniester. A key position of the 4th Infantry Division, near Żurawno. It was oppressively hot, and while waiting for dinner we dispersed among the village huts, just in time to hide from the storm that came from the Dniester, with a downpour and thunder. As soon as the last thick drops of rain stopped drumming on the hut windows, and the scorching sun flooded the plain again, startled messengers flew in from our supply camp with news that the Ukrainians were busy among the carts and already occupying the eastern part of the village. The storm had found us entering the village from the side of the front held by one of the Division's units, and our supply camp was temporarily closest to this front.

And here's what happened.

Some none-too-shabby *sich* battalion, I think from Kołomyja [Kolomyya], had cleverly exploited the storm and downpour and surprised the Polish garrison of the redoubt, and was now advancing through the village, swallowing our camp as it were.

There was no time for fancy manoeuvres. A reflexive counter-attack of one mobile platoon eliminated the threat in the village. Now, one platoon went straight ahead – to the redoubt, supported by the fire of all Lieutenant Walasek's heavy machine guns. The rest of the company moved quickly under the cover of the high railway embankment to attack the hill from the flank. Only a very well-coordinated detachment, with officers who understood each other in an instant, could mount this attack. After all, merely a moment before the soldiers had been dispersing among huts to hide from the storm.

But there it was!

Like a bolt from the blue, now clear after the storm, the guns of the Polish armoured train rang out just in time, signalling that it had come around the bend, alerted by the Division about the loss of the hill. And the boys of my platoon went like a shot, angry that their lunch had been interrupted. A hungry Pole is an angry Pole, apparently.

The redoubt was recaptured as quickly as the soldiers' legs could make it up the steep slope, and with minimal losses. Moving fast, they quickly found themselves in a blind spot of Ukrainian heavy machine guns, which were located quite high up.

While at the hillcrest I was busy organizing the troops, because there were too many soldiers in one place and the Ukrainian battery was now furiously biting back; a breathless messenger called me down to the armoured train, to see some senior officer.

I ran down.

With a machine gun slung over my back and two hand grenades under my belt, blackened, muddy, and generally quite menacing-looking, I reported to the commanding officer, who had reached the front by train.

It was Commander Józef Piłsudski. I write 'Commander' here, because that's how I had known him since the time of my university studies in Lwów and the times of the Riflemen's Association. This is how I had addressed him during our one and only previous face-to-face meeting in 1913, when at the premises of the Association at Kadecka Street in Lwów, I had reported as a guard on duty. The acquaintance was one-sided anyway – Piłsudski did not remember me. How could he remember one of his young riflemen practising cavalry skills on Sundays and in the evenings?

So, I reported by the book, with my rank, name, etc., and described the battle. Piłsudski's eyes scrutinized me, and finally he said with a smile, 'You look very dangerous, Lieutenant – you dealt with this mountain quickly! Just hold it until your Division's troops arrive.' Sweating more from this briefing than from the entire battle, I left the train. A few weeks later, I was awarded a promotion for outstanding action on the battlefield. But somewhere in the headquarters above, the staff had clearly blown it, because I was appointed 'Lieutenant'; I had already been promoted to this rank in November of the previous year.

For the time being, I ended up with the huge honour of a battlefield promotion, and the following year's verification fixed the mistake – I was backdated as 'Captain' to that battle in June.[6]

This incident had deeper repercussions.

Whenever fate would bring me into contact with Marshal Piłsudski, my menacing appearance near Czerniów, with hand grenades under the belt, came up in conversation. Many years later, I took part in the final Wilno [Vilnius] wargames led by the Marshal; I don't know whether his recollection of Czerniów had an impact then, and due to a kindlier attitude towards that lieutenant with the hand grenades, my analysis was put on top of the pile. At least that's how it seemed to me at the time, though perhaps I was too modest in my thinking, for I wrote nothing wiser in my report than my wargame companions.

The Flying Company became the favourite of the Division. When it passed infantry or artillery regiments, it was greeted by joyful and friendly shouts, despite the fact that, when being replenished, it sometimes stripped other units of their best soldiers, which does not always lead to popularity.

---

6. Translators: General Maczek's promotion on the battlefield at the hands of Marshal Józef Piłsudski himself on 26 June 1919 was the first of its kind in the Polish Army of newly independent Poland.

Two units especially, the 9th Lancers Regiment and Captain Riess's reconnaissance *dywizjon*, who were in constant cooperation with the Flying Company, made friends with my 'lancers on wagons', despite the sometimes fierce, though noble, rivalry. We played pranks on each other, as is often the case even in the most loving family. I remember how, after the battle of Kałusz [Kalush], when the road to Stanisławów opened and the forward cavalry unit was passing the leading platoon of my Flying Company. How my platoon commander then opened fire on some imaginary enemy on the edge of some forest; this halted the swift and eager cavalrymen and thus the platoon remained proudly at the front. Working with the 9th Lancers Regiment, I had the opportunity to meet and make friends with such commanders of squadrons and platoons as Captain Komorowski, commander of the heavy machine gun squadron, who had not yet taken on the pseudonym 'Bór', radiant with the fame of the Home Army's commanding officer; Lieutenant Tatara, who later died in a car accident in peacetime; Lieutenant Wania, Second Lieutenant Rzepka, and many, many others.

Cavalry Captain Borkowski, who commanded the regiment after Major Bartmański, later proposed to me the incorporation of the Flying Company as one of his squadrons. A very honourable proposition, showing appreciation for a mere infantryman, but I liked my rugged freedom too much to submit! [7]

The popularity of the Flying Company and its good name already spread beyond the Division. It was mentioned in orders, it was called the advance guard of the Division, it even made it into the official 'news from the front'.

All this led to a special visit from General Żeligowski's division, when we reached the town of Buczacz [Buchach]. Lieutenant Colonel Jaruzelski came from the staff headquarters with a request to borrow us as a specialist unit to carry out a raid on the monastery in Jazłowiec. This happened a week or so before the charge near this city brought lasting fame to the 14th Jazłowiec Lancers Regiment.

In this convent, under the wings of the Ursuline sisters, a handful of young ladies from the gentry had taken refuge and, among them, two daughters of the same Colonel Jaruzelski. Before our further offensive began, they would need to be evacuated, together with the Ursuline sisters. A special unit for this sortie had already been formed, but it needed to be 'professionally' led.

Summoned to the staff, I expressed my enthusiasm about the project, but on two conditions: the expedition would be led by the Flying Company, and

---

7. Translators: Literally, General Maczek states that he loved his 'Cossack freedom' too much to submit. It is yet another reference to Henryk Sienkiewicz's patriotic novel, 'Ogniem I Mieczem' ['With Fire and Sword'] in which the Cossacks are characterized by a tremendous and rebellious desire for freedom.

no sooner than on the second night, because I wanted to set aside the first one for reconnaissance.

So much 'noise' had been made about us that I did not want to risk an action in unfamiliar terrain and conditions, with soldiers who were not mine.

For the reconnaissance I chose my reliable Sergeants Kielar and Szponar, and two Cadets: Kazio Michalewski and I think one named Mrówka.

The ascent through the overgrown canyon presented no special difficulties, nor did the approach to the monastery, whose fruit garden was surrounded by a high wall, which descended to a stream. It seemed it would be more difficult to cover the whole sortie and, using wagons, evacuate as many nuns and girls as possible.

Therefore, I created two sub-units: one under Lieutenant Czerniatowicz, and another under Lieutenant Cadet Zawadowski, giving them the task of climbing quickly to two ridges that embraced the monastery buildings as if with arms on both sides – and engaging in battle for as long as I needed. I led the rest of the company myself, creeping up the ravine, straight to the monastery. We took the outpost, which we had spotted the previous night, by surprise. Before they managed to fire a single shot, we were already jumping over the high monastery wall. Sharp shooting from both sides reassured us that the plan was working and the attention of the Ukrainians was focused on the two ridges from which my platoons were attacking.

I quickly explained what was going on to the superior of the convent, who was as calm as a Spartan about the whole situation. We pulled up the wagons and started the evacuation.

There was some shooting near the monastery itself, which brought me forwards to the protection lines.

Our 'guest performance' was a complete success; we had no more than two or three lightly wounded, but for the life of me I could not later remember a single face of any of the maidens saved in such a romantic manner.

A new spurt in the offensive brought us back to the front of the division. Buczacz – Czortków – Husiatyń [Buchach – Chortkiv – Husiatyn]: small skirmishes, small successes, and so we reached the Zbrucz river. In the autumn, together with the Division, we were transferred to Volhynia.

Today, when I look back to the times over 40 years ago, I am full of admiration for the volunteer soldiers whom I commanded from the first days of November 1918 to the end of 1919; boys who often became soldiers only in the first fights, without prior preparation and methodical training. From the first moments, when the older ones among them (who had already come under fire on many fronts) declared that 'their lieutenant knows how to walk between bullets' – which was supposed to be a compliment on my behaviour in battle and my way of commanding them – from this moment they gave me all their heart and trust.

Without My Own Unit

During the winter of 1919/20, I was temporarily transferred to General Listowski's frontline operational unit. The chief of staff was Lieutenant Colonel Marian Przewłocki and it was his initiative. The head of the operational unit was Major Jabłoński, who would die at the end of the campaign as the commander of the 11th Lancers Regiment. This supposedly temporary assignment extended until the spring of 1920. I made it through the Kiev [Kyiv] offensive in the operational unit, but after the reorganization I was with the staff of the 2nd Army of General Raszewski when Budyonny attacked. With passion and zeal, I 'commanded' the flags on the map which signified the movement of his brigades and our troops. I understood and could tap into the psyche of General Raszewski, an officer of the former Prussian army, when one night I woke him up with an important report about the failure of one of Colonel Dreszer's cavalry regiments. His reaction to my report was one of surprise: 'What foolishness is this, Lieutenant? You were present when I gave the order to Dreszer to break up this rabble of Budyonny's, and here you are talking about retreating.' The old general did not comprehend that an order, regardless of the degree of feasibility, could sometimes not be executed.

Soon after, when Budyonny, despite these and other orders, was making continuous progress and threatening to tear apart the southern front, a chance occurred for me to escape from fighting on the map. Captain Benedykt, the commander of a division of the II Army, intercepted and deciphered a message from Budyonny which alerted the senior commanders to his complete lack of ammunition, especially artillery ammunition, and gave the exact location of the brigades in the area of Korzec [Korets]. A concentric strike was assembled with everything that the II Army had at its disposal. From the north, the 6th Infantry Division was to strike from the Ludwipol [Sosnowe] forests and from the west along the Równe [Rivne] – Korzec axis, the Legion's 3rd Infantry Division of General Berbecki, supported from the south by the 9th Lancers Regiment. Since the concentration of our forces did not take place before the attack, but was to take place only near the object of attack, i.e. in the area of Korzec, the concern of the army commander was the huge gap between the initial positions of both divisions, which was to be reduced as the attack advanced. Therefore, they halted the loading of the last two battalions of the 4th Infantry Division, one from the 37th Infantry Regiment, and the other from the 18th Infantry Regiment, which were the last to follow the Division to the northern front and the town of Głębokie [Hlybokaye]. One 75mm training battery was added to this, and the heavy machine gun squadron of the 11th Lancers Regiment, which was just unloading. I was to take command of this group, due to my knowledge of the units of the 4th Infantry Division. The group was to bind the attack of both divisions, striking through Międzyrzecz Korzecki [Wełyki Meżyriczi] to Korzec. At the last moment, the recently arrived Major Wolf of the General Staff of the 6th Army took command, and I volunteered as aide-de-camp to help him lead, due to my familiarity with the unit commanders. My only ambition was to get back on the line, to the real events on the frontline, and to escape the ones on the map, although they may have been just as real.

At dawn, if my memory serves me well, on 1 July 1920, our liaison group set off to Międzyrzecz Korzecki; it seized the town and thrust forward strongly, dislodging the Cossack troops. We reached the west of Korzec in the late afternoon, which promised a quick liaison with the 6th Infantry Division and the 3rd Legions Infantry Division and the full success of the planned operation.

At that time, two successive events occurred which radically changed the whole picture. First, we sustained artillery fire from the north, from the direction of the expected movement of the 6th Infantry Division, and then Cadet Wieleżyński, one of the boys from Borysław whom I had known since November 1918, came from the south with a patrol of the 9th Lancers Regiment with the following report. He had been sent, on his own initiative, by Lieutenant Adam Epler, commander of the battery of the 3rd Legion Artillery Regiment, whom I knew as a brave artilleryman from Chyrów, with a warning that General Berbecki did not intend to attack Korzec at all and that he had a dismissive attitude towards the Army's orders. In Eplers's presence he had given an order to the commander of the forward guard of the Division, Lieutenant Colonel Bończa-Uzdowski, that upon encountering the Cossacks and after an exchange of fire, he was to immediately return to Równe.

There was even more to be pessimistic about: Cadet Wieleżyński had barely managed to reach us, as the unfolding Cossack manoeuvre was encircling our group from the south.

A tight spot indeed!

And the battalions were weary from marching all night and heavy fighting throughout the day. Swift action was required. I suggested that we head north to the Ludwipol forests, where we would link up with the 6th Infantry Division, if it was already advancing and, in any case, we would not be scattered by cavalry in the forests. If it was indeed already advancing, because at that time our reconnaissance confirmed only the presence of small Cossack units, from whom we had already taken artillery fire.

In any case, these forests covered a large area all the way back to Horyń river, and were the perfect place to which to withdraw.

But Major Wolf lacked combat experience and, with probably the best intentions, applied one of the relics of the Austrian regulations, which in the event of retreat advised endless 'drawers' or the *'schwarm-weise zurück'* manoeuvre; one squad retreats, the other provides covering fire and so on, until either the training field in the garrison runs out, or the nerves and strength of the fighting men. And, add to that a completely open area, with thirty kilometres to the Horyń. After such tactics were employed almost until nightfall, battalions with good soldiers began to withdraw. Such a manoeuvre brings about a number of surprises, both tactical and psychological. At one point, there was commotion among the units. In this instance, Major Wolf, responding resolutely in order to prevent panic, sent me forward to the platoon of the 37th Infantry Regiment, which, as a rearguard, was covering the retreat of the heavy machine gun squadron of the 11th Lancers Regiment. When I rode to the platoon as fast as my horse would go and repeated the order, its commander, a non-commissioned officer unfortunately unknown to me, made a scathing remark: 'It is so easy to give such orders on horseback.' It stung me so much, and made me so angry, that I jumped off my horse, stayed with the platoon, and replied that I would now show that such an order could also be given on foot.

I took command of the exposed rearguard and came up to the front line among the tall blades of wheat. After giving instructions not to fire except at my command, I began to observe the approaches. To this day I am left with this impression from the vast fields of Ukraine and Volhynia: that our greatest enemy at that time was the tall wheat covering the fields. How to dig in and establish any field of fire? How to oppose a cavalry charge, when you had to stand, or occasionally kneel, to fire? Those platoons and squadrons, unable to see each other or coordinate their fire, lost in the sea of lush rippling grain of the rich lands of Ukraine or Volhynia! And with the situation changing constantly, there was no time to prepare this area for defence.

The rolling terrain near Korzec allowed the cavalry to approach the final rise undetected, about six hundred metres ahead of us. Half-obscured silhouettes of cavalrymen emerged from behind this ridge, shouting at us and waving their sabres over their heads, seemingly to intimidate us and to embolden themselves. Then they quickly hid behind the ridge of the hill. I only just thought, 'But they don't seem to have it in them to charge', when a hundred or so cavalrymen broke out from behind the ridge. I shouted, 'Attention, fire!' and I stood and fired a shot. Realizing at that moment that mine was the only shot that had been fired, I threw myself to the ground. Spattered with dirt from the hooves of the horses that flew past me on either side, I realized what had happened. While my attention had been fixed on the figures of the Cossacks appearing and disappearing behind the ridge, the nerves of the overtired soldiers had given in. After all, they were not bound to me by trust; this 'staffer' who had come came here for goodness knows what reason! Either at the sight of the charging Cossacks, or even a fraction of a minute before, they had begun breaking ranks, rising and retreating, which had provoked the Cossacks, restrained until now, to attack.

I lay in the crops, all ears, while several dozen steps away some troops were passing. Darkness couldn't come too soon, as the sun leaned lazily towards the west.

Just before nightfall, a Cossack battery came close and fired a few shots.

Then it was silent, and the only thing that could be heard were the conversations, laughter, and shouts of soldiers roaming about. When the night fell, bright moonlight made it very difficult to slip away.

I rose cautiously, with my rifle wrapped in my uniform and without a cap, so that my silhouette did not betray me. I began slowly, slowly to move away, not to draw attention to myself by too conspicuous an escape. There was some shouting in my direction, to which I did not react, and I moved away without rushing, although everything inside me was screaming to run.

The fires burning in the village and the sound of wistful Cossack song ruled out this direction as a possible route. I started to circumvent the village through marshes and thickets until, after a few hours of cautious progress, I found myself in the forest. My instinct for self-preservation drew me into these woods. Feeling more confident, with less caution and greater speed, I began to move forwards, choosing the paths leading west or north-west, surrounded by a tall forest, with moonlight seeping through the leaves. It was so strange, the silence all around – and within me – after the noise and emotions of the whole day, that I was able to relax in the knowledge that I was responsible only for myself.

When dawn broke, I hid in dense bushes and slept for a good few hours, awakened from time to time by the sounds of marching troops and distant artillery fire.

On the second night, I changed my tactics, knowing that the forests around Horyń were filled with Polish settlements. I went to the first isolated hut, where I was given food and drink, and then on; I trekked from point to point, passing from one helping pair of hands to another, from one guide to another. I reached Równe after three nights, and found that the city with the Army staff and the 3rd Legion Division had been almost completely sealed off by Budyonny's troops. I was greeted warmly at the staff headquarters. Everyone was happy to see me, as I had been considered lost since Major Wolf had returned from the unfortunate excursion with the remnants of the group. But there was no time for emotions. The situation was serious. I was entrusted with the command of two battalions which had been formed ad hoc for the task of shielding Równe from the west and, to my great surprise, I was assigned an armoured platoon with three French tanks.

Did I commit a great heresy using tanks as I did in those days of early July 1920? Not trusting these makeshift battalions, and having no means of command and communication, I rode with the platoon of tanks from one battalion's section to the other, sitting on the rear of one of the tanks. In this way, I could prevent crises arising constantly in these sections. Only once did these tanks actually fire and their appearance alone deterred the Cossack attack. In most cases, they served rather as moral support.

Exactly twenty years later, in June, as I was retreating from the Marne in France, my tanks were similarly festooned with men, mostly Senegalese. I wonder if back in 1920 I had not been the same, sitting on top of the tank. But kudos to anyone who could tell me how, in 1920, in my situation, I could have made better use of three whole tanks!

I have elaborated extensively on this incident, not only because of the novelty of this experience – after all, not often is one run over, or even leaped over, by a cavalry charge – but also because this incident strongly influenced my further fate. I had had enough of the staff and taking occasional command of unknown soldiers, I wanted my own unit, my own 'boys' with whom I would be bound by mutual trust. Had it been my own Flying Company with me at Korzec, would this whole incident have been conceivable? I had to get back on the line, I had to have my unit; I would still have my revenge.

At night, the entire Równe 'crew' broke through to Aleksandria and soon the Army staff was in Łuck [Lutsk]. Before long I was sent as a liaison officer from the Army to General Krajowski's Group, and I could not return to my staff because Budyonny had cut off the roads leading north. So I reported to General Iwaszkiewicz in Lwów, requesting the opportunity to form my own unit on wagons.

Captain Maczek's Assault Battalion of the 1st Cavalry Division

There were no objections to the creation of a detachment on wagons as a mobile reserve of the High Command. In the May 1919 offensive, the Flying Company had operated as part of General Iwaszkiewicz's army, and thus the attitude towards the creation of a similar but larger unit was positive at all levels of the Army staff. I left with the first organizational orders for Jarosław and the commander of the Reserve Centre, Colonel Kamionka-Jarosz. Yet, the months-long plan of organization and training imposed on me there was unrealistic in view of the blazing fronts and the fact that Budyonny was advancing on Lwów. My repeated appeals to General Kessler, chief of staff of General Iwaszkiewicz, saw me transferred from Jarosław towards Żółkiew [Zhovkva], with everything that could be squeezed out of the Centre (about four hundred soldiers in total). A few days later, an order from the command of the 6th Army directed me to protect the Lwów Infantry Division at Mosty Wielkie [Veliky Mosty]. In small skirmishes, my unit – not a battalion, rather a jumble of three companies with only two heavy machine guns, because the rest were still somewhere in transit – crossed one of the Bug's tributaries. We received an order to seize Hill 289, which dominated the area above the village of Oserdów, to cover the regrouping of the infantry division.

Thus the unit experienced the first ray of the same soldier's luck that had shone on the Flying Company near Chyrów. I reached the edge of this hill with the unit's picket and two heavy machine guns as a Cossack brigade advanced from the north-east, almost in a column. From eight hundred metres, the accurate heavy machine gun fire at the mass of cavalry felt like full payback for their charge near Korzec. However, it was just the beginning of the battle, as the Bolshevik brigade advanced quickly and, with the support of artillery and the fire of the *tachankas* [wagons mounted with a heavy machine gun] from both flanks, in part began to charge. However, before that happened, two companies were already firmly dug in around Hill 289 and, emboldened by the first success, they would not be pushed back.

The first battle of the Assault Battalion had been won.

Although not a huge success, for poorly trained recruits in their first battle with the cavalry, it offered a huge boost in self-confidence and zeal. This moment marked the beginning of the development of an assault battalion soldier.

Relieved at night by a detachment of the Lwów Infantry Division, we went to the village of Dzibułki [Zibolky], where we were met with an organizational order from the command of the 6th Army. It changed our future fundamentally.

We were drafted into the 1st Cavalry Division of General Juliusz Rómmel as its assault battalion.

The Division's commander was to give us the time necessary for reorganization, and to put at our disposal lancers who, for one reason or another, had lost their horses, with a proportionate number of officers and non-commissioned officers. He would also provide wagons, etc.

Simultaneously with this order, new soldiers began to flow in from all sides.

Although the 'traditions' of the assault battalion consisted of only a few days of battles or skirmishes, some form of an organizational structure had already been established, so I decided to mix the infantry recruits with these new cavalry soldiers. Having no quicker option at my disposal, I directed the reinforcements straight to existing companies.

This led to something resembling a rebellion. A very large delegation of about thirty non-commissioned cavalry officers came to me. Speaking on their behalf, a senior sergeant of one of the Wielkopolska regiments declared that 'They might, as a last resort, agree to fight on foot, but they would never agree to be merged with the infantry.'

This was a very critical moment which would determine the 'to be or not to be' of the battalion, even before it was truly born. I stood surrounded by a circle of non-commissioned officers, with my devoted Cadet Mrówka from the Flying Company at my side. After spending some time at the hospital, he had managed to get to the Reserve Centre. I had to remain calm, even though I was seething on the inside. I turned calmly to the Sergeant saying, 'Well, if not – then please take off your belt and give it to Officer Cadet Mrówka, who will escort you, Sergeant, to the Division's field court for refusing to carry out an order.' Suddenly, it was deathly still. The Sergeant handed over his belt. And after waiting a moment for psychological effect, I turned to the others with, 'Well, who else does not agree to be merged with the infantry?' When not a word was said, I snatched the belt from the Cadet and threw it to the Sergeant with the words, 'So you were fooled by the youngsters, and now no one is with you. Take the belt and take yourself off to the unit.'

This is how the specious antagonism between infantry and cavalry was nipped in the bud. Never again would it break out in the battalion composed of those two components.

And the same senior sergeant fought bravely near Waręż [Variazh] and was one of the first to be decorated in the battalion.

A similar situation repeated itself twenty-three years later, during the organization of the 1st Armoured Division, when it was necessary to fuse cavalrymen and armoured forces men into one. This time, the tank crews did not want to fight together with the 'cavaliers'. I solved this rebellion psychologically too, without getting a field court martial involved.

After all, young people were not to blame when they fell prey to chauvinistic slogans that praised only the cavalry, or only the armoured units, etc.

The next day, when General Rómmel came to me, the battalion was already assembled and divided into training groups practising the use of hand grenades and operating the light machine guns and heavy machine guns. General Rómmel understood that I needed time, but stipulated that in the current situation he could not give me more than two to three weeks to train and coordinate the battalion. 'God bless you even for that,' I thought. Yet, in the evening of that day, an operational order of the 6th Army set out the battalion's task for the following day: in cooperation with the 6th Cavalry Brigade, to break through the front of the 24th Soviet Division at Waręż, to pave the way for the Cavalry Division that was pursuing Budyonny, heading for the Battle of Warsaw.

I would have been able to report confidently that the battalion was absolutely not capable of such action, or any action, yet.

But could I really, in the heated situation of mid-August 1920?

It was still dark when, on the road to Waręż, the column of my battalion's wagons passed the 8th Lancers Regiment with a group of officers, in long dark Austrian coats, because the night was cold. Captain Krzeczunowicz, commander of the regiment, was at the head. The battalion also overtook the cavalry reconnaissance, and was joined at the rear by the 6th Battery of the Mounted Artillery *Dywizjon*.

The mood was like that before a morning sortie, when the lack of sleep and the freezing cold mixes with the feeling of jitters and anxiety, before the first shots even everything out.

The day had fully dawned, however, when I made my way to a reconnaissance group which was pinned under the accurate fire of machine guns placed on the northern edge of the forest and the hills on both sides of Waręż. One Soviet battery, and then another, began to harass the exposed section of the road coming out of the forest.

In front of me – Waręż, squeezed into a valley between hills lined by Soviet infantry. Somewhere far to the east, a small firefight in the direction of the advance of the 7th Cavalry Brigade. We were not alone! Between the hills with the fire of the Soviet heavy machine guns and the forest, there was an open, slightly uneven space: crops, potato fields, corn – typical small peasant fields. The machine gunner in me expertly assessed the effective distance at which to concentrate the fire of heavy machine guns at about 1,200 metres.

'It would not be easy to break away from the edge of the forest with this untested group of soldiers,' I thought.

Using runners, I assembled the commanders and the artillery spotter and gave orders for the forward companies to spread out on both sides of the road. The breakout of the troops from the forest was to be covered by all the heavy machine guns of the battalion and the assault fire of the Mounted Artillery *Dywizjon*'s battery. It was a pity that half of the heavy machine guns promised by the Army had not yet arrived.

On the face of one of the young company commanders, whom I had known for only a few weeks, I noticed an excessive sensitivity to the bullets whistling overhead, so I stood up and I finished giving my orders while standing in the road. Although I did not feel like it at all, and I know how showy and senseless it was to do so, something had to be done to boost morale. The effect was instantaneous. The young man stood up too, and I ended up scrambling back down into the ditch, pulling the lieutenant behind me.

Both companies broke away from the edge of the forest with losses even smaller than I expected, and slowly gained ground moving in packs, using the rolling terrain and thickets. They were already halfway between the forest and the hills, and even more advanced on the left flank. Even though the flank was more exposed, the greater unevenness of the terrain allowed for partially hidden approaches.

And they got stuck there for good.

The crisis of the battle was approaching and its first indication was the silence on the part of our battery, presently explained by the report that the battery had one dismantled gun and a lack of ammunition, and, following an order, was returning to its *dywizjon*. But the enemy's activity was also restrained. Here and there, an artillery shell exploded among troops who had been dispersed, and were therefore no longer as vulnerable. From time to time, heavy machine guns barked furiously from hither and thither.

The sun was getting hotter.

The Soviet fire was clearly weakening.

Did that signify anything?

I moved the reserve company along the approach already used by the forward units. They had the task of supporting the left, more advanced, flank of the battalion to attack. As this developed, a spotter reported to me from another battery, which had been sent to replace the one which had departed. And on this summer afternoon, sleepy and doused in the scorching sun, with the silence rarely interrupted by single shots, to which the ear has already become accustomed as if it had been the chirping of crickets, erupted an angry storm of assault fire, centred in front of the left flank of the battalion, synchronized with the fire of all the heavy machine guns. The reserve company, which had already approached the first line, roused the left flank, and then the entire battalion advanced quickly to the hills, all guns blazing.

What a surprise – or was it?

I never worked out whether, at that moment, the breakdown of the troops of the 24th Soviet Division, considered the 'Iron Division', was the result of being physically or psychologically overwhelmed. The fact is, it was not until we took the town of Waręż, forcing an opening in the Soviet front, and that we seized both hills in a flanking manoeuvre, that we found ourselves facing the Soviet response in the form of strong counterattacks, which were no longer working out for them.

Waręż had been captured. The road to the rear of Budyonny's advanced unit was open.

A few killed, a dozen or so wounded, was not too high a price for the vital success of the Division. A success which, in a speech to the soldiers a few weeks later, General Rómmel referred to as the battalion's Battle of Racławice.[8]

Despite the success, there were also severe losses, not the least of which was the loss of the field kitchen and the wagons of the battalion.

And here's how that happened.

Waręż was important not only for our Cavalry Division; it was also important for Budyonny and for the 24th Soviet Infantry Division which, through continuous counter-attacks for the rest of the day, tried to throw us off and close down the road. Such was the situation when, in the late afternoon, I received through Cavalry Captain Morawski an order from the Brigade staff to move out from our position and follow the 6th Cavalry Brigade, which had already passed through Waręż in the direction of Tyszowce. I explained that that would be impossible before nightfall. When it became dark and the contact with the enemy had ceased, I started to pull my troops together.

The weather had changed; it was raining heavily. It took a long time to bring in the tired soldiers and to finally set out on foot – because the wagons had still not arrived. After some time, I came across some Cossacks and had to change direction westward, following the cavalry which had also turned that way. And then a report from the 9th Lancers Regiment came to me from the rear areas.

---

8. Translators: General Maczek refers here to one of the first battles of the Polish-Lithuanian Kosciuszko Uprising against Russia in 1794, a victory that was subsequently promoted as a major success and helped in boosting the morale of the insurgents and spreading the Uprising to other areas of Poland.

The regiment was supposed to cover the divisional supply camps, and they reported that, immediately after leaving Waręż, some of the wagons had been attacked by the Cossacks. I ordered a part of the dismounted battalion to turn back, but I found only rubble: destroyed wagons and field kitchens, including all those of my battalion.

In a roaring downpour, drowning in mud on the road to Komarów, the battalion was abandoned, with communications cut off, without provisions, and without the possibility of immediately moving forwards due to the loss of the wagons.

It was only in the morning that I made contact with the commander of the 9th Lancers Regiment, Major Dembiński, who had also had no communication with the Division and could only tell me in which direction the Regiment was moving.

Therefore, the only thing left to do was to appropriate wagons and horses by ourselves. It was very difficult within the combat zone, because the cautious local population had evacuated all their horses to forests and secluded places.

And so the combat role of the Assault Battalion in the Battle of Komarów ended only with this useful prelude.

Transferred to Zamość, we entered the period of organization and training that we had been promised back in Dzibułki.

Those few weeks brought the battalion back onto its feet. I do not know how, but more and more non-commissioned officers and soldiers of the Flying Company would return to the battalion from their leave and hospital stays, instead of to their own units. There were several officers as well, such as Second Lieutenant Zawadowski and Cadet Michalewski. The adjutancy was taken over by an officer from the area of Chyrów, Second Lieutenant Alojzy Bartosz.

Finally, the rest of the heavy machine guns and mortars arrived, and an innovation similar to that Budyonny had had – *tachankas*. Captain Maczek's Assault Battalion of the 1st Cavalry Division, because it was what the official stamp of the unit said, was at the peak of its form and its willingness to fight.

But we did not take part in any further major action. With the Cavalry Division, we reached the river Słucz and there, the end of the Polish-Bolshevik War found us, to the south of Zwiahel [Zviahel].

A period of my life had ended which had more of an air of Sienkiewicz's *Trilogy* than Remarque's *All Quiet on the Western Front*, and its events were coloured by the aura of a foregone era.

After the end of the war, for more than half a year, we remained an assault battalion, but clearly no-one knew what to do with us.

We did not fit into the organizational framework of the Polish Army, with its clearly and sharply outlined division into infantry regiments on the one hand,

and the cavalry on the other. We spoiled the clarity and organizational simplicity as neither this nor that, and we were not conservative and traditional enough.

We were finally dismantled. It was only a few years later that the idea of creating battalions of riflemen for larger cavalry units would re-emerge.

The newly created 1st Riflemen's Battalion in Chojnice continued the combat tradition of Captain Maczek's Assault Battalion, and a young officer in charge, Captain Henryk Piątkowski, would collate the wartime history of the battalion in writing. It would be the first publication by this commander, who later became a staff officer and an author of military books.

Part II

Maczek's second section describes the two years between him assuming command of the 10th Motorized Cavalry Brigade and his arrival in Bristol in September 1940 following both the Brigade's withdrawal from Poland and the Fall of France. Maczek had wryly suggested that his memoirs be given the alternative title of 'Third Time The Charm'; while he himself famously never lost a battle, in both Poland 1939 and France 1940, he was tasked primarily with fighting a rearguard action.

In October 1938, after nearly a decade of commanding infantry formations, Colonel Maczek was given command of the 10th Motorized Cavalry Brigade. This first saw action in the autumn of 1938 when Poland demanded the contested region of Zaolzie from beleaguered Czechoslovakia. Over the next year, Maczek prioritized on improving operational cohesion within the Brigade, reinforcing the solders' basic training and further developing the Brigade's driving skills. The Brigade engaged in a number of exercises: those in June 1939 focused on halting the advance of the enemy's armoured units.

Intended to serve initially as reserve forces, the Brigade was thrown into action on the first day of the German invasion, fighting in the Beskid Wyspowy mountains to halt the enemy's advance through the mountain passes and into Poland's plain. Over the next two weeks, his Brigade would engage in offensive operations against German armoured formations, all the time fighting utter fatigue and the logistical difficulties of maintaining a motorized force: interruptions to supply lines, shortages of fuel, and a lack of opportunities for maintenance and repair. On 18 September, following the invasion of the Soviet Union from the East, Maczek was ordered to lead his Brigade across the Hungarian border, with the aim of joining the Polish Army being formed in France.

Having escaped internment in Hungary thanks to his wife's connivance, Maczek presented himself to Poland's new Prime Minister, Władysław Sikorski, in Paris; Maczek, promoted to Brigadier General, was tasked with commanding the Polish camp at Coëtquidan. At the end of the year, he succeeded in his lobbying for the formation of a Polish armoured unit. Incomplete and under-resourced when Germany invaded France in May 1940, Maczek was able to field only a section of the 10th Armoured Cavalry Brigade in early June. The military situation was rendered the more problematic by the difficulties in communication, disruptions to supply lines and the need to forge a path against the mass of refugees fleeing from the German advance. Maczek's Brigade nevertheless secured a number of victories, most notably at Montbard, before disbanding and scattering across France in an attempt to reach a port – and to continue the fight from Britain.

I Take Command of the
10th Motorized Cavalry Brigade

S tationed in Częstochowa at the end of October 1938, I received a telegram
from Warsaw appointing me commander of the 10th Cavalry Brigade –
and I was genuinely shocked.

At first I didn't understand what was happening; then, I didn't know whether
to be pleased, or proud, or sad. After all, a lot of time had passed since the times
of the Flying Company and the assault battalion, since that youthful *Sturm
und Drang* period, and the ideas of rapid mobile units, improvisation and the
seeking out of new routes.

During these eighteen years of peace, except for short assignments to staff
headquarters, I had served, successively, as the commander of an infantry
battalion in the 26th Infantry Regiment in Lwów, and I had completed a one-
year training course at the Higher War School in Warsaw, under the direction
of a well-known French officer, Colonel Faury. For a year, I was the deputy
commander of the 76th Infantry Regiment and for five years, with great
satisfaction, I had commanded the Grodno-based 81st King Stefan Batory
Infantry Regiment. I had learned a lot, both by myself and from my invaluable
divisional commander and friend, General Franciszek Kleeberg; no less did I
learn from my subordinates of various ranks. The power of solid preparation,
the importance of artillery and machine gun fire support, organization, more
art than technique: the art of prediction, the maxim: 'soldiers pay with their feet
for what commanders forget', and more. To be concise: solid and decent work,
with no space for improvisation. One lesson was perhaps the most important –
that, regardless of technical progress, inventions and improvements, psychology
does not change in any way, and under one's command there is always a human
being – living, breathing, and unexceptional – who is elevated to the heights of
heroism only on occasion and in very particular circumstances.

For the previous four years, I had been the deputy commander of the
7th Infantry Division in Częstochowa – the commander of divisional infantry,
as it was called. Only through reading did I come across the topic of rapid
mechanized units. I occasionally devoured news about Italian mobile regiments,
and later about the dangerous developments in German and Russian armoured

divisions and motorized-mechanized corps. However, when I was in charge of training, either on the map or in the field, I would try to add in improvised mobile units. It was called my 'hobby'. And it is well known that only the British are dilettantes at their professions, and experts at their hobbies. Here, I was rather a dilettante.

But an order is an order. I went to Warsaw, as I was told, to report to the Chief of the General Staff, General Stachiewicz (my previous commander in the first year that I had served with the 7th Infantry Division), and to the Minister of National Defence, General Kasprzycki.

At the staff headquarters, the 10th Cavalry Brigade was presented to me from various sides and in various contexts. As in a marriage, I would be bound to this unit for better and for worse, until the end of my military service and through three campaigns: September 1939 in Poland, the French campaign of 1940 and the Allied campaign of 1944–45.

The Brigade was the first fully motorized Polish unit. By tradition a cavalry brigade, now it was essentially machine-driven.

On my way to Warsaw, I was spinning in my mind mirages of a professional offensive unit, perhaps an armoured division in miniature … but my illusions faded very quickly. It was to be a defensive unit, running at fire-fighting speed – enough to locate a fire here and there in time. The concept of the Brigade was rather an attempt at a defensive response to terror of the enemy's rapid mobile units, or armoured divisions. An attempt only, because the military command still maintained it was to be an experiment. For example, General Stachiewicz pointed out to me that the Brigade had not 'proven itself' during the last inter-division exercises and, if I failed to demonstrate its usefulness during another round of exercises, then the attempt would have to be abandoned. I do not know how much of it was aimed at motivating me, and how much revealed a real doubt about the unit. In turn, General Kasprzycki, rather a fan of the unit, was mainly troubled by the length of the column. It seemed almost like psychosis, their worries that when the 'tail' of the brigade was still in Warsaw, its 'nose' would strike, for example, Poznań. They were afraid of six hundred machines on the move; meanwhile, later on, even four thousand machines in an armoured division never presented a problem. Hence, the idea of 'trailers' was born, that were to shorten the length of the columns. It was dangerous for the speed and manoeuvrability of the brigade, and fortunately, negative experiences from Zaolzie did away with this innovation. General Regulski gave me the most no-nonsense comments and help in this difficult period. Nevertheless, the situation was generally such that, among the less informed, we were considered a clumsy creation whose operation could be halted by a handful of infantry with an anti-tank gun or with bottles of petrol; or we were taken for a thoroughbred armoured unit running smoothly over any obstacles with iron and fire. In fact, we were neither. I would like to emphasize this is not a criticism aimed at our senior military command in Poland. I do not have enough knowledge to claim that in the poor conditions of 1938–1939 we could have afforded something better or greater. This is also no scientific analysis – it is too easy to be wise after the event!

From Warsaw I went directly to Zaolzie, where the Brigade was in action, temporarily concentrated in the area of Bielsko.

I was received very warmly indeed.

The surname of the commander of the assault battalion of the 1st Cavalry Division from 1920 was familiar to most cavalry officers, as the official name on that unit's stamps was 'Captain Maczek's Assault Battalion'. My kinship with the cavalry was taken for granted. Maybe I was a poor relative, but always a relative!

I, for my part, tried to define my attitude clearly and honestly.

While touring the troops on an official first visit, I shortened my speech to the officers to three slogans, more or less as follows:

- I salute your martial tradition;
- I will accept any cavalry tradition for which you are willing to pay in blood on the battlefield;
- I will do away with any mannerisms and bravado that prove to be empty beneath the surface.

At the time, it was hard for me to judge how these words were being received by the soldiers. I feared that, as cavalrymen, they were too polite and well-behaved to show me either approval or disapproval.

When fighting side by side brought us closer together and unified us, I heard from many of them how good an impression I had made with my approach.

It was only when I arrived in Zaolzie and spent some time with the troops that I realized what our motorized brigade actually was.

I saw it as follows:

The two basic cavalry regiments, i.e. the 24th Lancers Regiment and the 10th Mounted Rifles Regiment, transported on trucks, had the value of two infantry battalions which, not fatigued by long marches, and setting out into battle without being weighed down by knapsacks or backpacks, could be much more valuable in battle than normal infantry battalions. Subsequent combat experience showed me that ordering vehicles to move at night would offer these units a basic substitute for sleep (which infantry units would not experience) and this would significantly increase their physical and psychological endurance. Anti-tank guns, a large number of motorcycles for reconnaissance and communications, and a platoon of tankettes would give us more flexibility and freedom in various forms of combat. The troops did not have high trajectory fire capability, but they gained it before the outbreak of the war (not without my intervention) in the form of 81mm mortars.

By any standard, this represented a significant force magnifier, both in speed and in combat equipment, compared to my 1920 battalion on wagons…

For long-distance reconnaissance, the Brigade had a reconnaissance *dywizjon* equipped with motorcycles and tankettes – or at least modern *tachankas* rather than armoured vehicles. This set of tools was flexible enough, but was it strong enough, too?

The balance of the other units was as follows: for offence, a battalion of 7-TP tanks and a mixed motorized artillery *dywizjon* promised much in terms of supporting manoeuvres. Regarding defence, an anti-tank *dywizjon* with eighteen 37mm guns and an extremely well-motorized battalion of engineers offered reliable prospects for effectively defending against armoured units. However, the Achilles heel for fighting across wide fronts was the shortage of radio stations and their unreliability.

Having figured out what the Brigade was, I set myself and the Brigade three tasks for the immediate future:

- *to drive* (conduct vehicle operation training), which was already partly achieved,
- *to synchronize* in action (combat training at the brigade level),
- *to increase force* by putting the emphasis on the basic combat training of the troops. I continued to maintain the principle of the Flying Company and the Assault Battalion: our wagons were not intended to carry just anybody.

The formal establishment of the units, dotting all the i's and crossing all the t's, did not require further work, owing to my predecessor, the Brigade commander, Colonel Antoni Durski-Trzaska.

Without venturing a judgement on the Zaolzie operation from any particular point of view, at least the entire Brigade was finally brought together, and was all the better for it. Before, it would only gather once in a blue moon for manoeuvres, garrisoned between Rzeszów, Łańcut, Przemyśl, Kraśnik (the 24th Lancers Regiment) and Stryj (the artillery *dywizjon*). As there was little combat action (except for the Zdziarska mountain pass), it mostly practised transportation.

When, after a short break in March 1939, the Brigade was put into combat readiness by appointing reservists and through partial concentration in the Rzeszów area, I tried to complete the tasks set for myself: to drive, to synchronize and to increase force by improving combat training.

The goal was achieved with the outstanding help of my staff, whose officers included the chief of staff Major Franciszek Skibiński, Cavalry Captain B. Mincer, and a little later Captain L. Stankiewicz and Cavalry Captain A. Pieregorodzki, as well as the communications officer, Captain Grajkowski, and even the head of the staff office, Lieutenant F. Ferenstein; they all demonstrated their patriotism in various ways. Further first-rate help was offered by the commanders: the commander of the 24th Lancers Regiment, Colonel K. Dworak – my colleague and classmate from the Military Academy, Major Święcicki, commander of the reconnaissance *dywizjon*, Major Stachowicz, commander of the anti-tank *dywizjon*, and the tireless commander Major J. Dorantt, who arrived later with the engineering battalion.

The training period of several months was not wasted and unquestionably increased the combat value of the 10th Cavalry Brigade. However, the outbreak of war on 1 September 1939 found the Brigade dangerously weakened in other respects. A few weeks before 1 September an exchange of reserve units was carried out, delivering to us soldiers who had been poorly trained. What was even more painful, the Brigade was still without its tank battalion and the third artillery battery of the *dywizjon*. Both of these units were supposed to reach the Brigade during the mobilisation period, but in fact they never did, leaving the artillery *dywizjon* without one battery for the entire period of fighting. Therefore, we had eight gun barrels – terribly few for a brigade with ambitions for greater action – and instead of a battalion of 7TP tanks, of which we had heard nothing but promises, only one company of worn-out Vickers' (I think only nine) and one company of TKSs, which we rightly considered as rather *tachankas* than tanks.

Thus the Brigade was cut short by one-third of its artillery and two-thirds of its tanks: a good half of its striking power!

The pain of that was even greater as it was absolutely unnecessary! I do not know whose decision in the mobilisation unit, fractured by aerial bombardment, deprived the Brigade of its striking power! We were like a wasp whose stinger had been taken out. While it still buzzes, circles, and threatens to sting, it cannot deliver the killing blow.

Would bluff have to be our most important weapon, instead of strength?

The Outbreak of War
The Brigade's Battles in the Beskid Wyspowy Mountains

In mid-August, the Brigade, in good order and good form, moved to the Kraków region, to be at the disposal of the Kraków Army of General [Antoni] Szylling as reserve forces. The commander set Pszczyna, Bielsko, Zawiercie, and Katowice as my area of operations, so I explored the area with my chief of staff, familiarising myself with it and establishing communication with the divisional commanders on the different sections, including General Boruta-Spiechowicz, General Mond and General Sadowski.

On 29 August, I was directed towards a new region – Nowy Targ. So, on 30 August, leaving Skibiński to process the results of our exploration from previous days, I conducted a reconnaissance of the Beskid Wyspowy mountains and made contact with the commander of the 1st Regiment of the Border Protection Corps (BPC), Lieutenant Colonel Wójcik. That evening, I delivered my assessment of the area in the event of a threat to the Army from the south, which, in view of the news about German concentrations in this direction, seemed very likely.

But despite such news, and the preparations made on the map and on the ground, the outbreak of hostilities at dawn on 1 September was as much of a surprise to those of us who had firmly claimed that war would not happen, as to those who had prophesied its outbreak any day. Some said, 'And still, it happened,' and others, 'As I said,' which generally meant that everyone was agitated and surprised by the developments. Literally 'surprised', because the raid of German aircraft on Kraków also hit the accommodation area of the Brigade. Several bombs fell on us without causing any damage to people or equipment.

It was simply a peculiar wake-up call at dawn on 1 September, marking an end to the period of uncertainty which, for the Brigade, had begun as early as March.

On the same morning, around 8.00 o'clock, an order from the Army commander threw us immediately into action.

The Germans struck at dawn on 1 September 1939 across the entire sector for which the Army was responsible. In the face of being outflanked from the

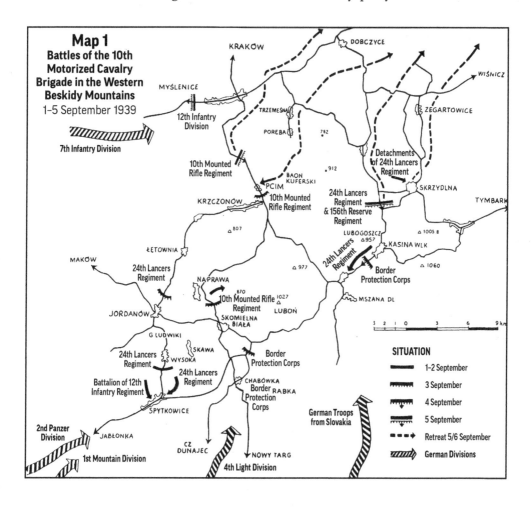

Map 1

Battles of the 10th Motorized Cavalry Brigade in the Western Beskidy Mountains

1–5 September 1939

7th Infantry Division

KRAKÓW
DOBCZYCE
WIŚNICZ
MYŚLENICE
12th Infantry Division
TRZEMEŚNA
ZEGARTOWICE
POREBA
782
10th Mounted Rifle Regiment
Detachments of 24th Lancers Regiment
912
BAON KUFERSKI
PCIM
SKRZYDLNA
KRZCZONÓW
10th Mounted Rifle Regiment
24th Lancers Regiment & 156th Reserve Regiment
TYMBARK
807
LUBOGOSZCZ
1005 8
ŁETOWNIA
957
KASINA WLK
MAKÓW
24th Lancers Regiment
977
24th Lancers Regiment
1060
NAPRAWA
870
10th Mounted Rifle Regiment
1027
LUBOŃ
Border Protection Corps
JORDANÓW
SKOMIELNA BIAŁA
MSZANA DL
G LUDWIKI
SKAWA
3 2 1 0   3   6   9 km
24th Lancers Regiment
WYSOKA
24th Lancers Regiment
Border Protection Corps
SITUATION
Battalion of 12th Infantry Regiment
CHABÓWKA
RABKA
Border Protection Corps
SPYTKOWICE
German Troops from Slovakia
2nd Panzer Division
JABŁONKA
1st Mountain Division
CZ DUNAJEC
NOWY TARG
4th Light Division

▬▬▬	1–2 September
▬▬▬	3 September
▬▬▬	4 September
▬▬▬	5 September
◼◼◼►	Retreat 5/6 September
▨▨▨	German Divisions

south-west by considerable armoured and motorized forces towards Nowy Targ and Chabówka, and shielded only by two BPC battalions with one artillery battery, and National Defence units, the commander of the Army threw his operational reserve, in the form of the 10th Cavalry Brigade, into battle with the task of protecting the southern flank and the rear of the Kraków Army. In particular, the Brigade was to prevent the enemy from emerging from the mountain gorges and, to this end, was to delay them as long as possible on the routes leading to Myślenice and Dobczyce, preventing them from advancing north from these villages into the open plains, which would be difficult to cover and which was also where the Army's main communication lines passed.

The order for the Brigade came down to the task of engaging in a fierce five-day-long battle in the Beskid Wyspowy mountains against an opponent identified only as 'considerable armoured and motorized forces'; as we captured prisoners and documents, these turned out to be the 2nd Armoured Division, and then the 4th Light Division. Finally, after encountering the 1st Mountain Division, we identified it as the full XXIII Corps of the 14th Army of General List, thrown into battle as the southern arm of the pincers, which were to encircle the Kraków Army. Bearing in mind the Germans' absolute advantage in the air, would it be an exaggeration to estimate the ratio of forces as at least 10:1?

But this data only surfaced in the course of the battle, once our successes allowed us to count the enemy. At that moment, one thing weighed heavily on our minds: 'As long as possible', and the names of two towns, Myślenice and Dobczyce. And since the depth of the terrain for delaying the enemy's action did not exceed twenty kilometres in one direction, and thirty kilometres in the other, it became imperative to act quickly in order to repress the first German push as far south as possible and as effectively as possible.

Therefore, leaving my chief of staff with orders to move the Brigade, I took Captain Stankiewicz and several motorcyclists and drove at full throttle to see the commander of the BPC Regiment, Lieutenant Colonel Wójcik. When I was still on my way, after reconsidering the situation, I sent a motorcyclist with an order to Skibiński to put one anti-tank squadron at my disposal, destined for Skomielna Biała. For I was aware how defenceless the BPC battalion, and even more so, the National Defence battalion, would be, facing an armoured-motorized unit, without a sufficient number of anti-tank guns. It seemed important to maintain some kind of front which would obscure the deployment of the Brigade in two long columns, which was restricted to paved roads, and with limited ability to descend into mountainous and wooded terrain.

What feelings did I experience on this short, full-steam ride to Zakopane along the railway track, which so many times in my childhood had carried me to my summer holidays and, later, to skiing trips in the winter season, most recently during the winter of 1938–39?

Was I amazed that, in the very first hour of the war, there had been a need to use the Army's operational reserves? Not really! I had already experienced my unit being moved into action unexpectedly quickly, although admittedly at a low level of command, in the very first days of my combat experience.

It reminded me of Żurawno in 1919 when, after being brought to rest in the reserves, I ended up organizing an improvised assault. It reminded me of Waręż in 1920 when, after having been given a dozen or so days to organize an assault battalion, I received an order to attack the same night. *C'est la vie et c'est la guerre* – such is the way of war that it often overturns both well- and ill-considered plans and projects!

My rather muddled thoughts were overshadowed by the satisfaction that I was moving at the head of such a rapid unit which, just a few hours after setting out from quarters near Kraków, would be fighting somewhere near the Tatra

Mountains. It was the satisfaction of having been given an independent task, and one suited perfectly for highly mobile units: 'Cover the flank and the rear of the Army'. Satisfaction with the importance of this task, one that left so much room for initiative. I never liked being shifted from point to point, being tied down by details of execution, and being dictated an often-imperfect course of action. A clearly defined objective, however difficult, as long as it clearly stated what was required of me!

In my mind I repeated the words of the order: 'As long as possible' and 'Myślenice – Dobczyce line'.

And as for the more personal feelings? Understandable stage fright before my first real performance after such a long period of stagnation. Would I rise to the occasion? Would all of my officers? My lancers and mounted riflemen, my tank crews and artillerymen, etc.? Would the whole Brigade manage, despite the deep conviction that, although weakened (I deluded myself that this was only temporary, hoping that any day an organic battalion of tanks and a third battery of artillery would join from mobilisation), the Brigade was a well-coordinated unit, full of enthusiasm and eagerness, as my Flying Company and my assault battalion had been in 1918–1920. One only hoped that a soldier's luck would be on our side as it had been back then, because without this ray of sunshine it would be difficult to fight!

One aspect of my personal life that I was not concerned about was my small children, who were under the care of my wife, my brave comrade in arms. They were to go, as we agreed, to our farm estate in Wołyń, where they would not suffer food shortages. This decision was made easy by the fact that my family had only moved to Rzeszów a few weeks earlier, and had not yet taken root in that unfamiliar city. On the farm, which was officially called Maczki Wołyńskie, there were a few of my old soldiers, who had fought alongside me back in 1918–20. They were warmly attached to us, and so were their families.

Isn't that what happened in Sienkiewicz's *Trilogy*? How unreliable all this turned out, we were soon to learn. But who could predict anything in the face of the tragedy that was approaching our homes? As it turned out, Divine Providence had a wiser and better path set out for my family.

The men of the two BPC battalions, and even those zealous, almost bare-handed Highlanders filling the ranks of the National Defence (since they were either too old or too young for the regular army); all turned out to be good army material.

They did not disappoint.

Around noon, when I joined Lieutenant Colonel Wójcik, the situation developed as follows:

From dawn onwards, in spectacular skirmishes with the Germans, during which they even managed to capture a tank, they inhibited the progress of the enemy and held him far from the approaches towards Chabówka. In the direction of Jordanów they delayed the German exit from Spytkowice, holding Mount Wysoka as the key to their position. I could confirm it myself when, joined by the chief of staff, I climbed the slope of this hill. I also breathed a sigh of relief when I heard the roar of the engines of the nine anti-tank guns, brought forwards from Skomielnia on my orders to immediately cover the hillside, because its western slopes, gently rolling towards the village, almost begged for a massed tank attack.

The barrier of the hills, dotted with observation points, obscuring the Jordanów-Skomielna-Chabówka road – a barrier which was so important for the deployment and organization of the Brigade for battle – was strongly held. That very day the barrier, reinforced in the Mount Wysoka section by a *dywizjon* of the 24th Lancers Regiment and with the support of the fire of our artillery, repelled, with serious losses, the first attack of German tanks, and held the initiative until the following day.

So when the chief of staff and his staff officers began to prepare the first general combat order of the Brigade, collecting and sorting all orders issued verbally so far, I had a moment to entertain some deeper so-called 'operational' reflections.

Already during the Spring exercises of the Brigade south of Rzeszów in the Subcarpathia region, a certain doctrine was emerging for units such as our Brigade in the face of the enemy's anticipated advantage in tanks and artillery, which focused on delaying operations.

You could put it this way:

From the outset, give up any notion of long-distance observation and exchanges of fire, because in such conditions the opponent would have an ideal opportunity to demonstrate their advantage in artillery fire and tanks. Instead, pitch battles in terrain with short horizons, drawing the opponent into ravines and gullies in which it would be difficult for them to deploy forces without losing time. Lure them into straits, in which they would have to fight us for a long time and with individual 'fingers', rather than the whole clenched 'fist'. To gain even more time and to make the opponent pay us more heed, constantly look for opportunities to bite back with short forays or counter-attacks. This would either force them to be cautious, which is time-consuming, or expose them to constant surprises which would delay them as well. I was well aware of the great demands such a method placed on commanders of all levels, demanding strong characters who did not flinch at the prospect of self-sacrifice.

We understood each other at the staff headquarters; we were harmonious and well-matched, and the commanders of all ranks also understood each other well.

The bare and distant slopes of Mount Wysoka and Mount Ludwika, which dominated the entire region, did not present a good position in accordance with this doctrine, since they were easily accessible to tanks. But as always, every tactical thesis has its antithesis, and so circumstances occurred that nevertheless led me to take up the first battle there.

These circumstances could be summed up as follows: these few kilometres would have constituted a large increase in territory for the Germans, and a painful loss for us; in addition there was little space to rebound. The entire valley of the River Skawa would have to be surrendered without a battle, making the opponent brash with too easy a success and diminishing their respect for us. This in turn could translate into bold, rapid action by the German units, which could be dangerous.

There was also fear of the inevitable mess; if the Brigade's units occupied positions in the rear, and the BPC and National Defence troops had to be withdrawn, they would be isolated and exposed to being overrun by German tanks.

This is how the battle for Mount Wysoka came about.

It began in the afternoon of 1 September with the tank assault of the 2nd Panzer Division being repelled by the Lancers, BPC and the National Defence, mainly thanks to our marvellous 37mm guns and motorized artillery. It developed throughout the rest of 1 September and the day after, with the deployment of increasing masses of tanks and motorized infantry and growing artillery support, which in the last thrust exceeded six light and medium artillery divisions.

Our men who were covering the mountain held up brilliantly. The destruction of forty-five German tanks was confirmed. Lieutenant Colonel Deskur, deputy commander of the 24th Infantry Division, was leading a squadron of lancers against the motorized infantry who were accompanying tanks; he suffered losses from the fire of the tanks, but his bravado inhibited the momentum of the attack.

Finally, on the evening of 2 September, we lost the very summit of the mountain, our two batteries of tanks being driven off over the ridge towards the Skawa, by concentrated fire.

The losses were painful both in the White Lancers Regiment and in the National Defence unit. Several of our anti-tank guns were crushed in their positions by tanks. Several field artillery observers and the commander of the motorized artillery *dywizjon*, Major Żmudziński, were killed.

It would take a great deal of fortitude and ferocity for my officers to complete a task that had begun with such bloodshed.

As compensation there was the fact that the losses were much greater on the German side; we had also gained two days for the performance of our difficult task and there was a huge boost to the soldiers' morale, who saw that it was possible to fight the Germans, and to do it well.

The night raid of 1–2 September on Spytkowice, a long, narrow village in which a large number of German troops were amassed, did not go as expected.

When I was preparing this foray, the commander of the 12th Infantry Regiment, Colonel Strażyc with his battalion (our neighbour from the west) came to me, volunteering his men, because it had been their training area before the war. They knew the terrain like the backs of their hands, so they had a better chance. For reasons unknown to me, the raid was delayed and was finally conducted after dawn, without achieving the intended result. It also had the effect of exhausting a squadron of the 24th Lancers Regiment which had been tasked with distracting the enemy's attention away from the actual direction of the raid. The aerial intervention, on the other hand, was successful. Several Łoś aircraft bombed the massing German troops in Spytkowice – at my request – via the Army commander. Too bad there were so few aircraft!

While the fighting against the tanks of the German 2nd Armoured Division was fierce in Colonel K. Dworak's section, the situation was much easier on the southern section commanded by Lieutenant Colonel Wójcik, closing off the Chabówka direction. A new large German formation, which we would soon identify as the 4th Light Division, was emerging laboriously out of the difficulties caused by the terrain, made perhaps even more troublesome by the damage wreaked by the sappers. It came up against the BPC defences only in the evening of 2 September. This was a comforting sign for us, but one should never overstep the mark. So, I quickly agreed with the staff and commanders at a briefing on a further plan of action.

The three roads leading north from the valley of the Skawa river constituted a route in the direction of the German pressure. They ran through three relatively narrow ravines to the Pcim-Mszana line: 1) Jordanów-Lętownia-Pcim, 2) Skawa-Naprawa-Lubień-Pcim and 3) Zabornia-Rabka-Mszana.

From Pcim there were only two roads: one to Myślenice, the other to Dobczyce. To the east of the latter, the terrain offered the opportunity to bypass Dobczyce and (by drawing a wide arc) to reach the rear of the Army. Therefore, I considered this direction operationally more dangerous for the performance of my task.

At that moment, however, on the evening of 2 September, I deemed the direction of attack of the 2nd Armoured Division dangerous and requiring special attention, while the situation in the direction of Mszana with Lieutenant Colonel Wójcik was not yet 'mature'.

The route towards Myślenice was shorter, giving us only about twenty kilometres to complete the task of setting back the Germans. In the first section from the Skawa to Pcim, the Myślenice route gave the Germans the ability to operate on two axes. By quickly reaching Myślenice they could separate the Brigade from the tactical wing of the Army, represented by the 12th Infantry Regiment in the area of Maków. More importantly, the Germans had already achieved success in this direction, albeit a costly one, in the form of seizing Mount Wysoka, and they had deployed forces for further action.

Therefore, leaving command over the movements of the 4th light artillery *dywizjon* with Lieutenant Colonel Wójcik – with his two BPC battalions, the National Defence unit and a 75mm battery, and reinforced only with anti-tank guns from the Brigade – I decided to pit the entire 10th Cavalry Brigade against the 2nd Armoured Division on the following day.

The reconnaissance *dywizjon* advanced on the Skawa in order to cover the withdrawal of the 24th Lancers Regiment and the National Defence unit and to allow for the gathering of the physically and mentally exhausted soldiers in Jordanów. These units were given the task of defending the Jordanów-Pcim route the next day, which I assessed to have been of secondary importance. The unit also covered the preparation of defences along the main route of Skawa – Pcim, near the town of Naprawa, by the 10th Mounted Rifles Regiment, which was supported by the whole of the artillery, i.e. the motorized *dywizjon*. Both groups, i.e. the 10th Mounted Rifles Regiment and the 24th Lancers Regiment, prepared defences at the entrances to the ravines, which were, in places, difficult for the deployment of tanks, as well as for supporting attacks with massed artillery.

A good route through Pcim enabled the operation of the reserve forces, which at that moment comprised a company of Vickers tanks and a company of tankettes, soon to be reinforced by the reconnaissance *dywizjon* once it came out of the screening line at dawn.

This clever manoeuvre, the authorship of which was collective – my own and my entire staff (as it always is in well-functioning leadership) – led to very positive results. The German artillery was well positioned because, by conquering Mount Wysoka by day, they had reached good observation points overlooking the entire Skawa valley. The Germans had covered the positions of the reconnaissance *dywizjon* at dawn, literally a few minutes after its retreat. And then, for a long time, they nervously fired at various 'geographical' points: intersections of roads, forests and towns, looking for their opponent, who seemed to have mysteriously disappeared. The penetrating German reconnaissance fell into ambushes and traps because, in the vacuum between the Skawa and our actual position, we had let loose the patrols of the reconnaissance *dywizjon* and the 10th Mounted Rifles Regiment. This is where the talent and the experience of Lieutenant Wasilewski had the chance to bloom. He was to become one of the best commanders and incursion specialists in the future Armoured Division, and went on to take command of the 10th Mounted Rifles Regiment, who by then were no longer on horseback or even in trucks! His bold offensive actions gave us our first prisoners of war, among them a German officer with a map, from which we first learned that we had two armoured divisions ahead of us: the 2nd Armoured Division from Mount Wysoka and the 4th Light Division, which was advancing on Chabówka. On the same day, 3 September, a German airman was shot down by the Brigade's anti-aircraft battery; he had been a part of a Vic formation which had spectacularly, but ineffectually, bombed the Brigade's column on the road to Zakopane. He bestowed upon us the gift of another map showing a large column behind both armoured divisions, marked as a mountain division. The armoured-motorized corps of General Kleist thus revealed its face, leaving no doubt whatsoever as to its identity. If I add to this what emerged from the first day, that is, the German tactic of setting houses on fire wherever they arrived for the evening and then being completely inactive at night, I had a faithful picture of a brutal German mass which was ten times larger than our forces. They moved like a fire raging in the forest. Smoke and flames marked where they arrived at nightfall and where they set up camp, which was not without its obvious benefits for our intentions and movements.

From that day, the Brigade began to show symptoms of controlling the situation from nightfall until late afternoon. Then there was crisis after crisis, survived with longing looks at the sun and an eye on the ticking clock: 'We just need to make it to the evening, and then we will pull it together and get out of this bind.'

The general plan of action outlined above, the terrain and the spread of the Brigade, the fractured communication due to the actions of the enemy – all this required great mobility and flexibility of command. You could not sit on your hands and wait for reports, because they might not come, or they might come too late, or they might come in a completely unexpected form, for example, as German tanks. It was necessary to be here and there – wherever a threatening situation arose or might become threatening at any moment – but it was also necessary to be at the command post in order to catch the often-ruptured threads of communication and not to be blinded by success or terror in one location and to lose sight of the general picture. And the situation became dangerous not only through actual facts, but also as a result of purely psychological symptoms which arose as a consequence of these facts. No report, no matter how well written, would capture what a face-to-face conversation with a subordinate commander, or the sight of a soldier full of enthusiasm or depression, could tell me. You can't command living men by paper!

In order to be able to afford such flexibility of command, you must first of all have a well selected and coordinated staff. Thank God I had that. The entire headquarters of the 10th Cavalry Brigade became, within a short time, one close-knit family. It united such disparate individuals as the chief of staff Major Franciszek Skibiński, Cavalry Captain Bogdan Mincer, the head of armoured weapons Captain Ludwik Stankiewicz, the head of Traffic Control Cavalry Captain Anatol Pieregorodzki, head of signals Major Jan Grajkowski and quartermaster Major Maleszewski, as well as liaison officers of the regiments: Lieutenant Ziółkowski of the 24th Lancers Regiment and Lieutenant Wąsowski of the 10th Mounted Rifles Regiment. We were like a well-matched tank crew. Only later, in part after the fall of France and then finally, after the end of the war, did different characters react differently to developments which pushed them beyond their mental endurance.

This also happened when the map in the staff headquarters, with its wonderfully optimistic depiction of our brave battle against the entire German armoured-motorized Corps, suffered its first lightning strike in the form of news that the defence of the 10th Mounted Rifles Regiment had collapsed under the attack of the 2nd Armoured Division; I jumped from the frying pan and into the fire to support the Regiment at Naprawa. I ordered a company of Vickers tanks to follow in my footsteps under the cover of a platoon from the reconnaissance *dywizjon*.

'Into the fire' was right on the money because, when I reached the Regiment's commander and his aide-de-camp, we found ourselves under strong artillery fire. I found the commander and the officers shaken by the following developments. After having had some success in the morning in the defence's approaches, since noon the Regiment had been repelling German attacks which, hour by hour, had been gaining strength, both in supporting artillery fire, as well as in the number of tanks deployed and motorized infantry. Sometime around 16.00, when the Regiment's reserves had readied themselves to intervene on the right flank, where the German advance was slowly gaining ground along the road, German infantry on the left flank (as it turned out later, from the Mountain Division, concealed within a forest on a steep rocky cliff), outflanked a squadron of the 10th Mounted Rifles Regiment and began to push it down towards the road. The situation was critical, because the opponent's movements threatened the defence, and we could respond with only one reserve squadron, commanded by brave Cavalry Captain Tomkowicz. I gave the commander of the Regiment, Colonel Bokszczanin, a company of Vickers tanks so that he could counter-attack on his right flank, while simultaneously attacking with the forward squadron which was valiantly holding position. This made it possible for Cavalry Captain Tomkowicz to eliminate the incursion through the mountains.

Conducted boldly and furiously, these two simultaneous counterattacks repelled the Germans and averted the first crisis of the battle that day. I call it the first crisis, because the second, more serious one in terms of its repercussions for the future, unfolded at the staff headquarters, when I delivered the triumphant news that the situation had been saved at Naprawa.

This second crisis had developed in the direction of Chabówka. The Germans – operating across the entire front, fielding not only their two frontline armoured divisions, but also parts of the Mountain Division's reinforcements – clearly and stubbornly sought to achieve full success, that is, to break through our forces and reach the rear of the Kraków Army.

The BPC Regiment, which had been fighting very effectively with the 4th Light Division since the morning, had been taken by surprise by some German tanks when changing positions and lost Chabówka. They were regrouping outside of the town of Mszana, reporting heavy losses and extreme fatigue among the troops, since they had been engaged in heavy action for three days and nights.

The situation had changed significantly in twenty-four hours.

The 2nd Armoured Division did not seem as dangerous at that moment, as it was doomed to move through tight passages and, from Pcim onwards, along the only road towards Myślenice, winding through the ravine. This Division, over three days of battle, had suffered serious losses in tanks and men both during the fighting on Mount Wysoka and at Naprawa. Up to and including Myślenice, there had been no convenient terrain for deployment, and the Division could only collect small tactical successes in a laborious fashion.

In contrast, the 4th Light Division was already emerging from the first group of gorges and entering an area which was much more convenient for its purposes, where it could outflank the Brigade's troops and proceed to the rear of the Army.

The threat could only be averted by a full response from the Brigade. Hence the decision to leave the 10th Mounted Rifles Regiment with an artillery battery and an anti-tank squadron under the command of my deputy, Colonel Łódź-Michalski, in the direction of Myślenice, while the rest of the Brigade consisted of the 24th Lancers Regiment, which was relatively rested since it had not been severely attacked on this day, along with a company of Vickers tanks, a company of tankettes, a reconnaissance *dywizjon*, an anti-tank unit without a battery, a motorized artillery *dywizjon* without a battery, and a battalion of sappers which would be transferred at night through the Myślenice-Dobczyce arc to Mszana, where, together with the BPC regiment with an artillery battery, they would strike at the 4th Light Division.

Strike, or bluff? Given that the combat equivalent of three battalions would be supported by only two artillery batteries and only one actual tank company? What a paucity! But even a bluff would at least win us some time – and that was the point.

During the day, when I was in the sector of the 10th Mounted Rifles, two incidents occurred at the Brigade's headquarters. The first was an air raid by a German squadron, which bombed my command post, i.e. the Brigade headquarters, this time with some losses in people and equipment. The second was a false alarm about the movement of a German motor column from Jordanów to Pcim, with the forward elements reported to have been already closing in on the command post. The chief of staff reacted vigorously with everything at hand to protect the post from this direction. Fortunately, the alleged German column turned out to be just some empty wagons of the 24th Lancers Regiment, which had moved to the rear.

This is always the problem with a command post. Either it is located at the most obvious point, usually at the intersection of roads, so that in rapidly changing situations and amid tension it is easy to find for motorcyclists or commanders with important reports, and is thus exposed to all kinds of aerial or artillery bombardments (it must be assumed that the enemy, like us, reads maps). Or, conversely, it is hidden somewhere in seclusion, in places not easily accessible and, thus, overlooked by motorcyclists and staff officers, but still not necessarily protected from bombardment.

From the two evils I chose the prominent locations, which risked the nuisance of bombing raids, but afforded a greater chance of actually being able to command the battle.

For armoured-motorized units, a night march of over sixty kilometres, without lights due to the threat of bombing, was already hard work in itself. But the real feat would be to push the columns of heavy equipment through the narrow roads along the ravines, which were filled with impossible throngs of cars, horse-drawn wagons, children's prams, all belonging to the people fleeing the burning villages. The motor column kept stopping and starting. Sometimes it moved at the walking pace of the traffic controllers and the staff officers working hard at the front; at certain moments, it got stuck for long minutes, in the face of some major commotion or confusion. Add to this the fatigued drivers and the constant horror of raids, even if only those by reconnaissance *dywizjons*. It was a true Golgotha for the Traffic Control Platoon, their energetic Cavalry Captain Pieregorodzki, the chief of staff of the Brigade and the officers who helped out. I have nothing but respect for their hard work, when, in the name of hard duty and soldiers' work, it was necessary to ruthlessly remove peasant wagons from the road, which had been stacked hurriedly with people's meagre possessions, or rather their remnants. The image of that night in Myślenice, brimming with real human tragedy, is difficult to erase from memory. I was later told how, at the end of the war, one of my old soldiers, hitting the fleeing Germans with rounds from his light machine gun, fiercely cried: 'For Warsaw, for the concentration camps!' and finally 'For the road to Myślenice!'

Due to these difficulties, the offensive action planned for 4 September was carried out only around noon and only by the units of the 10th Cavalry Brigade. The reason for that being that, when I found Colonel Wójcik before dawn, I saw with my own eyes that the BPC battalions, which had fought their way out of a difficult situation in the night, were in a state of complete physical exhaustion, incapable of immediate deployment. Despite this, I did not abandon the idea of a strike by Colonel Dworak's battalion, which was supported very efficiently by Vickers tanks and tankettes, as well as by the fire of two batteries. It was a complete surprise for the 4th Light Division, which was preparing for a further approach from the seized ridge behind the village of Kasina Wielka. In less than two hours, the Germans had been expelled from the ridge and pushed towards the Mszana area.

So with Dworak satisfied with his success and Wójcik licking his wounds and gathering his troops with the hope of a solid rest, I drove to the Brigade staff headquarters in the afternoon. I was worried by the lack of news from the Myślenice area, and about whether there had been a phone call from the staff headquarters, as well as my chief of staff's return from the Army headquarters with a new important order.

When I arrived at the new Brigade command post, which had been moved to Dobczyce, the situation presented to me by the chief of staff was as follows: the Kraków Army was in retreat. The part of it located south of the Vistula formed the Operational Group of General Boruta-Spiechowicz, who became our commander. The task of the 10th Cavalry Brigade remained largely unchanged: to cover the flank and the rear of the Operational Group. But the holding of Myślenice, in view of the retreat of the Group to the east, was only of importance until the night of 5–6 September. Then, for a while, the roles were to change. The 12th Infantry Regiment of Colonel Strażyc was to hold the area until the 10th Brigade's units had passed through Myślenice in the general direction of the Dunajec. A significant threat loomed in the southeast, where the Germans were circumventing the open flank of the Brigade and could cut off the Group's retreat. To execute this difficult task, the Group commander reinforced the Brigade by directing the following units to the Dobczyce area: Lieutenant Colonel Młyniec's 156th Reserve Regiment, which would reach the area by 5 September; a heavy artillery regiment; the rest of Lieutenant Colonel Gaładyk's BPC brigade troops, of which Major Kuferski's battalion was already advancing on Dobczyce; and two battalions of Lieutenant Colonel Strażyc, with the task as above.

If I had ever dreamed of completely crushing an armoured division (albeit a light one!) – I guess it was at the time of reading this order.

The forces gathered on the eastern flank of the Brigade were the following: the 156th Reserve Regiment, two BPC battalions and the 24th Lancers Regiment – in total the equivalent of six battalions – although supported by only three light batteries (the 16th *Dywizjon* of the Motorized Artillery Regiment and a BPC battery), but with the whole Heavy Artillery Regiment, a company of medium-sized tanks, a company of tankettes, and a large number of anti-tank guns. It all held great promise, particularly considering our previous considerable successes, which had been secured by much smaller forces. Our Achilles heel was being a kaleidoscope of various units of unequal combat value, units which were unfamiliar to me, and which were scattered all over.

A detailed analysis showed that it would not be possible to carry out this strike before dawn on 6 September, and only if we had assembled and directed the new troops to the right place in time.

While my staff bent over backwards to cope with the task of locating and directing troops, I convened a briefing of the liaison officers and those commanders who could make it, during which I gave orders for the transitional day of 5 September. Among the commanders in charge of the new BPC battalion was Major Kuferski, the former commander of the training company and, later on, of the Reserve Officer Cadet School attached to the 81st Infantry Regiment during the time I commanded this unit. I knew Kuferski very well, and I knew what to expect from him.

My message at that briefing was simple:

- To proceed in the direction of Mszana-Kasina Wielka for the purpose of defence, to distract from the gathering of forces to attack on the 6th.
- Commander: Colonel Dworak
- Forces: the 24th Lancers Regiment and the BPC battalions of Lieutenant Colonel Wójcik, two artillery batteries, one anti-tank *dywizjon*.
- The reconnaissance *dywizjon*: to scout in the direction of Skrzydlna and along the roads bypassing the defence from the east.
- To bite back in the direction of Myślenice with a raid by Major Kuferski, who would set out from the town of Trzemeśna, cross a ridge stretching along the Kraków-Zakopane road and preclude the attack of the 2nd Armoured Division by coming in from the flank, while simultaneously cooperating with the units of the 10th Mounted Rifles in the front.

When I was issuing these orders, General Boruta-Spiechowicz came into the room and, asking me not to interrupt the briefing, remained until it concluded. Then he stood up, warmly greeted me and asked if I was taking responsibility for these orders. Taken aback I replied, 'I would not have given them otherwise.' But the General quickly appeased me. For a short period of time, during which the Brigade was subordinate to him, he had always emphasized his faith and trust in us. And even if the situation was very difficult, there were several instances when he came to talk to me in person while I was in action, to do everything that could be done in a desperate situation. I greatly appreciated this attitude towards me and the Brigade. I only encountered similar behaviour in 1944–45, when the commander of the Canadian Corps, General Simonds came to me in difficult situations in his armoured car and, by making direct contact, clarified many complicated situations. General Boruta-Spiechowicz and General Simonds had a lot in common, even in terms of appearance: they cut a handsome, towering, soldierly figure. I was fond of them both. Such personal contacts with commanders make war much easier.

The briefing was over. Once again I went through the movements of the raid on the map with Kuferski and discussed details with him, giving advice from my experience as a seasoned commander of raids, and as an older colleague. For a moment it seemed to me as if this all were just the 'manoeuvres' of 1939 and that this excellent officer and I were just plotting 'pretend' action for the next day. I embraced him warmly and bid him farewell with a heavy heart.

How gladly I would have switched places with him!

The crises of the evening of 4 September did not change my decision. After my departure, Dworak bravely repelled the attack of the 4th Light Division, which had already shaken off the failure at noon that day. But the second attack in the evening forced the 24th Cavalry Regiment to bounce back to the starting line of that day, i.e. the hill of Kasina Wielka. In view of the threat of being bypassed in the south-east, Dworak had to use one of the less tired BPC battalions to extend his left flank.

At that moment this did not endanger the planned attack on 6 September. Dworak still had space up to the next horizon, i.e. the slopes of Mount Wiśniowa, beyond which troops were to gather to attack the following day.

The final balance of the Kasina strike, although with insufficient forces, was very positive. The 4th Light Division did not advance a single kilometre on this day, seizing in the evening as much land as it lost in the afternoon, and the way it cautiously engaged was proof that it had gained respect for its opponent.

The crisis on the western flank of the Brigade on the 10th Mounted Rifles Regiment axis was transient, eliminated by the counter-attack of our own reserve. However, in the face of the growing pressure of the 2nd Armoured Division, the crisis testified to the validity of the action intended for the dawn of 5 September, i.e. Kuferski's raid and the actions of the Mounted Rifles Regiment.

I decided to wait for the results of the action at dawn at the command post of the 10th Mounted Rifles Regiment, so that I could later switch to the eastern axis with greater peace of mind, to oversee the gathering of forces and to issue final orders to strike on 6 September.

The picture would be incomplete if I did not mention in the description of this four-day effort the dedication and courage exhibited by the Brigade's sappers in their meticulous work. The Engineering Battalion, the best conceived and most motorized unit in the Brigade, organized truly down to a tee, was commanded with flair and vigour by Major Jan Dorantt. In 1938, he literally built this battalion from scratch, engaging all the personnel and materiel, to the last sapper and to the last file and screw, and now he was lucky enough to command this first-born child of his. In these difficult days we all worked to the limits of human resilience, but our sappers were famous at the Brigade, and later at the Armoured Division for their willingness to work until their physical and nervous forces were exhausted… and then a few days more.

But we had a worse crisis on our hands – we had run out entirely of the explosives needed by the sappers. Dorantt cleverly remedied this by sending his patrols to all former military garrisons which, although evacuated and abandoned, always harboured some materiel in various warehouses, if one knew where to look.

The early morning hours of 5 September, after initial alarming and confused communications, finally brought news of a much-awaited success.

At night, Major Kuferski had reached the slopes of the hills which spread across the Zakopane-Kraków road in the area of Pcim and, using the firepower of all his heavy machine guns and four anti-tank guns, entirely obliterated a motorized column, driving the German *Panzergrenadiere* to the starting base for the attack. He burned several tanks and over a dozen vehicles. At the sound of gunfire, a squadron of the 10th Mounted Rifles Regiment forced the forward units of the armoured division back along the road.

Safe in the knowledge that this success would grant me a much-needed delay in the advance of the 2nd Armoured Division, and that the hinge (Myślenice) connecting the Brigade with the troops of General Boruta-Spiechowicz should hold until 6 September, I set out, via the staff headquarters in Dobczyce, to the eastern flank of the Brigade, to join the forces gathering for the attack.

The first rude awakening was the news waiting for me at the staff headquarters, that the heavy artillery regiment with horse-drawn wagons, whose arrival we had expected, was a hundred kilometres away from us, so would not make it in time. Although we had considerable strength in the 'light' parts of the intended strike, this regiment was intended to be the mainstay of firepower, affording an element of surprise with its heavy calibre shells. With it out of the picture, the situation changed completely.

The second bit of bad news was the final blow. Talking with Lieutenant Colonel Młyniec, the commander of the 156th Regiment, and my erstwhile subordinate in Grodno and, even more so, seeing his soldiers, dragging themselves around, tired and still in shock after the air raid that had struck them as they were unloading from the wagons; all this deprived me of any illusion that these troops would be able to attack the armoured division.

I returned to the idea of attacking with only the 10th Mounted Rifles Brigade, which I had assembled on the left flank, possibly with one BPC battalion, to achieve a limited success and to gain time. But in this case, the defence of the extensive Mount Wiśniowa ridge would have to be covered by the 156th Reserve Regiment, which absolutely did not guarantee either a successful defence or the protection of the regrouping of the 24th Lancers Regiment and the BPC battalion for the attack.

I succumbed to the insistent requests of Lieutenant Colonel Młyniec to leave behind a part of the 24th Lancers Regiment, which had already sustained enemy fire and was familiar with the realities of war, as the backbone of the defence and to interweave it with the units of the 156th Reserve Regiment, whose morale would soon be raised and then one would be able to count on its combat value. With such a purpose in mind, I placed this Regiment at the disposal of Colonel Dworak and withdrew only one *dywizjon* of the 24th Lancers Regiment, with Vickers tanks, to have at my disposal.

I could hardly do anything else.

At that time, although 5 September had started so nicely with Kuferski's raid in the west, the situation had matured in a dangerous manner for us.

On the western flank, while the Panzer Division had not shown much activity, a German unit from the Mountain Division or the 7th Infantry Division had achieved a temporary success at the intersection with the 12th Infantry Regiment, and now threatened to occupy Myślenice before the withdrawal of the 10th Mounted Rifles Regiment. A counterattack by the Regiment patched the situation up, but only a little, and only temporarily. In the centre, the advance of the units of the 4th Light Division was halted by a combined defence of the Wiśniowa hills involving a part of the 24th Lancers Regiment, the BPC battalion and the 156th Reserve Regiment.

On the eastern flank, German armoured and motorized units pushed back our reconnaissance *dywizjon* and advanced to Skrzydlna, into the open terrain and towards the flank and rear of the Dworak battlegroup, and the communication lines of General Boruta-Spiechowicz's Group.

My newly reconstructed reserve, i.e. the *dywizjon* of the 24th Lancers Regiment, supported with anti-tank guns and a company of tanks, under the command of Major Deskur to whom I had subordinated the reconnaissance *dywizjon*, was already in trouble, after a heavy battle, surrounded this movement north of Skrzydlna. However, the reconnaissance reported further signs of flanking manoeuvres from the east.

The hinge of Myślenice, the front at Window, and Skrzydlna. This situation stretched the forces of our Brigade, supported by the BPC and the reserve regiment, across thirty kilometres and three flashpoints, again: Myślenice, Window, Skrzydlna.

It is difficult to keep up when the speed of the enemy is the speed of motors, while the speed of one's own troops is the speed of the weary legs of infantrymen. It is also no wonder that, within twenty-four hours, our left flank at Kasina-Wiśniowa Góra slowly became the centre of our group. And the fabric of the units stretched beyond measure and began to tear.

In the evening when I was returning quickly to the staff in Dobczyce, I had a spell of bad luck.

A breakdown; and not a single motorcyclist in sight, because I had sent them all away, carrying orders, in various directions. I wasted precious minutes, a quarter of an hour, a good hour, marching along the road to Dobczyce, before a means of transport miraculously appeared and took me to Dobczyce.

After dark, I learned about all the turmoil in the Myślenice area. It was now definitely in German hands.

The situation was serious across the board, and it was vital that we responded quickly, sending liaison officers and staff officers to all units to pull the troops out of trouble.

The Myślenice-Dobczyce line, which I was not supposed to let the German armoured and motorized advanced formation cross, had finally ceased to matter. I say 'finally' because it was the strict execution of this order that had led to this critical situation of the Brigade and the assigned troops. The Operational Group of General Boruta-Spiechowicz in their retreat towards the Dunajec at night would pass the easternmost point of this line, i.e. Dobczyce. The Brigade's new task involved the seizure of the Wiśnicz area for further screening of the group's retreat from the south.

It was also in the interest of my motley group not to be truncated into still smaller groups and surrounded entirely by Germans, which at that moment was almost inevitable.

And so, looking from the west: the Myślenice 'cork', occupied by the Germans, cut off the retreat of the 10th Mounted Rifles Regiment, whom I ordered to break through in the direction of Dobczyce, bypassing Myślenice from the east. The Regiment would find their wagons on this road, withdrawn from the ravines in time. They would not now be a hindrance in action on terrain without good roads.

Kuferski's battalion was already in a stronger situation, marching through the forests from Trzemeśnia to the east, an area which was not threatened by tank manoeuvres.

I ordered the Dworak battlegroup to retreat to the forests around Leszczyna, in a race against the Germans who had squeezed into the gap between this group and Major Deskur's *dywizjon* of the 24th Lancers Regiments, which was returning to its unit.

The reconnaissance *dywizjon* was covering the Wiśnicz area from the south and monitoring further German movements on the flank.

There was nothing more to be done than to believe that the situation would not get worse, that the officers sent with the orders would find the troops, and that the troops would move in time to where they needed to be.

Nightfall would also probably lend us a helping hand!

All that was left for me to do was to collect and direct my 'clenched fist', i.e. my company of tanks and tankettes, part of the anti-tank *dywizjon* and most of the Engineering Battalion, as well as my entire staff, to Wiśnicz Nowy, as I had been ordered.

When assessing the outcome of the five-day battle in the Beskid Wyspowy mountains, it must be acknowledged that it was the result of a consistent execution of the order not to let the German advanced unit approach the rear of the Army or the Operational Group. We gave everything we could to fulfil this task. The commanders and the staff, the Brigade troops and the assigned troops – they all made the same effort, except for one reserve unit, from which it was difficult to expect more.

Perhaps our situation on the night of 5–6 September would have been much easier and the morale much higher, had we been able to attack on the eastern flank, as had been our plan, but this was not within our power.

For five days and nights of continuous operations by all the Brigade's units and the assigned units – a rather large, although strangely assorted group – we had been up against an armoured-motorized Corps which exceeded our forces tenfold. We had surrendered only twenty to thirty kilometres of terrain, reducing the pace of the German advanced unit to no more than four, at most five, kilometres per day. We had not let them approach the rear and flank of the Army beyond the Myślenice – Dobczyce line until the units we were screening had left this area.

We used all forms of action: raids and counterattacks, bending over backwards in our efforts, fielding the same company of tanks and two modest batteries of artillery several times over, pretending to be a large armoured unit and confusing the opponent as to the magnitude of our forces and our intentions.

Although in a temporary crisis, I solemnly believed we were still a unit fit for further use.

We had done much more than any infantry unit could ever have done in these conditions, and significantly more than a mounted unit could have achieved in our place.

We passed what had been announced as 'manoeuvres' in 1939 and which had turned out to be the test of real war, and passed it well.

And all our soldiers – the lancers, the mounted riflemen, the tank crews, the artillerymen, the sappers, the BPC soldiers – united in the struggle; they had all fought hard and fought relentlessly, with full conviction of their superiority over the Germans.

Was that any small feat?

The Dunajec, Wisłoka and San Rivers: The Stages of Our Retreat

The difficult day of 6 September began, and the Brigade's situation remained unclear. We still had not caught up with all the troops, or at least we had not yet received any reports to this effect. I was not sure whether the officers I had sent out had reached the units among the maze of Polish and German troops, or whether the units had moved in accordance with their orders. After the Brigade's staff reached Wiśnicz Nowy, a new alarm was raised by frightened refugees that a German motorized column was moving a few kilometres to the east of us, through Lipnica Murowana. It was possible that it was our own reconnaissance squadron, as the units of the entire Brigade wore German steel helmets and black leather jackets, characteristic of armoured divisions. We had often been mistaken for Germans.

At the moment, I had only an anti-aircraft artillery battery and communication and Traffic Control platoons at hand, so I immediately sent Cavalry Captain Pieregorodzki with a few volunteer motorcyclists to reconnoitre the column in Lipnica Murowana.

This reconnaissance did a great job; they drove along the hedges to the very road itself and even pelted the column with hand grenades, throwing it into confusion – after making sure beyond a reasonable doubt that it was in fact German.

I gave the order to defend Wiśnicz with what was at hand. The layout of this town was very helpful: four roads leading in all four directions, and solid brick buildings. The order was issued just in time, because immediately after taking up its position, the anti-aircraft gun at the exit to the south of the town started a firefight with the approaching German tanks and, after immobilising one of them, forced the rest to quickly withdraw. I rushed out to this tank to find out which German unit it was. Since the evening before, I had been plagued by the nightmare that maybe we were being surrounded by fresh German armoured units from Slovakia. (This did actually happen, but a little further to the east, where the troops of the Carpathian Army faced the newly introduced German Mountain Corps.)

A dead tank crewman's regimental number from the 4th Light Division, written down in his papers, brought me much relief.

My final decision was easier now.

Until the arrival of the Brigade's units, Wiśnicz Nowy would be defended by the staff, communications, traffic controllers, supply soldiers, an anti-aircraft battery and anyone with a rifle or hand grenade to hand. I gave an order to distribute the anti-tank rifles that had arrived in crates from the mobilisation department, and to remain at posts.

From the windows of the first floor of the school, two such long barrels looked out, providing direct protection for the staff at work. The problem was that, in these nerve-racking circumstances, we needed to read, and calmly, the enclosed instructions for the actual use of the anti-tank weapons. (The rifles were of excellent quality for 1939, incidentally.)

The commander of the Operational Group, General Boruta-Spiechowicz, came by for a moment, and was impressed by our improvised alcázar and our determination.

However, there was nothing else to do at that moment. In the *panta rei* of it all, Nowy Wiśnicz was at that moment the only fixed point which offered the possibility of bringing the situation under control. It was a point known to all units, so relocating the command headquarters would introduce even more confusion into what was already a chaotic situation.

But even in this mess, it was with great joy that I welcomed the liaison officer, Lieutenant Ziółkowski, who announced the arrival of the entire 24th Lancers Regiment. This regiment had had trouble in the evening and during the night, which could not have been solved by Austrian, French or Polish combat regulations: Colonel Dworak was the invaluable commander of the Regiment and a fan of employing these rules interchangeably. He had made it through thanks to the bravery of his White Lancers, and had appeared just when the situation was becoming critical. Then the artillery arrived, and the 10th Mounted Rifles Regiment turned up where they were ordered. There were comforting reports about the retreats of the BPC battalions and the 156th Reserve Regiment, a little more to the rear and through the forests.

The appearance of General Boruta-Spiechowicz was accompanied by an announcement of a further withdrawal, beyond the Dunajec, for which precise orders were later brought to me by Skibiński, who had been sent to the headquarters of the Operational Group.

The evening of 6 September ended with the same, if not even more confusing, situation as the previous day, except that the 'hinge' was not Myślenice, but Bochnia, and the role of Dobczyce had been taken over by Brzesko. The Brigade was in danger of being cut off from the north if the Germans defeated the rearguard of General Boruta-Spiechowicz too rapidly. On the eastern flank, the Germans had already secured complete freedom of manoeuvre to cut off the Brigade from the direction of retreat to the east, because they had wedged themselves between the brigade and… whom? I had some unverified information about the units of the Carpathian Army, about the 24th Infantry Division and the 11th Infantry Division, but I could not establish tactical communication with them. My reconnaissance encountered Germans everywhere.

In the evening, with the chief of staff and the operational officer, I went to observe Bochnia, as it was a vulnerable point. From there, I sent Skibiński to General Boruta-Spiechowicz with a proposal for some changes to the direction of the Brigade's route to the eastern bank of the Dunajec. The axis imposed on us had no petrol depots or filling stations; it was therefore worthless to a motorized unit. With the staff officer, I led the last infantry company retreating from the west to the ridge right in front of the first buildings of this village. This ridge obscured the view of the southern road, to where I had directed most of my units from the area of Wiśnicz Nowy. The company soon found itself under the fire of German artillery and of troops deploying for the attack. I persevered as long as I could, until I could no longer guarantee resistance. Only then, through a staff officer, did I change the route for the rest of the Brigade's retreating units onto rough paths which bypassed Bochnia from the east and (as I expected) were still safe from the Germans.

The Brigade was gathering near the town of Radomyśl. And again, on the night of 6 September, there was an impression that the unit would probably not extricate itself fully, if at all, from the obvious trap. My part of the staff was even now mourning the chief of staff, who might have been caught when returning via Bochnia, which had already been vacated by the troops. The other half of the staff, with Skibiński, was doing the same regarding our fate.

By noon on 7 September, all organic units of the Brigade had gathered across the Dunajec, having already risked crossing the long wooden bridge over the river in broad daylight, surprisingly unmolested by the Luftwaffe. Apparently, the aircraft had something more important to do that day than bothering with a brigade which, according to German calculations, should no longer exist.

The assigned troops removed from the Brigade were ordered to join the units assembling on the west bank of the river.

I returned these troops with regret, and I would like to thank them today, especially the three battalions of the Border Protection Corps led by Lieutenant Colonel Wójcik and Major Kuferski, for their diligent soldierly work and for having confirmed what this elite Polish infantry could achieve in battle. There had been no opportunity to thank them for that at the time.

As soon as the staff had gathered and we had secured a telephone connection with the Group command, I had a short conversation with General Boruta. Something was not going according to plan on the western bank of the Dunajec, which is why the General said the following: After what the Brigade had been doing and considering how tired it must be from constant fighting, he had no right to burden us with an additional order, but he kindly requested that, if possible, some unit might try to save the day on the western bank, in the southern section.

We formed a separate unit, which arrived at the designated place in time, relieving General Boruta of at least one of his worries, of which he had plenty on that day.

All through the night of 6–7 September, and into the afternoon, the Brigade's units broke through and disentangled themselves from the Germans – who were coming in greater and greater numbers from the west, from the direction of Kraków, and from the south and the Tatra mountains.

On the west bank of the river, the troops, already exhausted from six days and nights of uninterrupted action, set upon the petrol like dragons, and devoured the food and ammunition from waiting supply wagons. Even Skibiński was smiling good-naturedly on that day, especially since he brought me the most desirable gift from General Boruta's staff: the order to move the Brigade to the reserve. Not only did the men desperately need some downtime, but so did the neglected and barely maintained machines.

The immediate future looked bright. We even made preparations for an improvised warm bath and a decent dinner. It seems that it was the head of the Brigade's office, Lieutenant Ferenstein, who delivered the crucial message that there would be three courses and a table covered with a white tablecloth.

Into such an idyll, Lieutenant Colonel Monwid Olechnowicz from the Carpathian Army staff arrived with an order that immediately shattered our rosy prospects. The 10th Cavalry Brigade was to be placed at the disposal of the Army commander, General Kazimierz Fabrycy. He gave us an order to move to Rzeszów immediately, because the Tarnów-Rzeszów-Jarosław region was completely undefended. I was to receive further orders from the Army headquarters, where I was to report immediately after ordering the Brigade to march.

I had already received information via a reliable route that Tarnów was occupied by the Germans so, leaving orders for the Brigade to move through the forests to the area of Głogów (north of Rzeszów), I left for the headquarters myself, taking one staff officer with me.

Since I could not find General Fabrycy, I had to wait until another occasion to report to him in person. However, the chief of staff of the Carpathian Army,

Lieutenant Colonel Morawski, my good acquaintance from Waręż, introduced me in a matter-of-fact manner to all of the unexpected twists and turns of the situation. There was not a single Polish unit on the Tarnów-Jarosław-Lwów route that could oppose the armoured and motorized troops in their race to the River San. The San could therefore be crossed by the Germans before our troops could withdraw. The latest news reported that Dębica had fallen. It was of the utmost importance for the Brigade to bar the way for this advanced unit, which was possibly still in the region of Rzeszów. Essentially, the task of the Brigade was to win two valuable days on 8 and 9 September, which were required by the Army commander in order to prepare the defensive lines of the San.

So again, something was worth fighting for and something was worth the trouble. The San flows into the Vistula. I thought this was the general Polish front, where we would halt the first German advance for a long enough time to see signs of easing, as a result of the French attack on the Siegfried Line. I needed to return to Rzeszów, which was provisionally covered by some local mixed lot, gathered together by Lieutenant Colonel Latawiec, the city's commander, and to wait for the leading units.

In the morning of 8 September, the Brigade should have been making an arc from the north through the forests of Głogów, blocking the path of the German unit by getting ahead of them by one or two hours on the march to Rzeszów.

The plan was again simple, and only needed to be executed. A temporary defence of Rzeszów should give us one day, September 8. The defence of Łańcut, another day – the 9th. The third day would be gained by a retreat to Przeworsk.

We would win at least three days, allowing the Army's troops to dig into the San.

I realized that it would be very difficult to bring both wings of the Brigade back together, as I was completely isolated in trying to enforce the delay. On the right flank, the Kraków Army, in retreat across the Vistula, gathered and drew its troops northward, increasing the gap between us with every hour. The left flank of Boruta's Operational Group, which concerned me the most, departed with heavy losses, having lost most of its artillery on the Dunajec. On my left flank, the Carpathian Army was concentrating to the south, towards the bend in the San in the Bircza area, and moving away from tactical communication with my troops.

Even more dramatic was the loss of my tanks. On the sandy roads leading to Głogów, my remaining tanks ran out of fuel; all my veteran Vickers from the Brigade's training period and its first battles. (The petrol wagons, which miraculously pushed through with the quartermasters, later allowed the remnants of this company to join General Boruta's troops.) So, realistically speaking, there was only the one tankette company, that of Lieutenant Ziemski, reinforced with several of Lieutenant Polityłła's tanks, who joined us. The tankettes would have to be operated like tanks.

In my thoughts I send warm thanks to this brave Vickers company:

- For saving the situation at Naprawa,
- For an outstanding performance in the Kasina attack,
- For driving around like crazy on the eastern flank of the Brigade,
- For maintaining the morale of the unit with their mere presence,
- And for the fact that they did not try to get out of performing even the most difficult tasks by pointing out that their machines were just old training equipment!

8 September was another day of success for the White Lancers.

On the west bank of the Wisłoka river, the field conditions were not the best. We could not leave the city due to the ongoing evacuation of the ammunition and petrol depots, which were so crucial for the motorized Brigade, who nonetheless played the day-long battle very neatly.

They unleashed their full firepower, supported by our two batteries, and eliminated the threat on their southern flank with a counterattack bravely conducted by the squadron of Cavalry Captain Radziwiłowicz. Their northern flank was protected by the 10th Mounted Rifles Regiment on the edge of the Głogów forest, looming from the north over the Dębica-Rzeszów road. My hand was forced, but fortunately so – we worked with whatever we had. Deploying for battle with the column turning round to oppose the Germans, I approved such a grouping as time and circumstances allowed.

All this, together with the solid performance of the 24th Lancers Regiment and significant fire and reconnaissance support from the 10th Mounted Rifles Regiment in the north against the Germans on the road, made it possible to hold the city until noon the next day, as well as to push the Brigade's 'tail' through Rzeszów to the Łańcut area.

Therefore, it seemed that holding Łańcut until the night of 9–10 September would not be difficult. Meanwhile, the German 4th Light Division, forced to deploy near Rzeszów, was halted at the front by the 24th Lancers Regiment and flanked from the north by the 10th Mounted Rifles Regiment, and deployed where the resistance was weakest, namely in the south. After entering Rzeszów, it approached Łańcut, already spread out in an extended line. Thus, on 9 September, the threat to the southern wing of the 10th Mounted Rifles Regiment defences appeared in the afternoon, almost simultaneously with the Germans approaching Łańcut.

From my vantage point on the southern flank, I directed the fire of the 75mm gun, which fired straight at the armoured cars that passed us by.

Then, as in a war of a bygone era, I was able to personally direct a company of tankettes to attack the flank of the German tanks, which were charging on our reconnaissance *dywizjon* in Albigowa. This bold attack by Lieutenant Ziemski against the flank of the German armoured unit, already fighting in Albigowa, had a greater effect than we expected. The company's strongest asset was the possession of several of the heaviest 20mm machine guns on its tankettes. They penetrated the armour of the German tanks with ease. The Germans retreated hastily, leaving behind in the approaches a few tanks engulfed in massive flames. The rest was achieved by a counter-attack on Albigowa by the reconnaissance *dywizjon* and by concentrating our artillery fire.

The threat to the southern flank was averted just in time, as the alarm on the northern flank forced me to throw the tankettes one by one in that direction in order to salvage the situation.

The castle in Anicut was crowded and bustling that evening before the sun went down, and later, when darkness seemed to put a halt to military activity. The Brigade commander did not respect the castle's plenipotentiary's request to recognize the neutrality of his historical monument. German artillery would be pounding on this 'marked geographic point' anyway, so why make it difficult for one to command, and for the breathless messengers to find the commander – somewhere in the steward's house – when all roads led to the palace?

Isn't it a centuries-long tradition of the noblest monuments, that they are destroyed by deluges and the conflagration of war? Doesn't a cannonball from the Swedish siege embedded in the wall add splendour and a veneer of tradition to monuments today, even though the same cannonball was once only an instrument of barbaric destruction? One thing I assured him of: there would be no Alcazar. It was not my intention to defend every brick of the palace and bury myself under its ruins; I promised that the upheaval of war would pass quickly like a summer storm.

So, despite our host's concerned expression, we spread out across several rooms and bent over the maps, as the situation seemed to be quite heated.

The castle became even more crowded and bustling when its doors were opened wide to the crowds of officials with their families, and the townspeople who took refuge in its dining rooms, as in the old days.

The blind attack of the German artillery hit the castle tower with just one shell, and all the fire was concentrated on the park and the field kitchens of the 24th Lancers Regiment. The poor White Lancers would go without lunch that day. They could not even benefit from the spread on the tables which had been set for everyone, out of wholeheartedly typical Polish hospitality, as an order urged them to move to Reworks.

And the castle would remain crowded and bustling after the departure of the last soldier of the 10th Mounted Rifles Regiment – for whom our beloved Anicut had been a peaceful garrison – ... The rooms would resound – not for the first time in history – with the foreign language of guests from the 'retinue' of Herr von Kleist and Herr List, paying a haughty and arrogant visit to Count Potocki.

Another threat to the defensive flank – being bypassed from the north – was averted, but my distant reconnaissance on the southern flank reported a grim situation. Strong motorized armoured columns had bypassed us deep to the south and were moving east towards Raymon. The Germans would be able to forestall us on the San and even cut off our retreat beyond the river.

I decided to assemble the Brigade in the area of Reworks and to find out whether we would reach Jarosław before the Germans. Should this turn out to be impossible, the Brigade would have to be led in a wide arc northwards to another crossing of the San, near Leżajsk.

However, given the military situation in the area of Łańcut, the idea of 'bouncing back' to Przeworsk for a part of the 10th Mounted Rifles Regiment would involve heavy combat, attempting to break through the city at night. Contrary to their practice so far of ending combat operations around 19.00, which had so far been truly beneficial for us, on this ninth day of our fighting, the German attack on Łańcut went on into the night, which caused a lot of trouble for the Mounted Rifles. Part of this Regiment, bravely fighting for its garrison, was defeated during the night and driven away from the direction of retreat to the east. It only evaded being completely cut off by the Germans by moving north, temporarily joining up with General Boruta's troops.

Clearly, this strenuous German effort must have meant something; I reasoned that they must have wanted to stop us from retreating beyond the San. I had no insight into the entire operation of both the Polish and German side... I saw little more than what was going on in front of our noses.

In a state of nervous tension, we were pushing through obstacles on the roads to Przeworsk. Did we have a clear path to Jarosław or not?

I was not surprised that we were fighting alone, as a small brigade on the main Kraków-Lwów route, and that both Armies were going in opposite directions, leaving the shortest route to Lwów exposed.

But a painful surprise for me and all my soldiers was the moment when, after a nightmarish night spent on gathering the Brigade's troops and directing them to the still-free Jarosław, I found this Polish Maginot (or Siegfried) Line almost completely empty.

One infantry battalion in Jarosław itself, some two or three batteries beyond the San, news of several companies and – more often than not – platoons running about not knowing what their task was…

The front on the San was a fiction – no less a *fata morgana* than a vision of an oasis over a clear spring with lush vegetation, to the weary eyes of a desert wanderer. I didn't want to believe it yet! After all, not only had we imagined, ardently desired and fervently believed that the main Polish defence forces would be positioned along the river, but also the Carpathian Army command had clearly defined our role in delaying the enemy so as to give them those few precious days to solidify the defence on the San!

So..?

I gave the order to strengthen the Jarosław bridgehead with a detachment of the 24th Lancers Regiment, anti-tank guns and the support of the 16th Motorized Artillery *dywizjon* – all under the command of Lieutenant Colonel Moszczeński, the commander of the anti-tank *dywizjon*. I directed the Brigade over the long bridge on the San to the eastern bank of the river. With Cavalry Captain Mincer, I took myself along the river to see with my own eyes: what was the state of this defence? Indeed, apart from one battery of artillery in position, I encountered only loose groups of wandering and disorientated soldiers. Driving a car along the road on the eastern bank, somewhere north of Radymno, I got a burst from a heavy machine gun with the characteristic barking tone of a German rifle.

Germans on the eastern bank?

I turned back to a platoon from the 24th Lancers Regiment, which we had just passed on its way to the Regiment's assembly point, and I directed it to attack. German resistance was weak; they were pushed rather easily towards the river. They were probably a reconnaissance unit, and yet supported by artillery, because in a moment the road came under relatively strong fire. As we retreated towards Jarosław, we had to leave the car, which the driver was unable to start and which soon after burst into flames.

The bridge at Radymno had been blown up by the retreating troops, but the Germans now had a superb opportunity to build a new one. I didn't know what was going on south of Radymno, where there were numerous fords, or in Radymno itself. I was considering the appropriate Polish reaction – the 10th Brigade from the north and other Polish forces from Przemyśl from the south – not yet realizing that we would not find any forces capable of attacking within a radius of several kilometres.

In the meantime, I deployed whomever and whatever I collected on the spot, which came down to the equivalent of one company with several heavy machine guns – in order to stop the Germans advancing from the small bridgehead by the river.

As the only memento of this self-directed reconnaissance of San, I had the car I had acquired earlier. It was a German Adler Cabriolet. Parading around in it, wearing a black jacket and a German helmet, I sometimes looked rather like a German officer.

Retreating on foot along with Cavalry Captain Mincer, it turned out to be a lucky day for us. We were caught by a courier officer from the Army command going to the Brigade by car, with an order for me to report to the headquarters in Lwów. He took me straight there. I reported to General Fabrycy, who did not approve of my proposal, that I be given two battalions from Przemyśl in order to quickly eliminate the German bridgehead near Radymno, and to prevent attempts to cross the San between Przemyśl and Radymno. I wanted to do that before the Germans could get their armoured weapons through. Instead, I received a specific task for the Brigade to close the route from Radymno to Krakowiec, Jaworów, Janów, and Lwów. This task was then extended to involve cooperation with General Boruta's Group in the east, which was to attack the Germans crossing the San from the north. A very attractive idea… but completely impracticable for anyone who knew of General Boruta's desperately difficult situation on that day. The fact that he was in trouble was confirmed that night by a telephone conversation with the General, who had to retain my Vickers, a section of the 10th Mounted Riflemen Regiment, and my anti-tank guns, to act as a 'spine' (as he would call it) on which to hang the remnants of his units, which were slowly regrouping.

As a result, this attack from the north did not take place, and the Brigade's task was specified as hindering the German advance along the Jarosław-Jaworów-Janów-Lwów axis.

The Screening and Defence of Lwów,
12–17 September

The screening actually began on 12 September with us holding back units of the 4th Light Division on the Jaworów – Janów – Lwów line. We kept identifying it as such thanks to the regimental numbers given by prisoners captured from it.

We left Jarosław not entirely due to the pressure applied by the Germans, whose attacks had collapsed against the defence of a bridgehead by Lieutenant Colonel Moszczeński, but because of reports on the movements of an armoured-motorized column coming out of the crossings on the San near Radymno. We had been outmanoeuvred to the northeast, which posed a threat of being cut off from Lwów and from our task.

Again, ours was a paradoxical situation, because at the time of setting off for the task we had already been overtaken by German armoured-motorized units, cutting an oblique line from Radymno to Niemirów. As before in Rzeszów, the Brigade bypassed the Krakówiec [Krakovets] region in a wide arc towards the north and, despite an enforced break in the forests between Wólka Zapałowska and Lipina to wait for the delivery of petrol, we reached Niemirów, which was still free of Germans, before dawn. From there, we returned to the correct axis and, upon reaching Jaworów, managed to get out of this town to the west, to the region of Krakowiec, in order to block the Germans' advance at the most convenient position for the defence: amongst vast ponds and wetlands, although these had dried out a lot as the summer had been exceptionally arid. The reconnaissance *dywizjon* located to the west of Niemirów was to cover us from the north-west.

Again, I felt the breeze of childhood. My middle school years, carefree summer holidays spent at the estate of my uncle, a lawyer from Lwów, Karol Czerny, who was the owner of the Wielkie Oczy lands, the same that featured in Sienkiewicz's trilogy. There were four of us boys, brothers by birth (my three brothers died in the wars of 1914–1920), and two cousins of ours. One of them was Staszek Czerny, a future lieutenant in the 10th Mounted Rifles Regiment in the Armoured Division, who fought his way through the entire 1944–45 campaign with grit and humour.

Did I ever think as a young boy, playing and building forts in these woods on sandy dunes, that one day I would fight here for real?

I drove to the observation point of the Regiment's commander, Colonel Bokszczanin. Obscured by fences, among the scattered peasant cottages, we waited for the German attack, the first chords of which hit the village with torrents of artillery fire, especially the causeway and the mill by the pond.

I hardly knew Colonel Bokszczanin. He had come to the Motorized Cavalry Regiment against his will, almost on the eve of the outbreak of the war, but he had already shown bravery and character during these twelve days of heavy fighting. But it was too short a period of time for him to become a true motorized cavalryman. For decades he had been firmly rooted to the traditions of a mounted unit. He turned to me at one point and said, 'And yet, how wonderful and different it would be, if I was sitting in the saddle commanding my mounted regiment right now.' I began to list for the Colonel the kilometres marched by the Regiment since 1 September, the number of battles and skirmishes and combat achievements. I also drew his attention to the fact that, after 12 days of fighting, despite the opponent's significant quantitative and technical advantage, he was still at the head of a regiment that was unbeaten and capable of action. He seemed to have known this well himself, but reason is one thing and sentiment another.

On 12 September, we successfully defended Krakowiec – temporarily – with the 10th Mounted Rifles Regiment and at night we held an intermediate position in Porudenko with the 24th Lancers Regiment. We were only pushed out from Niemirów, the possession of which exceeded the strength of the reconnaissance *dywizjon*.

The remnants of this stubbornly militant *dywizjon*, commanded by Major Ksawery Święcicki, regrouped in Magierów. This was the end of one of the Brigade's newest units. The remnants would supplement the reduced numbers of the 24th Lancers Regiment and the 10th Mounted Rifles Regiment.

At some point during this period of crises and fighting, I was called to Lwów, to the commander of the southern front, Lieutenant General Sosnkowski.

I reached Lwów after a nightmarish night drive along roads, some parts of which were congested with everything that war can throw into motion, while other stretches loomed devoid of any signs of life and made me keep my hand constantly on my rifle in anticipation of a sinister 'Halt – Leute.'

What a different Lwów it was.

Lifeless, skulking and resigned, like someone expecting a beating. It was dark and dirty, with people creeping by, illuminated only with dying fires after the bombings.

It was not the Lwów of 1918–19, it was not the Lwów of 1920 – a proud and confident border city, standing heroically against the blows from the east.

It was not the fortress that had shielded the Republic of Poland with its breast in the hope that the country would awaken – as she needed time to awaken – as had been the case so many times in the rich history of this *semper fidelis* Polish city.

It was no longer the vanguard of the Republic of Poland.

This time it was the crumbling Republic which approached Lwów from the west to perform its final act of resistance with its dying breath, if only for the sake of posterity.

And yet a half-open gate here and there, people watching and listening… that maybe still?

People coming up to my car, with hope in their questioning eyes at the sight of my tank crewman's black jacket, hoping that perhaps some armoured units might still work a miracle. Others pressed into my hands their last cigarettes, chocolate and fruit for the Polish soldiers. Others still silently marked us with the sign of the Holy Cross.

It was no longer the vanguard, but the hopelessly abandoned rearguard. But I too did not want to face reality yet.

The 10th Cavalry Brigade was not yet defeated, the feeling of joy in fighting for Lwów still carried us, the feeling that like in 1918–19, that we were coming to the rescue.

Knowing that we could still fight, belied and stifled all black and gloomy thoughts.

I reported to the commander of the southern front, General Sosnkowski, at the headquarters of Corps District No. 6, a building which was so familiar to me.

A long conversation with the General, undaunted, full of faith in the future, despite everything. The subject was the proposal of the General, or in any case proposed by him, to break through to Przemyśl with a part the 10th Cavalry Brigade, because he wished to personally take command of the divisions abandoned by General Fabrycy (which included the 24th Infantry Division, the 11th Infantry Division and the 38th Reserve Division) and break through to Lwów with them.

Would I guarantee the success of the first part of the operation, i.e. breaking through to Przemyśl?

I was sorry to extinguish his faith and enthusiasm; it was difficult for me to disappoint raised hopes.

But this first part of the plan was completely unfeasible. We had neither the minimum of strength nor the minimum of time.

Even the entire Brigade would have been too weak to perform this task, let alone a section of it. I briefly told the General how the Brigade stood at that moment.

The two cavalry regiments represented the value of two overtired infantry battalions, with depleted numbers (50–60 per cent of establishments), eight artillery guns, and a complete lack of tanks. The Vickers were stuck with General Boruta. There was one improvised unit with ten tankettes, doing everything they could to pass for a company.

And the time restraints looked even gloomier. Even if I was not relieved by some other unit, but just left by breaking contact with the Germans and leaving Lwów undefended in the Janów – Magierów section, it would take at least twenty-four hours to assemble the Brigade for action, to gather the necessary materiel, and especially replenish the constantly low levels of petrol and ammunition. This meant that I could be ready for the dawn of 14 September, with a chance to start the operation in the evening, because only at night could I use the surprise factor to my benefit.

The 10th Cavalry Brigade was still a formation capable of fighting, performing dynamic manoeuvres and striking, but only under the condition of surprise. The effect of the surprise would last for several kilometres – with luck, over a dozen.

Generally speaking, any breakthrough is usually an act of despair, which can lead to success – or not. I could not guarantee that this act would bring General Sosnkowski in one piece to Przemyśl in time.

General Sosnkowski agreed with my arguments. A more reliable and faster route would involve flying by aircraft with his staff officer to the Przemyśl region.

With Lwów's safety in mind, General Sosnkowski subordinated the Brigade to General Langner, the commander of the defence of Lwów, with the task of screening the city from the north, because both the last battle of the 10th Brigade and the news from other sources confirmed the circumvention of the Lwów area by motorized German troops north of the Janów forests. In the future, General Sosnkowski would be able to count on the cooperation of the Brigade with the divisions from Przemyśl, when they broke through to Lwów.

In the already-functioning Lwów Defence Staff headquarters, I became acquainted with the details of the situation. Everyone there was still recovering from the recently concluded battle on Gródecka Street. In the afternoon of 12 September, some motorized German units with tanks or armoured cars had broken into Lwów from the direction of Rudek and Lubień and created a crisis on the south-western edge of the city, which was finally brought under control at 19.00 that day.

Lwów had a whole range of loose infantry and artillery units – quite difficult to coordinate – and the 35th Reserve Division of Colonel Szafran, a former commander of 41th Suwałki Regiment from back when I was in command of the 81th Grodno Rifles Regiment. Part of this Division was already in Lwów, and part of it was still on the road. The estimation of the opponent's forces was the following: one large armoured formation – probably the 2nd Armoured Division on the axis from Gródek Jagielloński, i.e. from the west – and the 4th Light Division, which was attempting to circumnavigate Lwów from the south- and north-west, and with which the 10th Cavalry Brigade was already in contact.

Lwów should have been able to hold out with the forces collecting within the city. The 10th Brigade was tasked with screening Lwów from the north and northwest.

As we later found out, the assessment was too pessimistic, with exaggeration especially in the estimation of the enemy's armoured units. At that moment, in the near and far approaches, there were actually only two German formations: the 4th Light Division, encircling the Janów forests, and one mountain division, the motorized part of which had created the first crisis in Lwów.

I agreed with General Langner, that with the current task in mind, and considering the tired Brigade units' need to rest, and the need to re-establish severed liaisons and to meet the need for materiel, it was necessary to gather in the area of Żółkiew. Therefore, General Langner subordinated to me the Polish forces that were located north of the so-called Kanał Rządowy, assembled and vigorously commanded by my colleague from the War College, Colonel Iwanowski. These units, defending their assigned areas, were the following:

- The reserve battalion of the 53rd Infantry Regiment which was holding Żółkiew,
- Colonel Gołaszewski's group – reserve infantry squadrons and a heavy machine gun squadron which were holding Majdan,
- one improvised 75mm battery,
- one improvised battery from the 6th Heavy Artillery Regiment
- and, as the only mobile units, Cavalry Captain Murasik's three squadrons of cavalry with a heavy machine gun platoon on *tachankas*.

Upon returning before dawn to the Brigade, which had already been directed towards Żółkiew, I already had some outlines of a plan of action with my now-strengthened formation.

First of all:

- to organize the troops and give them the minimum time to rest,
- to restructure them so that they would be able to perform the minimum task, that is, the defence of Lwów from the north,

but:

- to keep the option of proceeding to offensive action against the 4th Light Division, based on the fixed defence positions of Colonel Iwanowski's units – among which I did not make any changes, in accordance with the principle that whoever had been there on the job for a long time probably knew more than I did.

The mounted squadrons of Cavalry Captain Murasik could constitute a reinforcement of the active operations of the Brigade, as could a part of the artillery, provided it could be deployed – regarding which I did not have any data.

From the dawn of 13 September, my exhausted units, the men and the machines, were emerging from the Janów forests, and slowly, almost until the evening of that day, crawled to the area between Żółkiew and the valley of the Kanał Rządowy, separating us from the defence of Lwów. Only at the forest junction of Janów did a *dywizjon* of the 10th Mounted Rifles Regiment, under the command of Major Słatyński, engage in skirmishes with elements of German units. Meanwhile the second 'skirmisher,' Major Rakowski, with a *dywizjon* of the 24th Lancers Regiment advanced towards Rawa Ruska, to the town of Dobrosina, and was ambushing individual enemy cars with a German officer in one, some cooks or some petrol in another; he grew very passionate about this job.

Reports on the squadrons of Cavalry Captain Murasik and the infantry units of Colonel Iwanowski started coming in.

They began to form a coherent picture.

Major Słatyński's prisoners of war from the western side came from the technical and supply services for the Division and the Corps. The prisoners and materials taken from the northern side by Major Rakowski and Cavalry Captain Murasik came from the engineering and anti-tank units of the 4th Light Division, which clearly aimed to go through Rawa Ruska to Mosty Wielkie, i.e. the northeast, and was concealing itself from us behind obstacles.

An incredible opportunity opened up: we could hit the communication lines of this division based on our fixed defensive positions in Żółkiew, and through this diversion stop its advance, the purpose and end of which was not clear to me at that moment.

The screening of Lwów from the north would not suffer and, if this operation succeeded, it would grant me greater freedom of action once I needed to turn to the southwest to cooperate with the Przemyśl Group. I cherished the thought and had high hopes for the operation's fruition. But every bullet has its billet.

At war, besides one's own will, there is the will of the enemy, which bends or completely changes even the best laid schemes.

It all began innocently. During the night of 13–14 September, there was a slight panic at our rear, in the Brigade services, south of the Kanał Rządowy, and therefore outside of my zone of operation.

The Germans pushed some Polish support units down from the hills above Zboiska; they even seized the village itself with a company of cyclists, led by an officer in a Polish uniform.

The chief of staff, Major Skibiński, respecting my need for sleep, moved our rear units so that we were in no danger for the time being. What worried me, however, was the fact that the main road between us and Lwów was cut off, but establishing a connection with the Lwów staff calmed me down, because some units from the city were already engaged in a counter-attack. Indeed, these troops regained Zboiska, but they got stuck on the slopes of the dominant hills. A complex of elevations west of Zboiska, the highest of which was Hill 324, towered over the area between the outskirts of the city and the eastern edge of the Brzuchowice forest, over the road from Żółkiew to Lwów and as far as Dublany – Malechów, and the entire valley of the Kanał Rządowy. The hill represented the key to all operations. It was a true bastion for the defence of the city – and an ideal starting point for attacking it.

This brought me back to 1923, to a discussion of extensive exercises conducted by General Thullie and the logical premises resulting from the characteristics of the terrain. I still remember how a colleague of mine, a major from the eastern borderlands of Poland, and a soldier of the former Russian army, who was ordered at the beginning of the discussion to orientate us in the terrain, looked at the 1:100,000 scale Austrian map, got lost in the tangle of contour lines and whispered to us, 'What an Austrian map!' Then, manipulating a Bezard compass, 'What an Austrian compass!' And finally, looking despairingly at the vast landscape of hills and forests: 'What Austrian land!'

But sixteen years had passed since then!

I did not want this incident with the Germans in Zboiska to change my plan, but when, despite the still reassuring news from the Lwów staff, Zboiska returned to German hands, and my depleted reconnaissance unit got stuck there, I sent the chief of staff on a roundabout way to General Langner, to get approval to shift the Brigade's operation to this area. Connecting with Lwów through Zboiska was of paramount importance to me at that moment.

In the meantime, I issued preliminary orders aimed at increasing the concentration of the Brigade by withdrawing the allocated units from Janów and Dobrosin, shifting the entire support from the north to Colonel Iwanowski's troops and assembling a raiding unit for the action in Zboiska. It looked quite modest so far: a squadron of the 24th Lancers Regiment, an anti-tank squadron reduced to a few guns, an infantry company, which had joined us from Dublany, and the support of the motorized artillery *dywizjon*.

I appointed Lieutenant Colonel Moszczeński, who led the anti-tank *dywizjon*, as commander, and decided in favour of an attack at night, due to the unobstructed lines of sight in the approaches to both Zboiska and Hill 324.

Since the dawn of 15 September, I had been at the observation point between Grzęda and Grzybowice with the chief of staff, who had joined me on his return from Lwów with the consent of General Langner. The night assault of Lieutenant Colonel Moszczeński started at 02.00 precisely, surprised the Germans and easily drove them out of Zboiska, but it halted on the slopes of the hill when faced with the enemy's well-entrenched and well-hidden heavy weaponry.

I pulled the third battery from Żółkiew and directed the three squadrons of Cavalry Captain Murasik through the forests, so that they would engage the German formation from the west.

The action was very lively throughout the day, with varying success for both sides, and did not bring about the desired result, i.e. the control of Hill 324 over Zboiska. It did result in serious losses: Lieutenant Colonel Moszczeński and his aide-de-camp, Lieutenant Patolski, came away wounded. We lost Zboiska again. But it gave us a full picture of German forces in the area. We were not dealing with a company of cyclists as the reconnaissance had reported so far, but a considerable part of the Mountain Division. The prisoners, taken from two regiments of this division, the 98th and the 99th Infantry Regiments, talked about the support of four artillery *dywizjon*s, which I doubted very much, because the concentration of fire from the German artillery seemed of a rather middling intensity.

Later on, the dropping of containers with food and ammunition for the Mountain Division, some of which fell on our territory, as well as the testimony of further prisoners solved the puzzle: the German Mountain Division was in a supply crisis, with shortages of ammunition and no food.

Wasn't this the same situation as in 1920 in Korzec?

Our own battlegroup encouraged a concentric strike even more than it did then. I decided to strike with the whole Brigade reinforced with the squadrons of Cavalry Captain Murasik and our own company of cyclists, with the support of three artillery batteries.

The Brigade attacked in the half-dark early hours of 16 September.

The 10th Mounted Rifles Regiment with the company of cyclists and an anti-tank squadron marched to Zboiska and towards the eastern part of Hill 324.

The 24th Lancers Regiment, with an anti-tank squadron from Grzybowice, attacked the Michałowszczyzna ridge and continued to the northern slopes of the hill.

The company of tankettes remained at my disposal and established communication between the two advancing groups with short excursions along the Grzybowice – Zboiska road.

The squadrons of Cavalry Captain Murasik attacked the German rear located on the western slopes of the mountain from the eastern edge of the Brzuchowice forest.

The concentrated fire of the three batteries was in my hand.

The attack quite easily seized the first objectives and emerged on the ridge directly above the road to Lwów, as well as the extended Michałowszczyzna ridge. But beyond that, we only had minor success in the field until the evening. The capture of Zboiska cost us the loss of the wounded commander of the Regiment, Lieutenant Colonel Bokszczanin, who went to the hospital in Dublany, and the Regiment's command was taken over by Major Słatyński. The German artillery demonstrated significant firepower on occasion, which no longer made me doubt the four squadrons; but the most cumbersome and intrusive were the heavy machine guns, the firepower of which inspired full respect, even among those of us at the observation point of the Brigade and artillery command.

On the evening of 16 September, when I gathered the staff and took all the factors into cool-headed consideration, my decision was very difficult. We were clearly attacking a much stronger opponent. The prisoners of war from the battalions of all the regiments of the Mountain Division spoke to that, since in addition to those from the 98th and 99th Infantry Regiments, new ones had arrived from the 100th Infantry Regiment. This was emphasized by the fourfold advantage of artillery fire. This opponent, although stronger, was on the defence, perhaps deceived by our relentlessness, or perhaps for reasons completely unknown to us at that moment.

For equally obscure reasons, the 21st Tank Battalion, whose commander, Major Łucki, had reported to me the previous day, did not show up; it could have changed the situation so significantly, had it arrived. Such bad luck! This was the second time that a tank battalion had not arrived (the first time was from the mobilisation)! As it turned out later, Major Łucki had received different orders from the headquarters.

I had nothing specific with which to reinforce the attacking units, except the strong willingness to conquer Hill 324.

This was already dictated by the task itself. The success of the attack would ideally involve the duality of the task: the defence of Lwów from the northwest (defence, because moving south from the Kanał Rządowy already connected us with the defence of Lwów), and lending a hand to the forces of General Sosnkowski, whose battle by the River Wereszyca could be heard when the tumult and roar of the fighting on our section subsided for a moment. It was like the distant thunder of an oncoming storm.

A storm indeed, but for the Germans!

We had to conquer the hill. So the order for 17 September was an order for a general attack by all the Brigade's forces and assigned units, except for Colonel Iwanowski, who was left in Żółkiew on guard, so that we would not be threatened from the north.

The beginning of the attack was planned for 05.00, but in order not to give respite to the Germans, and because of their particular dislike of it, both my regiments would conduct night-time raids with squadrons. The foray of the squadron of the 10th Mounted Rifles Regiment had a particular terrain-centred purpose – to capture and hold, until the day-time attack, a small transverse ridge on its right flank, from which well-hidden heavy machine guns, eluding our artillery spotters, had seriously inhibited the movement of the left flank of the 24th Lancers Regiment from the Michałowszczyzna ridge. Such was the request from Colonel Dworak and it was very justified from a tactical perspective.

Both night raids went well and resulted in many prisoners, and confusion among the German defence.

For a long time into the night, German artillery rained down fire into an empty area – at an imaginary all-out Polish attack.

I do not know by what misunderstanding the squadron of the 10th Mounted Riflemen returned from the night raid, instead of remaining in the field. It might have also settled in the wrong place, despite the fact that Słatyński reported the execution of the order. This resulted in severe losses to the left flank of the 24th Infantry Regiment in the first hours of the morning and inhibited the initial momentum of the attack.

For a long time I held a grudge against Słatyński, a very combative and energetic officer.

However, on that day, all the Brigade's units competed to give of their best. It was not the stubbornness and hardiness of the lancers and the mounted riflemen, but that of elite infantry that won us one heavy machine gun after another, one source of firepower after another. They were supported by our artillery's targeting of fire, which the commander, Captain Pawłowski, who was based next to me at the observation point, moved masterfully on demand from one point to another.

The arrival of the squadrons of Cavalry Captain Murasik and a platoon of motorcyclists from the 10th Mounted Rifles Regiment with Lieutenant

Wasilewski to the eastern border of the forest beyond Hill 324 also did the job, as it confused the advance of the German battalion.

Around 16.00, Hill 324 west of Zboiska was finally captured. The fact of its capture could be both seen and heard. It brought to mind an artillery training ground, with intense fire from both sides and visible silhouettes of soldiers, jumping over the ridge, and a murmur of 'hurrahs' coming from here and there.

The hill was taken.

As it later turned out, it was the key position, through which the German commander, Colonel Schörner…

Leaving only one battalion on the western periphery of Lwów, the rest, that is, a group consisting of two battalions of the 98th Infantry Regiment and two battalions of the 99th Infantry Regiment, with the support of light artillery and two heavy *dywizjons* Colonel Schörner intended to have conquered Lwów from the north by 13 September. Judging by the prisoners from the 100th Infantry Regiment, a battalion from this regiment was certainly added here. The rest of the mountain division was already engaged in Wereszyca against the forces of General Sosnkowski.

At the moment of seizing the hill, the commander of the infantry battalion sent to me by General Langner as reinforcement, reported at my observation point. I was to have fresh troops to relieve the tired units at night.

It all seemed to have gone too well and too smoothly. This was not typical in war!

And sure enough, an alarming order to immediately cease fighting came soon after. My units were to be relieved by infantry, and I was to personally report to Lwów for further orders.

A commander would not be torn away from battle for an insignificant reason and troops in direct, close contact with the enemy would not be relieved – and by day at that!

And all that at a time when it seemed that maybe the next day we would unite with the divisions of General Sosnkowski, for whom, after capturing Hill 324, we would finally be able to do something!

I took the shortest route through Zboiska, and I went to the staff headquarters in Lwów, taking Skibiński and the quartermaster with me.

I found the staff of the defence of Lwów – although located at the same building on Bernardyński Square as before – strangely changed!

Not the walls and not the windows; these were still in place, despite the air raids and artillery bombardment. And not the personnel; they were still the same.

Then what?

An immeasurable depression was hanging in the air.

No one was interested in the report of the three-day battle for the hills around Lwów, which had ended an hour ago in total success.

Something had happened that transcended the ordinary triumphs or failures of everyday soldier's life at war.

General Langner with Colonel Rakowski, the chief of staff of General Sosnkowski, who remained in Lwów, asked me to come to the commander's office.

Lo and behold! General Langner, a well-known abstainer and hounder of officers who abused alcohol, pulled out a bottle of cherry liqueur from a cabinet, and poured four big glasses.

Although it was 18.00, I swallowed the contents of my glass almost on an empty stomach, choking on it severely. There had been no time for meals that day.

But what really gripped me in a chokehold was the grave news.

On the night of 16–17 September, the Soviets had crossed the Polish border. Intention: unknown! In the south, a defensive bridgehead had been created on the Dniester and, on the order of the Commander-in-Chief, the Brigade was to immediately move south to the region of Halicz. There was every chance for the Brigade to slip between the German and Soviet armies. However, in the event of contact with the latter, one was not to open fire immediately, but to first examine their intentions, etc.

The Brigade was gathered around Jaryczów.

The officers were convened for briefing at the manor of Major Krzeczunowicz, once a commander of the 8th Infantry Regiment in the Battle of Waręż in 1920, absent at that moment, driven somewhere by the maelstrom of war. I only met him later in Scotland and was able to thank him for the dinner and the hospitality shown then by the representative left on the estate.

In the car, returning from Lwów, we had a 'war council' of our own with my chief of staff and the quartermaster, and we decided that for the time being we would not breathe a word about the Soviets crossing the border. I would lead the vanguard myself in the car with the chief of staff, right behind the picket of three tankettes, to be able to figure out what to do quickly if need be. After all, I could not let the Brigade be taken by surprise by the actions of German or Soviet troops, but I also could not take upon my conscience an imprudent act that would provoke a Polish-Soviet war.

We really had no idea what was going on in that regard!

The Brigade marched through the night from Jaryczów through Kanał Rządowy to Bóbrka – Bohorodczany. It was painful to see the villages illuminated for the first time after eighteen days of war and blackouts.

How much more welcome it would have been to trudge on in the dark, even with the accompaniment of gunshots.

Major Grajkowski, the Brigade's head of signals, came up with a superb idea for the most effective reconnaissance. He attempted to communicate in the direction of the Polish-Soviet border at each crossing, and surprisingly, communications were not down. Polish telephone operators answered at posts A, B and C to inform us that they were free or that the Soviet army had already entered.

That showed us that the Soviet troops had stopped for the night, at about a day's march from the axis of our advancement.

Therefore, we would arrive unmolested. No trace of the Germans either.

At dawn on 18 September, I crossed the bridge over the Dniester in Halicz, where an officer from the Commander-in-Chief handed me another order: to continue the march to Stanisławów, where further orders would be given.

The fact that the transmission of orders was functioning offered the hope that comes with being under someone's command. I thought that the Brigade would probably become a reserve mobile branch of the huge bridgehead on the Dniester and Stryj rivers, beyond which there would be large Polish forces.

Nightmarish thoughts plagued me all the way.

On the eve of the war, it had seemed so sensible to send my family east to Wolyń, and to put them under the care of my old soldiers, the veterans of 1918–20; yet by doing so I pushed them right into the gaping Soviet jaws.

What would become of them?

Stanisławów early in the morning, when I was looking for the Commander-in-Chief, seemed so familiar to me and yet so different.

Some people, whom I had never seen before, roamed the streets looking suspiciously at my car. On that very day there would be attempts to stop and disarm a part of the Brigade by supporters of Soviet 'liberation'. In the abandoned school building, I found only Colonel Rudka with a telegraphed order of General Stachiewicz for the Brigade.

An order as short as it was tragic and, despite everything, unexpected. The Brigade was to cross the Polish border, remaining at the disposal of the Commander-in-Chief. The choice of the direction was left to the Brigade's commander – a passage to Romania or Hungary. I went down the stairs as if in a dream. I fretted about whether to go to my wife's mother's apartment, and what to say to her when asked where her daughter and grandchildren were.

At that moment, despite his wounded leg, Colonel Rudka quickly ran after me, shouting, 'Colonel – do you know that your wife is in Stanisławów?'

I got into the car and soon found myself in my mother-in-law's apartment; I almost pulled the family out of bed and gave them a dozen or so minutes to pack. I loaded them into the car which my wife had in Stanisławów, and I instructed the chauffeur to join the Brigade's column. It was all the work of one impulsive thought and execution.

How had they ended up there?

My wife and my two young children had set out on the second day of the war from Rzeszów to Wołyń, as we had previously agreed. They were bombed along the way and got stuck for good near Tarnopol. When the driving conditions northwards turned out to be very difficult, she had followed the advice of my officer from the 81st Regiment, Lieutenant Kazio Chojnowski, and travelled instead to Stanisławów to see her elderly mother.

And in Stanisławów she decided to stay, having received no news from me for eighteen days, except rumours that the Brigade was still fighting.

It must have been Divine Providence that directed the fate of my family, because my wife could have shared the fate of her sister, who was later shot by Ukrainian troops serving under German command.

The Brigade spent their last night in Poland from 18–19 September in Tatarów, a resort town in the Subcarpathia region, well known to me from the good old days.

On 19 September, in the afternoon, in a column arranged as for a parade, with all the artillery guns except for one stray one (which had rolled into a ravine on a sharp turn) and with all the anti-tank guns that had not been crushed by German tanks, with its numbers diminished from over 3,000 men to fewer than 1,500 – the Brigade crossed the Polish-Hungarian border.

Hungary

In a quiet village beyond the Carpathians, now on Hungarian soil, I fell into a blessed slumber that lasted for a whole day and night. I wasn't awakened by the roaring of engines, or by the sound of air raids and artillery fire, or by the ringing of telephones or the monotonous voice of the operator, or by the tramp of messengers' feet, or by murmured orders punctuated by loud shouts. I was not concerned for my family, because they were safe and sound nearby.

Those eighteen days and nights without any, or with little, sleep, in a state of constant tension, had entirely exhausted me, and had dulled my sensitivity and ability to embrace the scale of our defeat.

To sleep – to sleep – and think of nothing, that was the one thing I wanted.

It was only after a few days that these worries returned and settled on my mind, like flies on empty plates in a country cottage.

What next? Where next?

Where was the Polish army, regrouping on Hungarian territory, to whom we were linked by alliance and by brotherhood? 'Pole and Hungarian – two brothers!'[9]

But soon after, even the semblance of a decision was to be taken away from me. I wouldn't have to concern myself with whether to attack or to defend, on the left or the right flank.

Namely, a brigadier from the General Staff, who had been sent from Budapest, requisitioned the Brigade's anti-tank guns – gently at first, as if from a child. Apparently, there was a fear that enemy tanks would creep through the mountain gorges behind us. (Whose?) 'The Hungarian army has no anti-tank guns. You want to help us, don't you?' In return, the brigadier provided the Brigade with supplies, and very well indeed. However, only two days later, he appeared again with an order that the brigade should hand over all small-calibre weapons, to avoid the prospect of Polish and Hungarian blood being shed if the soldiers started to wander about. Only officers were allowed sidearms.

I didn't appreciate such 'concern' for us and our 'mutual bloodshed'. I refused to carry out the order unless I received it from my commanding officer or from the Polish authorities.

---

9. Translators: In Polish: Polak, Węgier dwa bratanki. A popular proverb reflecting a celebrated historical bond between Polish and Hungarian nations, dating back to the 18th century.

There was a long conference, adjourned until the following day, with a further brigadier who bore the initials IB (Istvan Batory) – like the infantry regiment which I had commanded in Grodno. It was held in the presence of a delegate of the Polish Legation to Hungary. In the end, Hungary would have no choice but to intern us, and Hitler's pressure would soon demand much more from them.

However, back then, we cherished certain illusions.

In a private and confidential conversation with me, the delegate of the Hungarian staff promised that the Hungarian authorities would turn a blind eye and not interfere with the evacuation of the Brigade to France, as long as it was careful, quiet and carried out in stages.

There was to be no more bargaining or, indeed, commanding.

After acceding to my request that the Brigade's units be interned together with their officers, the Hungarian officers who had been sent to us started to 'command', directing us to various barracks and camps.

Although the Hungarian brigadier's assurance had calmed my misgivings about the future fate of the Brigade's soldiers, the large numbers of Hungarian officers who were clearly pro-Nazi raised some doubts. I remember a colonel who tried to explain to me the 'absurdity' of going to France, to wander needlessly, since my whole brigade could potentially survive the war in quite bearable conditions – as snug as a bug in a rug. He argued that he was especially surprised that the officers were so active as, in his view, the officer rank lived and died with the government and the state. The best proof of that is that they ceased to receive salaries. He didn't want to understand, when I corrected his reasoning, that the officer class lives and falls with the nation, and the Polish nation, however difficult its situation might be, had not fallen. This was evidenced by the fact that even the most miserable slacker in my Brigade wanted to continue fighting for Poland, from no matter which country.

But at the same time, the wonderful Hungarian people welcomed the 10th Cavalry Brigade warmly. We were hosted and fêted, fed and watered everywhere and at all times. The sun-drenched Hungarian landscape was a joy to behold. It is hard to forget so much hospitality and such kindness.

One day, the Brigade's staff was transported by truck to a small town, which we reached late in the evening. The entire population of the town had come to the market square and in no time they had snatched us away and divided us up among themselves. My family and I ended up at the expensive home of the post office owner. The hosts took themselves elsewhere so that we could have the best rooms.

We hardly ever got up from the table, which was always set with delicious food and wine, because whole processions of people came to see us and to greet us.

When, after a few days, the moment of parting came (because I had decided to head to Budapest, breaking free from the care of the 'guardian angels', i.e. the Hungarian officers assigned to me), the lovely hosts, weeping, showed us around their rich pantries and hiding places, pointing out the wealth of provisions and begging us to stay with them throughout the war, if only because my children were so small. Their cordiality and hospitality did not cease. When the escapade to Budapest ended with our being interned in an officer's house on the Austrian border, we received by post a whole package of food supplies, fruit, and sweets for the children, in exchange for our letter of thanks for having hosted us.

Once in the camp, I was trying to liaise with the camps where my Brigade's units were located; Major Słatyński was the easiest to find. The chief of staff Major Skibiński and quartermaster Maleszewski had escaped Hungary relatively easily and were already on their way to France.

The colonel, who was the camp commandant, was extremely charmed by Hitler. It took some doing to escape from his care within a few weeks.

We managed it as follows:

My wife, to whom the ever-polite commandant had also extended the principle of internment, obtained a pass to Budapest under the guise of needing to consult a well-known doctor. At the Polish Legation, she had false passports with visa made for us, as well as for several officers and my chauffeur, Corporal Kochański. Most importantly, she found us some civilian clothes. She brought a whole package of these with her, as a 'gift' from some Hungarian aristocrat for the poor internees. Armed with a certificate of admission to the hospital in Budapest and a letter signed by the same aristocrat promising that she would take the children into her home for the duration of my wife's treatment, she officially left the camp on the following day, escorted with all the honours by the unfailingly courteous colonel.

In the evening, dressed in civilian clothes, together with Major Bittner, Captain Pruszyński and others, we crawled through a hole in the rickety fence of the park, and walked a few extra miles to the next railway station, as gendarmes would have questioned us at the local station. And then, simply by purchasing tickets, without being bothered by anyone, we arrived in Budapest.

After that we were skilfully helped and guided by the officers of our Legation until we were seated in a Pullman headed for Italy.

Each party of soldiers from the 10th Cavalry Brigade went through something similar, with greater or lesser difficulty, depending on the attitude of the Hungarian officers assigned to them.

And so, Colonel Dworak completely won over the Hungarian colonel who was 'also from the erstwhile Austrian Army' and from the Theresianum Military

Academy, with reminiscences of the highs and lows of the Imperial Austrian Army and the First World War.

Major Słatyński, although he did not speak much German, let alone Hungarian, nearly drank himself to death every night with the Hungarian colonel who was the commander of his camp, in order to consolidate the friendship between the Poles and Hungarians. Every night before midnight, a sergeant of the gendarmerie approached their table in the officers' mess with a report about what time and in what direction his patrols would be going; or rather, emphasizing when and where they would *not* be. To which the Hungarian colonel, leaning towards Słatyński, would add: 'Only, no more than thirty men.' Thus, after a few weeks, the 10th Cavalry Brigade, after the September Campaign in Poland and internment in Hungary, found itself travelling slowly and in 'instalments' towards the new assembly point in France.

*　*　*

I seem to recall that on the evening of 21 October, I found myself, along with my family, at the Italian-French border station, already on the French side.

France!

The French Campaign –
The Period of Organization

On the night of 21–22 October 1939, my family and I arrived in Paris. At ten o'clock the next day I reported to the Commander-in-Chief at the Hotel Regina.

I had not served under General Sikorski either in the war of 1918–20 nor in peacetime. I had started my university studies in Lwów at the same time as the General was completing his, and I was a small pawn on the growing political scene when General Sikorski was already a well-known activist.

In the years 1925–26 the General was the commander of Corps District No. 6 in Lwów; after graduating from the War College, I was appointed as the head of the local branch of the 2nd Department, in Lwów. I reported directly to the head of the 2nd Department in Warsaw in matters of intelligence, but I was obliged to make occasional reports on the situation in the eastern approaches to the corps commander.

It was only then that I got to know the General personally, both during my official reports, as well as off duty.

General Sikorski welcomed me very warmly. He already knew the story of the 10th Cavalry Brigade's involvement in the September Campaign and was full of praise for the bravery of its soldiers. He offered me the command of the 1st Polish Infantry Division, which was being formed, and made much of the honour of commanding the first Polish unit on French soil.

For the time being, he appointed me as the commander of Polish troops in the Coëtquidan camp in Brittany – to replace General Jerzy Ferek-Błeszyński.

Promoted to Brigadier General, I took command of the camp, which was the centre for the formation of the Polish units.

At the beginning, everything was in short supply in this camp: accommodation, uniforms and armaments. Everything except for two things: men pouring in from all sides, who were to constitute the infantry units, and unsolicited advice from the French on how to make an army out of all of this.

The influx began with volunteers from France, with the tremendously patriotic sons of Polish emigrants; then came men from all over the world, mainly officers and non-commissioned officers who had been evacuated from Hungary and

Romania, and finally came Poles from French immigrant communities; the French government had extended to General Sikorski the right to military conscription among these communities.

The few dozen barracks quickly became very crowded and soon the Coëtquidan camp absorbed the humble local Breton villages, which provided very primitive and poor accommodation for the winter, in granaries and attics.

But the 'eagerness' was there, so the Polish soldiers endured these poor conditions with admirable patience, dreaming of the front – as if it had been the height of comfort and convenience.

We prioritized the infantry, since the French had only agreed to the formation of such units. There was a vision of creating Polish infantry regiments, from which, by adding French artillery regiments and technical troops, infantry divisions would be formed. There were various reasons for choosing this path, some of them perhaps correct from the French point of view, such as the time needed for training and the fact that there were already large numbers of French artillery units available, etc. But those reasons were unacceptable for the Polish side. Soon General Sikorski succeeded in securing the artillery and all the units that were coherent parts of an infantry division.

In addition to excessive French administration, the camp was also flooded with French instructors who had a satisfactory level of expertise – for peacetime. They were very eager to teach us how to fight – us, some of whom were veterans of the first clash with the Germans and were willing to share these recent combat experiences with our allies. Wrongly identifying the reasons for the Polish defeat as the inadequate basic training of the soldiers, they perceived the manoeuvres of the fusilier and grenadier sections within the infantry formation as the height of military philosophy. It looked completely hopeless! This manoeuvre wouldn't have worked in an actual attack against tanks, such as at Wysoka or Kasina Wielka – or even in the attack on Hill 324 near Lwów!

But soon, more open minds such as General Faury, a former director of the Warsaw War College and my professor from 1923–1924, understood the paradox of the situation. And, as it turned out later, they tried to help as much as they could.

When was the idea of the Polish armoured division born?

As early as 1 September 1939, in the course of the battle with the German 2nd Armoured Division at Wysoka?

Or did it grow steadily during the September struggle against the overwhelming armoured advantage of the Germans?

Or was it in Hungary, when my unencumbered mind was reviewing the course of the September Campaign and hope was stirring in light of the news that General Sikorski was establishing a Polish army in France?

It is very difficult to pinpoint the exact date in the calendar!

I certainly raised the matter in my first conversation with General Sikorski in Paris and, perhaps on the basis of this, I obtained priority for the evacuation of the 10th Cavalry Brigade from Hungary, although at that point without a clear commitment from the Commander-in-Chief as to the possibility of a Polish armoured division.

And I certainly didn't want to talk to General Faury about anything else but our September experiences and about the future Polish *division légère mécanique*, slowly infecting him with my enthusiasm.

At the same time, the staff and officers of the 10th Cavalry Brigade promulgated the idea of a future armoured division at every step, both at the Staff Headquarters of the Commander-in-Chief in Paris and at the camp in Coëtquidan.

As the evacuation of the 10th Cavalry Brigade from Hungary progressed, I obtained the consent of General Sikorski to ringfence it entirely, protecting this discrete formation full of valuable soldiers from being scattered throughout the emerging infantry division.

This is how a centre for cavalry and armoured weapons was created near the camp, in Paimpont and Campeneac, into which I incorporated, under the guise of the 10th Cavalry Brigade, not only every cavalryman and tank crewman I could lay my hands on, but also every mechanic and technical specialist, and even the more proficient car drivers.

Meanwhile, our talks with the French slowly began to show results. Slowly, because General Faury himself had been coaxed out of retirement, and his friend, General Boucherie, an armoured forces theorist, had long since retired. It took a long time before our report on the September Campaign made its way into the hands of French military decision-makers. We had gone to a great deal of trouble over this report – mainly Skibiński and, as far as I remember, Stankiewicz – but it was worth it, because when I was summoned to the staff headquarters together with General Faury, I finally received an answer: 'You will have your *division légère mécanique*, but only for your return to Poland and to conditions of mobile warfare; we, the French, have the Maginot Line – and at the moment we do not need a Polish armoured division'.

Although the answer was negative, it left a door open for the future, and this was certainly in large part due to the talks which were proceeding simultaneously between the staff of the Commander-in-Chief and the French staff.

One aspect of our position, however, was severely weakened. It became increasingly difficult to hide away the specialists, and we even needed to give up a certain number of them, especially the car drivers, to divisions whose formation had been prioritized.

As time passed, the organization of the Polish infantry division progressed methodically. We went through a tense period during the formation of the Finnish 'expedition', for which the Campenéac centre had to come up with a tank company.

The Polish Independent Highland Brigade had begun to form when, in February 1940, we saw the first modest developments in relation to our armoured future. The centre for cavalry and armoured weapons was moved south to the area of Avignon – the village of Orange-Bollène.

The centre was supposed to constitute the beginnings of an armoured motorized brigade, but soon a decision was made to create a *division légère mécanique*, albeit with a very distant date set for its formation: the spring of 1941.

When I was concluding my service at the Coëtquidan camp and assuming command of the newly-created centre, I reported to the Commander-in-Chief in Paris.

General Sikorski was visibly disappointed that, as he put it, 'for my beloved 10th Brigade, I was giving up command of the 1st Infantry Division, which would fight the Germans sooner.' But in fact, he understood well the need to create this armoured division, as well as the fact that I was already personally connected with it.

We received a dozen or so elderly but functioning tanks, a tank firing range, and a dozen or so cars and motorcycles, more for administrative purposes than for combat training.

From March 1940, the crews of four tank battalions began to train on these tanks. New recruits from old cavalry regiments, as well as from reconnaissance and anti-tank divisions, were being trained on drivers' courses.

But the combat training situation for everything other than tanks was much worse. Neither the motorized cavalry units, nor the motorized or anti-tank artillery units could secure even a dozen or so heavy machine guns or light machine guns and field or anti-tank guns. And so, in April, during combat exercises, among the already budding vineyards of Avignon and Châteauneuf-du-Pape, a thick stick represented a heavy machine gun, and a thinner stick a light rifle.

Did we waste a lot of time on this? Undoubtedly. For the motorized units the two-three months of training without weapons were a sham. And the loss of these two, three months would soon turn out to be irreparable.

The German offensive of May 1940 broke through the French front in the north, allowing German armoured divisions to reach the Somme. Simultaneously, in the south near Avignon, it smashed through the front of French ignorance and reluctance towards the Polish armoured division. Suddenly, the creation of this division became almost a matter of saving France, and sending at least part of the not quite ready armoured-motorized brigade to fight on the Marne became a matter of 'to be or not to be' for the northern front in France. That's how the

French put it, or at least that's how it was presented by General Denain, the head of the Military Mission at the staff headquarters of the Commander-in-Chief, and then in talks with General Sikorski, General Weygand and Marshal Pétain.

Now they wanted a Polish armoured division – immediately, and desperately. In the second half of May, we received an order to accelerate the formation. We had to dissuade the French from enacting a different dangerous idea – creating a dozen or so anti-tank companies out of the entire centre at Avignon and dividing them among the units along almost the entire French front. In the end, the earlier idea of the formation of an armoured division prevailed.

To speed up the organization, our entire motley crew was moved north to the Paris, Versailles and Arpajon areas at the end of May, bringing us closer to the main armoured and motorized vehicle depots.

Up to this point we had had problems getting even one heavy machine gun or an old car or motorcycle for training, but from then on, from dawn to dusk and even at night, materiel began to flow our way: tanks, anti-tank guns, heavy machine guns, cars, motorcycles and, from various Polish centres, surplus soldiers from the infantry, artillery, aviation and other units.

A great deal of work was on our hands.

But an armoured unit – a technical unit – is not built in a day, or improvised.

One had to contain the continuous stream of surplus soldiers, assigning the men, with some sense of their suitability, to appropriate units; to organize new units, to secure the equipment and the weapons, to get acquainted with the handling of new, unfamiliar ordnance.

All this was too much in such a short period, even with twenty-four-hour long days.

Therefore, when, after two weeks of struggling with this organizational and training chaos, I was ordered to immediately detach a part of the *division légère mécanique* and hand it over to the frontline commander as an armoured-motorized brigade, I simply did not want to believe that this was a serious order.

And the order was given by the military attaché, General Denain, in a manner close to blackmail: Either carry out the order, or return the weapons which had already been collected, for which unarmed French units were supposedly waiting.

This second alternative, considering the morale of the soldiers who had been waiting for guns for six months, and who would now have to give them back almost immediately after receiving them, was absolutely unacceptable to us.

I went looking for help in high places to find a way out of this difficulty.

I sent my chief of staff to General Sikorski and asked for intervention.

We could neither give up our weapons nor send something so ridiculously unprepared to the front. We needed at least a few weeks to muster a half-decent armoured brigade. We understood the tragedy of the situation, which forced the French to summon everything that could counter the German pressure.

But the intervention of General Sikorski, asking for these several weeks of delay, ended up having the opposite effect. In response, Marshal Pétain urgently requested that the armoured brigade be placed at the disposal of the French army. There was no choice but to agree.

Only one tank battalion was just completing the collection of its equipment and was ready to deploy, along with the commander of the armoured regiment, Colonel [płk. dypl.] T. Majewski. The second tank battalion awaited its tanks and it was estimated that they would arrive within a week. The readiness of these battalions was only based on there being a sufficient number of trained crews, which constituted the nucleus of four battalions. The rest, i.e. the motorized part, was in utter chaos, due to having been rapidly replenished from surpluses with different types of weapons, which were only now being sent to us.

After very careful consideration of the options available, so as not to ruin forever the possibility of the future creation of full regiments of motorized cavalry, motorized artillery and anti-tank artillery, we decided we could field, with great detriment to the units under formation, the following:

- One squadron of the 24th Lancers Regiment with a motorcycle platoon;
- One squadron of the 10th Mounted Rifles Regiment with motorcyclists;
- One anti-tank battery;
- One anti-aircraft battery;
- One communications platoon;
- One traffic control platoon.

From 24 May, when the first news of the formation of the first *echelon* of the *division légère mécanique* had arrived, to 6 June, the day when this 'improvisation' was ready, only fourteen days had elapsed.

Who was to lead this avant-garde – this improvisation?

There was no doubt in my mind that it had to be me personally. I left my deputy, Colonel Dworak, to organize the rest of the units and to send them to me gradually, as they formed and became ready to enter the field. The first one to join me was supposed to be the second battalion of tanks.

As core staff, I took with me the officers with whom I worked best: Major Skibiński, Captain Stankiewicz, Cavalry Captain Pieregorodzki and Cavalry Captain Mincer.

I was rather an incorrigible optimist, still believing that I would build an entire armoured brigade at the front, as the materiel was eventually sourced. But even the greatest pessimist among us did not foresee a complete collapse of both the front and the whole of France before we had the chance to carry out this plan.

As I was departing, I had a long conversation with Colonel Dworak; we settled everything that could be settled in this chaos and, overtaking the railway transport of the Brigade, I went with the chief of staff to the commander of the Army Group, General Huntziger.

Hours of sitting passively in the car have always been conducive to reflection, a calm mulling over of the situation. A comparison sprang to mind with the 10th Motorized Cavalry Brigade setting out on 1 September 1939 towards the battle for Podhale. Back then, nine months ago, we were missing one tank battalion, which was supposed to emerge out of the mobilisation process and did not reach us until the end of the action. Now I had a battalion of good, if slow, tanks, poorly balanced by only two squadrons of motorized cavalry and anti-tank weapons. Apart from that, the artillery and support services were completely lacking. We were a typical mayfly of a unit, existing for a single tactical use, after which we would be spent, if the rest of the units did not arrive. And even assuming there was a rapid reunion with the others, how much time would elapse before we synchronized and merged and formed a brigade as capable of independent action as the 10th Cavalry Brigade had been back in Poland?

But the fact was that the premature collapse of France upset all our calculations. Nothing would come of the units formed around Paris. Even the second tank battalion would not come to us!

As for our support in rescuing the critical situation on the French front, it would be nothing more than a gentlemanly gesture on Poland's part, demonstrating that, to the very end, the Poles had given their all to save France.

* * *

This 'improvisation' of ours was called the 10th Armoured Cavalry Brigade, and this name, and not our actual qualitative and quantitative force, or rather lack of it, determined the manner in which we were employed. We were given tasks suited to a normal armoured-motorized brigade, and even tasks that exceeded the capabilities of such a formation. After all, we ourselves, the actors in these events, also use this name when talking about the past. We wanted to attempt missions which conformed to the name, which sounded so sweet to our ears.

The 10th Armoured Cavalry Brigade. Let's emphasize this difference clearly: 'armoured', not 'motorized', as it had been in September in Poland. All in all, this was a big step towards creating an armoured division!

Approaching the front at the Marne, I could hear from a distance the hollow but continuous pounding of guns and aerial bombardment. I had left Colonel Dworak near Paris, with an indeterminate amount of people and equipment in order to form the rest of the Brigade; I had already left General Regulski near Avignon with a core of units: our hope of developing a full *division légère mécanique.*

We had also left behind all our families, who were in the care of General Sikorski and were to be transferred to the Mende region.

The French Campaign – The Front

After reporting to General Huntziger, the Army Group Commander, and to General Requin, the commander of the 4th French Army fighting for Reims, I received my first combat assignment. A weighty task, designed for a large armoured motorized formation: to cover the army's flank due to the huge gap that existed between this army and the one defending Paris. We found ourselves between a division on the left flank, part of General Requin's Army – the 20th Infantry Division – and, lost somewhere to the east of us, the 59th Infantry Division, a formation on the left flank of the neighbouring army. We twice tried to make contact with the headquarters of the 59th Division, but its units existed only on a map overlay at the staff headquarters. Wherever we sought contact with them in the direction given to us, we encountered Germans. Thus, it was impossible to accomplish the task of linking the diverging flanks of the two armies and filling the gap between them. The operational task of covering the army's flank needed to be extended to covering its rear and its lines of communication, because no one was blocking the Germans from a deep encirclement manoeuvre from the west. We absolutely did not have the forces for that. The only thing we could offer was a tactical cover of the flank and the rear of the 20th Infantry Division on the right. That we managed to do. At a critical moment in the Division's retreat through the Saint-Gond marshes, we saved it from being cut off by a German advanced unit – by attacking Champaubert-Montgivroux. The battle itself was a short clash of our tank battalion with German tanks; Lieutenant Colonel Zgorzelski with two motorized cavalry squadrons covered this manoeuvre from the north. We suffered in the raids of German *Stukas*, which returned twice and, constantly dive-bombing, bombarded the group which consisted of the tank battalion with the anti-aircraft battery – and what passed for a staff headquarters, though it fit comfortably in two cars. Our anti-aircraft battery took down one German aircraft and did not stop firing for one moment, even when fiercely attacked by the *Stukas*.

Their first raid took me by surprise just as we reached the tank battalion and the two anti-tank and anti-aircraft batteries gathering in the sparse forest undergrowth.

A line of French infantry was retreating in our direction, which compressed our forces in the forest even more and blocked the only road available for motor vehicles with equipment.

The tanks slammed shut their hatches and the crews were relatively safe from the showers of shrapnel.

But in the open field we had to look for some shelter, the more so since an ammunition truck from the anti-tank unit, hit directly, would burn like a torch and scatter exploding shells around.

I shared a hollow in the ground with a French infantryman, who later couldn't get over his admiration at having had such a high-ranking comrade in arms by his side.

The German dive-bombers kept returning and, for an hour, tormented the poor forest and us with it.

The effect of aerial bombs, targeted with relative accuracy, was heightened by the acoustic effects: the characteristic whistling of the aircrafts' nose-diving and the projectiles' fall, as well as the howling of the aircraft lifting almost right above our heads. Anyone who goes through such an air raid has the impression that they are the personal target of such a dive, and that the German airman wants to strike them directly. This unpleasant feeling is increased due to the passivity of waiting for it all to finally end.

But despite this incident, our tanks, less sensitive to such air strikes, came out in time to do their job.

This battle, although fitful and short-lived, halted the German tanks, which belonged to what was most likely some reconnaissance unit, for twenty-four hours. The 20th Infantry Division made its way out of the danger zone unchallenged and passed south of the Saint-Gond marshes. Later, in the zone unoccupied by the Germans, General Weygand and General de la Porte du Theil (commander of the VIII Corps and of the 20th Infantry Division) would openly express how thankful they were for that rescue.

However, as regards the operational task of covering the rear of the 4th Army, I was aware from the beginning that it exceeded any of our capabilities against German armoured raids, the scale of which was still unknown to us.

Aligned parallel to the 20th Division in a general direction towards the south, in light contact from time to time with German reconnaissance, on roads clogged with the evacuation of military equipment and civilians, with the Brigade fragmented among this avalanche of people and machines, I tried to do everything possible to not become entangled with this helpless mass of refugees. First of all, my staff and I, through the French liaison officers headed by Colonel Duchon, were seeking out contact with the commanders of the French units, begging for tasks and cooperation. Through Colonel Duchon we received an order to concentrate the Brigade on the Seine. We were in contact with the staff of the XXIII Corps for twenty-four hours.

Then we arranged a parallel passage across the Seine to the west with the 2nd Infantry Division. On 15 June, we crossed the bridge at Bar-sur-Seine, which was intact, and reached a more wooded area, despite being harassed by the German air force. There, finally, we came across the commander of the French 42nd Infantry Division, a general equally lost in the mass moving south, but full of initiative and the will to escape from the impasse. His idea was to break through to the west and stage what he imagined would be the Battle of the Loire. I don't know if he had any grounds for it, but we accepted his illusion with 100 per cent faith, looking to the French resistance to get a foothold somewhere and counterattack the enemy in great style. The fall of Paris (which we had only learned about that day) would not determine defeat in the war after all. There was still a huge stretch of country up to the Pyrenees; there were also overseas colonies. The general, commander of the 42nd Infantry Division, left, gladly accepting our cooperation, and promised to send us detailed instructions after consulting the Corps with which he was trying to liaise. While we were waiting for these, we assembled the brigade in the forest of Chaource and devoted all our efforts to one overriding concern – to provide the tanks and vehicles with petrol. Having no Brigade supply columns, we lived haphazardly on petrol which we took from whichever depot was nearest; as a result of the French retreat, we faced the prospect of a complete lack of supplies. All the depots to which we had sent our supply trucks were either in German hands, or had been bombed by the German air force – and were therefore a sea of flames – or had otherwise been destroyed prematurely by the first wave of French troops in retreat. The vehicles sent out came back empty or did not return at all, the officers and non-commissioned officers sent out returned with nothing or did not return at all. We learned about their fate, such as that of Major Mincer, much later, probably only in Great Britain.

When orders came from the Corps for the Brigade to take the town of Montbard on the Burgundy Canal, acting as the vanguard and securing a passage west across the Canal, we were faced with reality.

Taking into account a sixty-kilometre-long march, a short fight and a minimal reserve of petrol, and assuming very optimistically that some petrol would be found afterwards, we could take with us only a minimum of tanks and motor vehicles. So, despite the protests of Colonel Duchon, who was lost and confused about the whole situation, we refuelled seventeen tanks and all the vehicles needed for the motorized troops, destroying the rest of the tanks and vehicles – useless now that they were out of petrol.

The Brigade, such as it was, had been reduced to the strength of a reinforced tank company, with two squadrons of motorized cavalry, sappers and anti-tank and anti-aircraft artillery. It plunged once again into an avalanche of retreat and evacuation, and pushed laboriously towards the Burgundy Canal. There was no reconnaissance, as there was no one to conduct it. The two platoons of motorcyclists, whose numbers were melting like a candle stuck to a hot plate, did their best to ensure communication between the troops, to protect their movements, especially at the intersections with roads leading from the west, from the German side, and to look for supplies, petrol, etc. It would have been impossible to maintain communication with any reconnaissance, in view of the complete absurdity of them having to return to us against the current.

What served as a substitute for reconnaissance was instead the rather exaggerated, often panicked, news about the Germans from here and there. We had to sift through it calmly to get at a grain of truth. The most obvious warning sign was the sudden emptiness on the roads and an ominous silence just as before a storm – when the Germans were already close.

Several kilometres before Montbard, French military and civilian vehicles, sometimes returning in panic from that direction, announced the presence in that town of German motorized units with artillery. We received relatively accurate information from the retreating artillery battery under the command of Captain Borotra, a well-known and celebrated tennis ace, and later a less famous minister in the Pétain government. In a roadside ditch, Borotra shared with us the chicken we had offered, and washed it down with some decent wine, but he excused himself from cooperating with us in the Montbard operation because he had different orders from his superiors. However, his single battery of artillery would have been of great help.

With the emptiness of the roads ahead, there was even room for tactical reconnaissance, but the possibility of betraying our position, foolishly and prematurely, warned against it. We were only a small handful, certainly smaller than those we aimed to strike, completely without field artillery. The night was approaching. The only hope of success was through complete surprise. One had to take that risk. I gathered the officers and entire tank crews on the road in front of the tanks and briefly explained my plan:

'Success lies in surprise!

You were taught, and have come to take it for granted, that under normal circumstances tanks do not attack at night, and that tanks do not attack forests or towns. But in our circumstances, that's all we can do. Let us remember Warsaw and our unsettled score with Germany. Let the tanks drive into the town, carving a path for the motorized squadrons behind you, and the element of surprise must yield results.'

Whether I used those actual words, I don't remember – but that was what I meant, and thank God I was understood, on this route to Montbard, with almost the final gallons of petrol, and the final chance to fight and, God willing, to break through to the west.

As I anticipated, our night-time tank attack on Montbard was a complete surprise for the Germans, a battalion from the 66th Regiment of the 13th Armoured Division. Their guards posted along the road ran off, almost without a shot being fired. Tanks quickly slid down the steep bend of the road towards the first buildings of the city, dragging in their wake both squadrons of motorized cavalry, which were energetically commanded by Major Zgorzelski, Major Ejysmont, Lieutenant Niepokojczycki and Lieutenant Kamil Czarnecki.

At the bend of the road, next to the captured German 88mm gun, and illuminated by a telephone pole burning like a torch, Lieutenant Colonel Majewski with aide-de-camp Captain Stefanowicz, chief of staff Skibiński, Captain Stankiewicz and myself experienced every part of this battle which was to decide our breakthrough. We could hear the distinct roar of our tanks' guns and the crackle of the cavalrymen's hand grenades. Somewhere from the deep dark, in our direction, but blindly and much too high, came the fire of German heavy machine guns and anti-tank guns, so that for some time we found ourselves under a luminous shower of shells. It was clear to me that the surprised Germans, not yet well versed in the situation, were setting a firewall in front of their own support positions, which had been taken out by us long before.

The fight slowly moved deeper into the town, with increasing German resistance. We took many prisoners, but our own losses also began to increase.

We received the comforting news that the bridge over the Burgundy Canal, which remained intact, had been taken, but it soon turned out that it was just a bridge on a branch of the Canal, and that the actual important one was still in German hands.

In this tense situation, word came from (I believe) our liaison officer to the corps commander that the French Division was not following the Brigade, but had changed its direction of march south towards Dijon.

Soon after, a loud detonation. It seemed that the Germans had blown up the bridge over the Burgundy Canal, afraid that it might fall into our hands undamaged. As the quantitatively weaker opponent, we treated it as a compliment. Very bitter satisfaction indeed!

In the end, it turned out we were wrong. In fact, as we later learned, the bridge remained intact, but the units of the 13th Armoured Division, on high alert, were already in firm control of the western bank of the Canal, ruling out any chance of our 'handful' breaking through to the west – in view of the already evident disparity between the size of the Polish and German forces.

It was 2 o'clock in the morning. And the blessed nights are always so short in June!

I paid a high psychological price in changing my decision. I had been too emotionally attached to the idea of breaking through the Germans. Also, I was too close to this battle from start to finish, caring about its every detail.

We needed to change our plans; we had neither the forces nor, above all, the artillery to cross the Canal.

Perhaps it would be possible to overtake the Germans and cross further south, and then to head west.

The kindly dense morning fog obscured both our withdrawal from Montbard to the forest and the evacuation of the wounded, including Major Ejsymont. A new regrouping meant a further reduction in the number of tanks to just a handful, for the spearhead of our little vanguard.

The race with the Germans was lost from the start; while we were fighting a unit of the 13th Armoured Division, other German divisions were already advancing on Dijon, cutting off our chances of extricating ourselves from the encirclement – as we were soon to find out.

Probing almost every crossing along the Canal and finding them in German hands, we reached the Dijon area. We were still desperately looking for a route through which to escape with any suitable vehicles; we continued to collect leftover petrol cans left here and there on the roads.

When all else failed, one final tragic alternative remained.

Dijon was occupied by the Germans, and the roads leading to this city were full of German tanks and motor vehicles. From the north, the constant advance of the German troops had reduced the unoccupied area to several square kilometres.

I had about five hundred soldiers with firearms remaining. Tanks and cars, anti-tank and anti-aircraft guns no longer played any role due to the lack of petrol and ammunition. Another five hundred had been lost – partially due to deaths and wounds after two battles and reconnaissance actions, but mostly these were losses from the march, due to the fact that various parts of the Brigade had been cut off – sometimes by French units, sometimes by the actions of German units. For example, a part of the column with a company of sappers did not reach us before the Battle of Montbard. Thanks to the quick-thinking and courage of Captain Neklaws when attacked by the Germans on the march, the unit wasn't destroyed and even took prisoners but, being diverted from the direction of the advance, it did not manage to reach us. We learned about it later, in the unoccupied part of France.

It was hard to take the final decision to destroy the remaining equipment – already completely useless – and to try to break through the ring of German armoured and motorized troops on foot. The hilly terrain, partly forested or covered with vineyards, prompted us to try to get out of the trap along roads unsuitable for motorbikes, or straight across the fields. After a night spent dismantling equipment in a place we called the Moloy Cemetery, we started our march in the early morning of 18 June.

I set out, leading the way with Skibiński and Stankiewicz, and others followed in units, led by their officers. By noon we had covered a dozen or so meandering kilometres. The mood was generally good, despite fatigue and a difficult situation. The Battle of Montbard was very uplifting for the soldiers. However, when I heard more pessimistic rumours that it was all for nothing and that not a single soul would come out of this trap alive, I gathered the officers and asked them to put on a show with cheerful faces, whether they believed or not that we would make it through – because the soldiers were looking at us and their morale depended on us.

Soon, however, the most important problem came to the fore: how to feed our five hundred people, when the success of our attempt depended on us avoiding even small settlements? Only individual isolated houses or farms turned out to be free of Germans, and the poor farmers offered a loaf of bread, a litre of wine, or a few eggs – far too little for five hundred hungry and thirsty mouths. Another practical problem emerged as well: how to hop over the roads along which German troops were advancing, with so many people walking in single file (as the terrain and forest paths made it impossible to form compact formations).

In the evening, when we stopped in the woods right before the main route to Dijon, clogged with German troops, I called a short briefing. Everyone agreed with my idea, as there was no other way out. I ordered them to divide into small groups and to advance further south-west under the guidance of officers or the most energetic soldiers. We distributed money and scarce supplies. My staff vigorously began to draw hundreds of sketches of roads and towns, based on their single Michelin road map. We agreed on how to find each other once again and where to go once we were in the part of France unoccupied by the Germans.

Each took the minimum of his belongings so as not to burden himself on the march, adding a few trinkets of sentimental personal value. From my car, I took a small statue of Our Lady of Lourdes which my wife had given me for the road, and which would then go on a long journey with me before it was able to come back home.

Among German Troops

There were five of us in my group: Lieutenant Colonel Skibiński, Captain Stankiewicz, an officer of the French army, Lieutenant Bonvalet, and my platoon driver Kochański.

We crawled to the edge of the forest.

Overhead, along the *route nationale* to Dijon, came the noise of a column of German motor vehicles flowing like a river.

Perhaps some armoured division?

The road intersected the direction of our planned route, and it would be necessary to cross it in order to start moving.

From time to time, there was a break in the clatter and roar of slow-moving German vehicles, but before we could exchange furtive glances and decide whether to risk dashing over the road, a new wave of vehicles would arrive.

We had to wait patiently until dark.

However, when the dark, the benevolent protector of all the oppressed, did finally arrive, several cars stopped close to us and the sounds of a conversation in German assured us of our obvious bad luck.

Again we waited.

Summer nights are short; a decision had to be made at last.

At the agreed signal, I jumped up and ran across the road, amid the screams of the Germans, 'Leute – halt!' Out of the corner of my eye I caught a couple of the silhouettes of my colleagues running alongside me.

I tumbled into an unimaginable thicket and a tangle of branches and bushes, through which I barely forced my way, quickly moving away from the road.

I was alone.

I thought to myself that this was nothing new, that had happened before, twenty years ago, in June 1920, when we were fighting against Bodoni. The bright moon, the light of which penetrated the dense forest here and there, intensified this memory.

I walked for a long time – maybe three hours, in what I thought was the right direction – but I was still alone.

Either I had got lost or the rest of my group had. But the terrain, descending ever more steeply towards some valley, seemed to confirm the belief that I was going in the right direction.

Resigned that I would be wandering among the Germans on my own, as I had done in the past, I lay down under a bush to rest and began to fall asleep. I was startled by the clatter of rolling stones on the slope and what was clearly a Polish swear word.

Silence.

Who would clamber up the rubble at night there, if not Poles? I got up and started calling their names, 'Franek! Ludwik!'

Well, we found each other.

First Ludwik Stankiewicz, and after an hour, the rest. We rested until dawn and started marching together by day, using forest roads inaccessible to motorized units.

Later, things changed.

We walked through forests by day, and through open spaces (and worst of all, towns) by night.

We thought that it would not be difficult to cross the terrain, currently swarming with rapid armoured and motorized units. All one had to do was be logical: to turn our backs on ease and comfort, to choose roads which motorized vehicles would not use, and to avoid towns like the plague. And to repeat the same ritual over and over again when crossing the *route nationale*. We had no maps of the area – only a Michelin map showing the numbers of major roads on a road network, and sometimes a river.

However, on roadside stone pillars, marking hundreds of metres and kilometres, were carved the numbers of given roads. There could be no mistake which road we were crossing, there could only be a (sometimes serious) mistake *where* exactly. A rather unpleasant surprise: the Michelin map often did not indicate rivers which were wide and deep.

When, much later and once we were in Great Britain, we recounted this escapade in conversations with soldiers, the validity of our course of action was confirmed 100 per cent. It was only in towns and when using paved roads that any of us had got into trouble. One entertaining episode stuck in my memory, because all's well that ends well. Captain Borys Godunov, commander of our anti-aircraft battery, had lost his group somewhere and, exhausted by the night march through the forest, had fallen asleep under some bush. Suddenly he was woken up by German voices so close by that he thought they were spoken directly into his ear. He jumped up, lunged forward and crashed onto the road, straight into the hands of Luftwaffe officers, whose car had stopped on the other side of the bush due to engine failure. Fortunately for this brave officer, he managed to avoid being captured and, without further incident, reached the unoccupied zone.

When I recall the days and nights of this march through the hills of the richest vineyards of Burgundy, Mayonnaise and Beaujolais, it brings to my mind a similar carefree passage during my journey among Budyonny's cavalry in 1920. 'Carefree', because the biggest worry had disappeared, the one that stems from the fact that one is not only responsible for oneself, but for the entire formation.

The burden of dealing with problems beyond one's capability had disappeared: leading a formation when everything was collapsing around, when our ally was at their very weakest, when one had to take actions without faith in the result. Back then, the only concern was how to extricate oneself from the situation with a few colleagues, rather than subordinates.

If it wasn't for the conviction that there were Germans all around (we didn't see many of them throughout the march), that we could fall into their hands and that we didn't know how long our journey would be... If it wasn't for the nights in the wet grass, in clothes soaked to the skin, it would have been a nice sightseeing hike.

If it was a feat at all, then it was one for boy-scouts, and for very junior boy-scouts at that.

*   *   *

It just so happened in our group, as if by agreement among friends, that I was the one to lead, especially at night, believing in my 'nose' and my sixth sense of direction in the dark. And although the oldest, I was by no means the least physically resilient. Many times during the march I was stopped by the shouts from behind that it was enough – time to rest, time to set up camp for the night, or day – depending on whether we were marching in the daylight or in the dark. Then, I would deliberately add a few more kilometres on the pretext that being further away would be better or safer. I was driven not only by instinct, but also by the calculation that, as long as we marched among motor and armoured troops, everything would be simple and easy. Their paths were not our paths. It was to be worse and more difficult when the infantry divisions came in the second wave, and when a clear distinction between their routes and ours would no longer be possible.

This was bound to happen sooner or later, for we moved only at walking speed and walked mostly cross-country, meandering and overcoming various obstacles.

We had become too modern in our thinking after the recent campaigns, and did not expected to run into mounted cavalrymen, yet it was these that we encountered on our march, and twice.

The first time was on 24 June, in the area of the rich vineyards of Pommard, when, led by a guide along the steep slope, we approached a forest near Volnay.

The day was hot, dull with the atmosphere of the storm hanging over us, and dull with the monotony of long, uninteresting trekking behind the guide, when a warning shout from Skibiński from behind alerted me to a German soldier climbing ahead of us. A quick glance behind him revealed another, who had joined our column from behind, carrying two canvas buckets of water for the horses to drink. Without hesitation I turned sideways into the vineyard, followed by the rest, heedless of the cries of 'Halt! Leute!' and the tall vines quickly hid us from the sight of these 'innocent' cavalry water-bearers.

The second time was less dramatic, but much more unpleasant. I remember prolonging our walk that night for a relatively long time, simply unable to find a suitable place to stop for the day's rest. Finally, we reached a tall forest thickly lined with bushes, and without going too far, we set up our wanderers' camp. No sooner had we fallen asleep than we were sprung to our feet (I don't know why one says 'to our lively feet' in Polish) by the sound of a cavalry reveille, trumpeted almost straight into our ears.

What was that?

This 'towering forest' was only a grove, several metres deep, behind which a meadow stretched, with a Burgundian village further beyond, full of prosperous houses and smoking chimneys – sadly not for us, but for some German cavalry squadron.

All day long, huddled under the bushes, we observed the squadron's daily schedule, heard and saw mounted platoons leaving and returning, overheard shouts, laughter, orders, and singing. Despite having tea in our bundles, we dared not build a fire, and munching dry bread with some fat, we survived that unfortunate day in hiding.

To make matters worse, the only road among the steep hills and terraces of vineyards falling towards the valley led through the village, densely built-up like a fortress. The road and the village were a genuine trap for the likes of us; should we have encountered the Germans, our retreat would have been blocked.

Bypassing such an obstacle was neither easy nor quick, and sometimes practically impossible. Then, we had to wait in hiding for the night and creep, ghost-like, through the sleeping village, which soon came to life with the furious barking of the dogs we aroused, walking like spirits – with revolvers in hand.

Once, we had passed halfway through a village, cautiously and on the shadowy side of the street – for the moon was full – when a young Frenchman spotted us and raced out to ask how we had managed to get into the village with all the houses occupied by German artillery quarters. The boy, however, had a knack for adventures and cleverly led us through some fences and shortcuts through the village... and almost joined our pack for good.

Speaking of revolvers, we had them as a last resort and didn't need to use them in the end. Only once, at the beginning, before crossing the road for the first time, Skibiński used his weapon, not so much out of necessity as out of temperament.

When it came to supplies, things were sketchy.

Teams of two went hunting for food each day, but I was courteously excluded from the task. Great ingenuity was shown in reaching isolated homes and farms, and even greater in obtaining food and wine. I have to give fair credit to these bands of two that I was never really hungry or overly thirsty, and some 'feasts' were quite impressive, precisely because they were improvised.

Credit for this belongs not only to my comrades, but also to the French people in this part of the country.

Aside from a few exceptional cases where we were refused, at every step we encountered an appreciation of our situation, we received help in providing us with food and getting our bearings, and in warnings about where the Germans were. In return for the food, they rarely wanted to accept money from us. Even elderly people volunteered to be guides – or, in safer areas, they gave us lifts by car – and I am certain that they understood what awaited them if they had been discovered by the Germans.

For them, the fact that we were Poles rather worked to our advantage, encouraging their cordiality and kindness. To this day, I am full of admiration and gratitude for those simple French citizens, who expressed their genuine patriotism in such a dignified way. It gave me faith in the future of France, despite those dark days.

The behaviour of many of them reminded me of 1939, in Hungary, with the great difference that, at that time, the Hungarian citizens were not yet in danger from the Germans.

The heroic figure of the lady from Tournus, who drove us for fifteen kilometres, despite the German military vehicles patrolling the road, as well as the heroic post office official who transported us hidden in a semi-truck over the Loire bridge manned by Germans, and the manner with which he did it, aroused in me great faith that France would soon recover and be restored to life, faith in the eternally immortal France.

We walked for eighteen days and nights and slept no more than two or three times under some kind of roof. But one of us, it seems Stankiewicz, prophetically stated that our worries and troubles would only begin in the 'French' France.

What did we know then about this 'French' France?

When we started our trek, we believed that, somewhere on the Loire, a French front was forming and we would be able to reach it. We would join up with the rest of the brigade which, with luck, had probably avoided being drawn into this chaos, and we would reconstruct our formation. Then we heard with disbelief about the armistice. The news was soon confirmed to be true. Much later we learned that there were two Frances, one occupied by German troops and the other free. Was it free? Maybe not but, in any case, not occupied by the Germans.

We also heard secret whispers from the French that England was at war, and even that some Polish troops had escaped to Great Britain.

That all was not yet lost!

Escaping France

O n the eighteenth day of our journey, we found ourselves in a small town in the unoccupied zone. We almost didn't notice that fact. The sun did not shine brighter, nor were the people different (they were just as preoccupied with the details of everyday life), nor did we experience a great shock and burst of joy. Long before, during our wanderings, we had felt sure that we would make it. We were alive and healthy, looking somewhat theatrical as we were in uniform and carrying weapons, but with a certain amount of personal satisfaction. Maybe that first glass of wine at the table outside the café tasted a little better, maybe the bed on the first night was a little more comfortable, and certainly a hot bath in a real bathroom was welcome.

Nothing more.

Yet all of us, if I'm not mistaken, first went to the village church to thank God for His protection. Most were driven by conviction, though one or two did so in order not to offend their colleagues who, in the course of the journey, had become friends.

* * *

We were given a lift to Clermont-Ferrand.

There, while reporting to the French military authorities, having come straight from the road, we ran into General Weygand, by chance. The General was just coming down the wide stairs in the staff headquarters while we were going up. He stopped, responded to my salute, realized who we were, and expressed his joy that we had been able to get through the Germans unscathed. He apologized that he could not return with us to the office as he was in a hurry, but thanked us warmly for the military contribution of the brigade, and especially for covering the retreat of the 20th Infantry Division through the swamps of Saint-Gond, which had saved the division. He directed us to the staff headquarters, who were to be instructed to help us with anything we needed.

But neither his staff nor our friend General Faury, who was gathering us Poles together in the Puy-de-Dôme camp, were willing or able to give us the only help we wanted: assistance in getting to Great Britain, where we wanted to continue our mission. They adopted a strictly formal attitude towards us: we were to be treated as French officers.

That is why we quickly shook off this official tutelage and, after a few nights' sleep, we found ourselves in Mende, ready to make inquiries about the evacuation of General Regulski's and Colonel Dworak's units, and to obtain information about our families. On 14 July, the day of the French national holiday, already wearing civilian clothes, we went to Marseille to seek out a window to the world.

*   *   *

Marseille, the largest port in southern France. As windows to the world go, this one was closed for good.

Memories of the recent evacuation of British and Polish troops were still vivid, not only from this port, but from almost all those in the southern zone – evacuation on any type of vessel, even Royal Navy warships. But that was in the past.

Now the sea route was permanently closed. You could pass through the Pyrenees to Spain and continue on from there, but only individually, and in one of two ways: illegally, led by smugglers, or legally, with a civilian tourist passport. The illegal route was very risky, and most often ended in internment. Obtaining papers for the legal route required know-how and involved a complicated procedure.

Namely:

You needed to get a passport. Fortunately, our Polish consulate in Toulouse was operating and the passports it issued were honoured by the French authorities.

You needed to get a visa. Since Spain only gave transit visas, you had to make an effort and apply for or purchase a visa to some exotic destination, such as Latin America, Congo, China, etc.

But in order to obtain these visas, you had to have permission from the French authorities in the form of the so-called *visa de sortie* – an exit visa. It was sometimes granted, but not for people of military age. So, you needed to either rejuvenate or to age your passport. A very complicated process, which was also very time-consuming, as it meant standing in endless queues in front of French consulates and prefectures.

Back then, Marseille had taken on special colours.

A mass of soldiers dismissed from the French army, a mass of refugees from the north, an incredibly overcrowded town.

All of them filled the boulevards and avenues, basking in the sun in front of various establishments, and swelled the crowds in cafés and bistros.

More and more Poles were arriving: from the 1st Division of General Duch, from the 2nd of General Prugar-Ketling, from various directions and, in the final wave, from the fighting echelon of the 10th Armoured Cavalry Brigade.

I don't know how they had managed to acquire their new clothes, but by their elegance, and by their soldierly posture and poise which could not be concealed by new clothes, they stood out among the swarm of other nationalities. All were obsessed with one idea: to get out of France, to continue the fighting and pursue new adventures.

But unoccupied France was already under constant, though seemingly invisible, German control.

Warnings came from other Polish authorities, consulates etc. not to stand out and not to appear in groups, but rather to blend in. Comrades in arms did not greet each other when meeting in public places; they pretended that they didn't know each other.

This led to many farcical events. For example, one day, accompanied by one of the officers, I showed up among the tables set out in front of the largest café in Marseille. It was crowded with a good hundred of my soldiers, pretending not to know each other. As if by magic, the spell of conspiracy and camouflage broke at the sight of me. The entire café stood to attention as one man. One didn't even need the thunderous 'Good morning, General!' to further clarify the situation.

Slowly, however, one by one, my boys, soldiers from the 1st Grenadier Division of General Duch and from other divisions, disappeared from the area of Marseille and Toulouse, travelling through Spain to Portugal, and from there on to Great Britain.

I was the only one to run into trouble. Despite the fact that I had already learned my new passport name, had a destination visa to Brazil and a transit visa through Spain and had borrowed money for travel from the Belgian former consul in Gdynia, I was repeatedly, politely but firmly, turned away at the prefecture, being told to report again in a few days. And so on, week after week.

Concerned about this, I went to a French major I knew from the 2nd Branch of the Marseille Corps Staff. I had met him back in the Orange-Bollène area when we were administratively subordinated to the Corps. He explained the situation to me: namely, German 'guardian angels' controlling traffic from France were already in place at the prefecture. I was well known in Marseille, so a false name in a passport couldn't disguise me. At this moment, I wasn't in danger, but they wouldn't give me an exit visa. However, he went on, if I didn't care about certain inconveniences, etc., he could smuggle me to Algeria among some Arabs who had been demobilized from the French army. Over there, the window to the world was truly open and I would be able to go where I intended without any problems.

That's how I found myself after a few days at Fort Saint-Jean, a depôt of the Foreign Legion, with a ship's boarding pass bearing my name, but with the military rank reduced to a rifleman. The document read: 'Discharged from the Foreign Legion, returns home to Casablanca, Morocco via Oran, Algeria.' Escorted by the corporal on duty, with a suitcase in hand, I found myself on board a transport ship among a colourful crowd of my new Arab 'colleagues'. When I boarded the ship, the pass was taken away from me, but I thought I wouldn't need it anymore. I made the acquaintance of some enterprising individuals from the air force and, with their help and a little cash, I was given a bed in a cabin and the right to eat in the second-class restaurant.

In Oran, I found my 'window to the world' significantly blocked by crossed bayonets. I left the dock in the port, handing over my suitcase to a kid who had won the battle for it against a band of ragamuffins. When I set out for the city, I was stopped by a cordon of black soldiers with bayonets on their rifles and white non-commissioned officers, who were identifying visitors. As mentioned before, I didn't have any French papers, but I hadn't ploughed through the Germans only to get stuck with the French! Calmly, with an air of superiority, I took out my only memento from Poland, the Virtuti Militari card, and handed it over to the NCO. He clearly struggled with it. He turned the card over and over for a long time. It was obvious that he didn't understand anything and didn't want to admit it. I wasn't too surprised, therefore, when after a while, handing me back my card, he saluted briskly and let me through the cordon. I hurried to a travel agency to buy a train ticket from Oran to Casablanca, and from there proceeded to the train station.

I don't know why the charm of my Virtuti Militari card expired at that moment. At the crossing to the platform, which was also manned by the army, it was explained to me that I needed to have a proof of demobilization and, since I had arrived today by sea transport, I would probably find this document at the office at the port. I went by taxi to the port for a demobilization document that I knew didn't even exist. Another long conference with an NCO at the port followed, until finally my ship's embarkation card was fished out of a pile of papers and I was given an NCO's escort to take me to a distant Foreign Legion depôt, where my papers had probably gone by mistake. On the way, over an aperitif, I explained to the NCO the nonsense of two of us both going for a single piece of paper, and I set out with my embarkation card, but back to the station instead, to try my luck. It still eluded me. They explained to me what I already knew: that the card was just proof that I had embarked the ship, that I should have a demobilization document with a photograph on the front page, etc.

While I sat in despair at a table outside the restaurant, opposite the entrance to the station, watching the traffic in front of the station in a melancholy state, my luck returned – quite unexpectedly. I saw the NCO dismissing the guards in front of all the entrances because the train I was supposed to take had already left, and there were three hours until the next one. I took advantage of the breach, and opportunity. No longer guarded by anyone, I reached the platform and crossed to the other side of the entry gates, undisturbed even when the guards returned before the arrival of the next train.

Perhaps the window to the world was finally open!

How pleasant, after so much trouble and annoying ordeal, to sit in an elegant dining car and study the menu with its exquisite dishes and wines.

Unfortunately, the pleasure didn't last long. At the border of Algeria and Morocco, the French gendarmes entered, examining documents and visas. It turned out that regular visas were required to travel from Algeria to Morocco, which no one had warned me about.

I showed my card but, needless to say, it wasn't sufficient.

Kicked off the train at the border station at midnight, into the sultry African night, I stood in a kilometre-long queue for visas issued by the border authorities. After an hour of slow progress, I realized that I was standing in the wrong line – the one for officers, while, according to the card, I was only a rifleman. I joined an even longer queue for privates. When I reached the window, my card provoked an outburst of fury from the NCO in charge. 'Can't you read?' he shouted, pointing to the writing above the window.

Fortunately, the inscription he indicated did not refer to the issue of granting visas, but to the times when holidaymakers and demobilized persons were to apply for them, namely only from 10 am. I answered in an equally raised voice that I was neither a holidaymaker nor a demobilized person, but a *libéré* from the Foreign Legion. I was going home and I didn't care about anything else.

With some juicy words, which my knowledge of French prevented me from understanding fully, the NCO stamped my paper, and thus the final hurdle was cleared.

I found my family in Casablanca. In Mendes, I had already heard that my wife and children were headed there. Not knowing what had happened to me in the chaos of France's collapse, she had not wanted to go with friends to Great Britain, but chose Morocco, where she thought it would be easier to find something out. She was guided by the fact that, in Casablanca, we knew some families of Polish officers – who, by the way, had behaved very badly towards her while I was gone. The only exception was Lieutenant Zaleski, who had been an architect in Casablanca before the war. Thanks to him, she found both an apartment and the protection of the French authorities.

In Casablanca, everything was as bright as the scorching African sun and as azure as the cloudless sky and the depths of the sea – except for one thing. The window to the world was already closed. The British evacuation ships had long since left port, and all traffic out into the free world had stopped.

It took a good few weeks of effort and toil before we managed to secure a place on a small inshore boat, which normally carried sand, to risk an ocean passage to Lisbon. For a place on the bottom of the ship, on seagrass mattresses bought from the Arabs, without a kitchen or bathroom, we were to pay double the price of a first-class ticket on a luxury ship that until recently had run on this route. We arrived in Lisbon with upset stomachs because, throughout the voyage, the ship had been tossed about by storms at sea.

All that just to be interned, while still on the boat, by the Portuguese authorities, who wanted to send us to Fort 10.

Fortunately, I managed to make contact with the Polish Embassy through some English people who had been travelling on our boat, but who had not been affected by the threat of internment.

After two hours of uncertainty, my friend from the War of 1920, Colonel Mally, the Polish military attaché in Lisbon, extricated us from the boat before we were sent to the fort with the interned Spaniards and Czechs.

Thanks to his intervention and care, after a few days of rest amid the luxury of a pretty war-free city without blackouts, seats were found for us on a plane bound for Bristol, UK.

On a bright and clear September day, after six and a half hours of swerving over the Atlantic Ocean to avoid German fighters, we landed in the United Kingdom.

It was 21 September 1940.

Stanisław Maczek during his time at high school in Lwów. (*PISM*)

Major Stanisław Maczek in 1924. (*PISM*)

Lieutenant Colonel Stanisław Maczek soon after his marriage to Zofia in 1930: 'My brave comrade-in-arms'. (*PISM*)

The family's last skiing holiday in Zakopane before the outbreak of the war, 1939. (*PISM*)

A panoramic photograph of the Polish camp at Coëtquidan in France 1939/40. (*NAC*)

A young Polish man reporting to the Polish Army in France, October 1940. The civilian clothing does not help to identify him as either a volunteer, a Polish soldier or a conscript from France's Polish communities as soldiers had to adopt civilian clothing in order to escape to France. Sympathetic Hungarians had to be ordered not to wear Polish uniforms and insignia too obviously in public, having exchanged their own clothes for the uniforms of escaping Polish soldiers. (*IWM*)

Documents bearing false names which were issued by Polish authorities to facilitate the Maczeks' escape from Hungary and later France. As Maczek writes, it was wise for older men to give their age as above 45, to avoid being drafted into military service. (*Karolina Maczek*)

Polish soldiers building coastal defences on Scotland's East Coast, 1940/41. (*PISM*)

A life ring from ORP Piłsudski, formerly a Polish ocean liner on the Gdynia-New York route. She was commissioned as a troop transport ship but sank off the Humber coast in November 1939. The life ring washed up on a Scottish beach guarded by Polish troops. (*PISM*)

The visit of King George VI and Queen Elizabeth to the Polish forces in Scotland, March 1941. General Sikorski stands on the left. (*PISM*)

'Matildas, Valentines, Churchills, fine for our "teething" period; then Covenanters and Crusaders, and finally, in the armoured regiments, Shermans, and in our reconnaissance regiment, the magnificent Cromwells.' Training in Churchills in Scotland, 1941/42 (NAC) and Covenanters and Crusaders in 1944. (*IWM*)

The Division's final exercises in Yorkshire before embarking for Normandy, July 1944. (*NAC*)

General Montgomery, still wearing his driving gloves, addresses Polish troops in Lanark, Scotland, March 1944. (*PISM*)

Polish troops preparing to embark from the London docks, July/August 1944 (*PISM*)

The Division's vehicles disembarking at Arromanches, Normandy. (*PISM*)

General Montgomery briefs officers of the 1st Polish Armoured Division on 6 August 1944, shortly before the Division first saw action as part of Operation Totalize. General Maczek is seated on the left by the table. (*IWM*)

The closing of the Falaise Gap as symbolized by the handshake between Private John Wellington and Corporal Grabowski on 19 August 1944. (*PISM*)

Holy Mass is said for soldiers of the 1st Polish Armoured Division; the bonnet of the Jeep serves as the altar. August 1944. (*IWM*)

The aftermath of the Battle of Mont Ormel: a knocked-out Polish Sherman on Hill 262. (*PISM*)

Two Faces of War: German soldiers captured by the Division in France, August/September 1944, and the graves of Polish soldiers with their temporary white wooden crosses prior to their reburial in Polish war cemeteries. (*PISM*)

General Eisenhower visiting Polish troops in the Netherlands, November 1944. (*PISM*)

General Maczek is decorated with the insignia of the Légion d'Honneur by General Juin at the Arc de Triomphe, February 1945. General Maczek's medals are on display in the Sikorski Museum in London. (*PISM*)

General Crerar, commander of the 1st Canadian Army, and Field Marshal Montgomery, commander of the 21st Army Group, with General Maczek. Breda, November 1944. (*PISM*)

Group portrait of Generals of 1st Canadian Army. L. to r.: (seated) S. Maczek, G. Simonds, H.D.G. Crerar, C, Faulkes, B.M. Hoffmeister; (standing) R.H. Keefler, A.B. Matthews. H.W. Foster, R.W. Moncel, S.B. Rawlings. (*Library and Archives Canada/Department of National Defence fonds/a137473*)

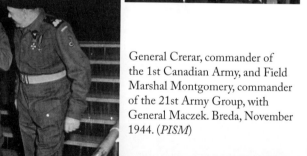

Four of the Polish women imprisoned in Strafflager VI-C in Oberlangen. They had fought in the Warsaw Uprising and, in accordance with General Bór-Komorowski's terms of surrender, were treated as prisoners of war. The camp was liberated by the 1st Polish Armoured Division in April 1945. (*IWM*)

General Maczek visiting the German naval base of Wilhelmshaven soon after its surrender to Colonel Grudziński (foreground), May 1945. (*PISM*)

General Maczek described Breda as 'the most Polish town in Holland'. Here, a street in the city is renamed in General Maczek's honour – General Maczekstraat. (*PISM*)

General Maczek speaking at the inauguration of the monument at Grainville-Langannerie Polish war cemetery, 1954. (*PISM*)

Simonne Brugghe visiting General Maczek at his home in Edinburgh in 1982. (*Karolina Maczek*)

Part III

'I can assure you that the newly formed as well as the re-equipped Polish units will repay [...] this new debt of gratitude towards Great Britain by bringing into battle against the common enemy effective strength and mobility in addition to their eagerness and experience. It is their greatest desire to equal the standards set by our Air Force and Navy in the common struggle for victory.'

General Sikorski to Prime Minister Churchill, 28 October 1941

Britain in the aftermath of Dunkirk not only had to contend with a German-occupied European mainland and the prospect of invasion, but also the challenges posed by the arrival of thousands of exiled servicemen, from the Norwegians to the Poles. Only a quarter of the Polish Army in France succeeded in reaching the UK; Polish units were initially sent to Glasgow and the surrounding area, and the newly-formed 1st Polish Corps was then tasked with preparing and manning the coastal defences between Montrose and the Firth of Forth. The future formation and strategic priorities of the Polish Army in Scotland were the subject of fierce debate: in February 1941, Sikorski gave permission for the formation of a Polish armoured division on the British model: Lend Lease offered the Poles an unprecedented opportunity to create a fully-modern armoured division which could be used in the liberation of Poland and then form the core of the rebuilt Polish Army in the post-war period. In February 1942, with the approval of the British, the 1st Polish Armoured Division came into being, commanded by Maczek.

Following Field Marshal Montgomery's inspection in March 1944, the Polish Division was now included in the Allies' invasion plans for the summer; difficulties in recruitment and the shortage of reserves meant that the Division was not scheduled to arrive in Normandy until a little later in the campaign, with the first units landing at the end of July. On 1 August, the Warsaw Uprising began; on 5 August, the 1st Polish Armoured Division joined the 2nd Canadian Corps, commanded by General Guy Simonds and first saw battle during Operation Totalize on 8 August. Throughout the Normandy campaign, the Polish Division would be ever-mindful of the fate of their friends and families engaged in fighting against German forces in Warsaw. By mid-August, the prospect of cutting off the German 8th Army from its retreat to the Seine had arisen: as the eastern-most Allied formation, Maczek's Division was tasked with sealing the Falaise Gap, at Chambois and at Mont Ormel, becoming, in Montgomery's later phrase, 'the cork in the bottle.'

The Polish role in the campaign had been costly and Maczek was offered the prospect of withdrawing the Division from the frontline for a number of weeks: the new dynamics of the campaign, however, offered the prospect of easier victories. For Maczek, it was all-important to stand in solidarity with those fighting in Warsaw and to ensure that 'the name of the fighting Polish soldier remained on the lips of the world.' Across towns and villages in France, Belgium and the Netherlands, numerous memorials now stand in grateful acknowledgement of their liberation from German occupation by the Polish Division, and countless friendships, marriages and children. After a hard-fought campaign across narrow waterways and in worsening conditions, the Division wintered in Breda, a city which was deeply appreciative that Maczek had secured its liberation with minimal damage to its medieval architecture: for Maczek, preserving European culture was as much a part of the fight against fascism as the military effort.

In the spring of 1945, the terms of the Yalta Conference were announced. Maczek describes with dark humour the awkwardness with which Simonds, Crerar and Montgomery addressed the question of whether the Polish forces would continue to fight: 'Of course we would keep fighting Germany was still Enemy No.1. Just because a new enemy – an Allied one for a change – had reared its head from the East, were we to forget about September 1939, about Warsaw lying in ruins, about Auschwitz and Dachau?' The campaign would have at least one more joy in store: the liberation of Oberlangen, which held over 1700 Polish women who had fought in the Warsaw Uprising. 'Poles were liberating Poles!' declared Diana Napier, the actress-turned-ambulance driver for the Division. In May 1945, moreover, Maczek's glee was unmistakable when the surrendering German officers recognized the presence of a Polish officer: a representative, no less, 'of one of the Polish formations which had never laid down its arms.' The Poles would be forever grateful that Simonds, the Corps commander, tasked the Polish Division with accepting the surrender of the German naval base of Wilhelmshaven. The Polish eagle from Gdynia, taken at the start of the war, was reclaimed, and the town tasked with the sewing of Polish flags for the upcoming visit of Polish Commander-in-Chief General Anders.

The Formation of the 1st Polish Armoured Division

The Fight For The Name

With my arrival in Great Britain, the second campaign to create a Polish armoured division began. Just as with the first one in France, the second also needed to be won on two levels: with the Polish authorities, and with those in the country in which we found ourselves; the British.

The state of affairs was as follows:

- The Commander-in-Chief, General Sikorski – who was apparently already convinced of the need to create an armoured division.
- The officers in the staff headquarters of the Commander-in-Chief – except for the chief of staff, where Colonel Kędzior had been replaced by General Klimenko – remained almost the same.

Our French experiences had proved a very important lesson. Back then, after months of neglect, the division had been very hastily improvised and miracles had been expected within a few weeks.

The shortage of soldiers evacuated from France was an even stronger argument for raising their value through specialisation.

And yet!

My first impressions from my short stay in London were that the traces of the 10th Cavalry Brigade had been rapidly erased. Back in November 1939 in France, when taking command of the Polish army camp in Coëtquidan, I found even my officers who were most attached to the cavalry and to motorized arms, particularly the chief of staff, Major Skibiński, harnessed to the infantry philosophy of how the war would be won, through manoeuvring two sections in the formation. Furthermore, statements by the French officers assigned to the camp left no doubt that the French wanted us to form only infantry units. In Scotland as well I found the 10th Cavalry Brigade stuffed into the ill-fitting mould of an infantry unit.

There was no 10th Armoured Cavalry Brigade, only the 2nd Rifle Brigade; no 24th Lancers Regiment nor the 10th Mounted Rifles Regiment – only the 4th and the 5th Rifle Battalions. The third formation, the Podhale Rifles Battalion, was the only one that consisted of true infantrymen. The cavalry and motor surpluses gathered so diligently in France, then united in the 14th Lancers Regiment and evacuated with it, had now been transferred to General Paszkiewicz's 1st Rifle Brigade, also as an infantry battalion.

It made no difference that the commander of the 2nd Riflemen Brigade – General Rudolf Dreszer – was a cavalryman, and that his deputy – our own Colonel Dworak – had bravely evacuated to the UK the entire group which had been so painstakingly assembled in France to create an armoured division; this was of great service to the Polish Army.

And when the train on which I had travelled from London to Glasgow arrived at the station, the crowds of soldiers who greeted me spontaneously and carried me out of the carriage were not riflemen from some 4th or 5th Battalion; they were my old lancers from the 24th Lancers Regiment, mounted riflemen from the 10th Regiment, motorized sappers and tank crewmen. It was symbolic that, at the railway station itself, they dressed me in a black leather jacket and a black beret, rather than the British Warm overcoat and the field service cap in which I had travelled from London. This left no doubt as to how the soldiers from the lower ranks had reacted to the administrative changes from on high.

A modest change was made just after I took command of the Brigade: the restoration of the 10th Armoured Cavalry Brigade's historical name (we did not let them remove the 'armoured' addition, hard-earned in France) and the historical names of the regiments, thereby removing the glaring anomaly between the official name of the formation and the one on the banners with which we had arrived in Great Britain.

For the sake of historical justice, I must confess that our situation, that of the Polish army reborn on British soil, was difficult without a doubt.

First of all, there were so few of us, and there was no émigré community from which we could draw recruits, whether voluntarily or by conscription. What improved the matter was the steady drip of some of our soldiers who had taken part in the battles for France, the modest influx of Polish volunteers from all over the world and, finally, a serious injection from the Middle East, the Polish army brought out of Russia by General Anders. The numbers finally improved only at the last minute; the richest source of recruitment became the Poles straight from the German army, into which they had been forcibly conscripted after the incorporation of the western part of the Republic of Poland into the German Reich.

For the sake of prestige and propaganda, it was necessary for the Polish soldier to be employed effectively. Hence the defence, by Polish troops, of a considerable section of the Scottish coast from Aberdeen to Edinburgh, which made us a valuable ally on the British Isles. Perhaps this passion for turning everything into infantry stemmed from the need to man the defence sector? Fortunately, I found an appreciation for the historical names with the Commander of the 1st Polish Corps in Scotland, General Marian Kukiel, and his staff officers, including the ever-devoted and helpful Lieutenant Colonel Jerzy Krubski. After all, under the name of the 10th Armoured Cavalry Brigade, we performed the same task of defending the sector from Montrose to Dundee, and yet so far we were fighting only to preserve the name.

The Fight For The Thing Itself

The 10th Brigade spread across the Angus coast, with its headquarters at Forfar.

Families of some of the soldiers of the 1st Polish Corps arrived by various routes from all parts of the world. Settling around the Polish garrisons, they soon made a little Poland out of this piece of Scotland.

We had the Polish press.

Dziennik Żołnierza, or *The Soldier's Daily*, was initially edited at the staff headquarters of the 10th Armoured Cavalry Brigade in Forfar, and later moved to the Corps; it was the source of various problems for me.

We had Polish theatre groups.

The *Lwówska Fala* [Lwów's Wave] was particularly popular. Was it because of Lwów?

Our family occupied a large house in Cairnhill near Forfar, offered to us by the Right Honourable Nancy Arbuthnott, who was genuinely devoted to the Polish predicament. Since the house was extremely spacious – like a Polish manor – it is not surprising that after each performance of the *Lwówska Fala*, all the actors and some of the spectators from Forfar would end up at ours. Guests included our Lwów singers Wada Majewska and Mira Grelichowska, Budzyński, Wieszczek, Szczepcio and Tońcio, Strońć, Rapacki, Bojczuk, Henio Hausman with an accordion and my cousin, Staszek Czerny, before he switched from the theatre to the tank, among mounted riflemen.

Warsaw, Wilno and Lwów were brought to life in the songs, particularly the latter. Budzyński's captivating song entitled 'Even in Edinburgh You Will See A Part of Lwów' was particularly moving.

At the same time, the units were engaged in intense military work.

In the first months, the 10th Brigade divided into working teams, which, under the leadership of Lieutenant Colonel Dorantt's sappers and the Corps' supreme authorities on fortifications – Colonel Bisztyga and others – fortified, laid down barbed wire and mined the coast in anticipation of the German invasion. But the Brigade put only as much time, effort and heart into these works as was required by the standard set by the Corps. The rest of our energy went towards mechanization. It became a universal truth in the Brigade that every soldier without a specialty must undergo a driver's course; every single driver must undergo a course in mechanics or electrical engineering, or any other higher specialty – and, where possible, they would undergo armoured warfare training. 'Private' brigade schools retrained the entire formation in instalments. The instructors – such as Captain Czekalski, Captain Wąsowicz, Lieutenant Lenartowicz, Lieutenant Bohdanowicz, Cavalry Captain Lesser and many others – were true professors in the field and they gave it all their knowledge and undying enthusiasm. General Kukiel came to the rescue, ensuring we had some space at the tank training centre in Blairgowrie for the training of instructors of the armoured training sections. All tank crewmen from Poland, i.e. those who came from tank or armoured vehicle units, were taken for intensive training as the rearguard of the Corps under the name of the 16th Tank Regiment, which later developed into the 16th Armoured Brigade.

Certainly 1941 was not a lost year for the future armoured division, despite guarding the Scottish coast, despite being organized as an infantry brigade, despite constant visits by persons of high and the highest stature, distracting us from training. These were required by the need for publicity, to show that the Polish soldier, here on British soil, remained ready to fight for Poland.

The 10th Brigade was visited by a whole series of British Generals: General Officer Commanding Scottish Command Thorne, General Grasset, the Commander-in-Chief of Home Forces General Paget, General Martel and others. We had high hopes for General Martel, the chief theoretician and practitioner of British armoured weapons.

We were also visited by a number of politicians, including the Foreign Secretary, [Anthony] Eden, and the Minister [of Economic Warfare] [Hugh] Dalton. Churchill himself came only to the sector of the 1st Brigade, where we went with a delegation. The American ambassador, General Biddle, a great friend of ours and of our formation, came as well.

From among the European personages in exile, there was King Peter II of Yugoslavia with ministers, and General S. Ingr, Czech Minister of National Defence.

The true highlight was the visit of King George VI and the Queen on 7 March 1941. On Barry Links, they went around the entire defence sector of the 14th Mounted Rifles Regiment, which had already joined the 10th Brigade under its reclaimed name. The royal couple was very interested in bunkers, anti-tank obstacles on the beaches and the soldiers, to whom they directed various questions. Once, the Queen asked one of the riflemen via which routes and through which countries he had eventually found himself on the British Isles. Laughing, she added that the Germans called us 'General Sikorski's tourists' on the radio. Unabashed, the fellow replied, 'But very dangerous tourists!'

The royal couple had a modest lunch in the officers' mess with the 24th Lancers Regiment. While spending the night in their Scottish castle in Glamis (the historic one haunted by the ghost of Banquo), they were under the guard of honour of the 1st Motorized Artillery Regiment, quartered in the town.

It was the first time in English history, rich in all manner of strange things, that on British soil, the honour guard of a royal couple was carried out by a foreign unit. A year later, in Forfar, at the place where the royal couple received the parade of the Polish army, the city council built a commemorative plaque registering this fact, so important for the small town. When invited to the unveiling of the plaque, I had to speak to a large audience in English. I don't remember that speech, but my son had by then been in a Scottish nursery for a year already. When asked, he loudly assured me that I was great, but in his mother's ear he whispered that 'Daddy spoke very badly, but it shouldn't be said out loud'. He was undoubtedly correct.

The section of coastal defence at Barry Links would later, once again, be marked out in a rather mystical manner. A year after the torpedoing of the Polish ship, ORP *Piłsudski* during the Allied operations off the coast of Norway, a lifebuoy with the inscription 'Piłsudski – Gdynia' washed up on the beach of the sandy peninsula.

The entire Brigade saw this as a happy omen for the future.

Even before Hitler attacked Russia, the invasion psychosis had subsided and the Brigade was officially supplemented with British motor equipment. We perfected our skills in this direction in larger exercises organized by the Corps and the Scottish Command.

That wasn't enough for us anymore, though. We were unofficially pushing for armoured training.

In the second half of 1941, it became obvious to everyone that the defence of the coast was changing into its peaceful garrisoning, and the expected German invasion would be replaced by the impending invasion of the continent by the Allies.

The outbreak of the Russo-German war and General Sikorski's pact with the Soviets meant that a Polish Army was being created in the East. It gave us the hope of drawing thousands of our soldiers away from Russia and strengthening our small numbers in Great Britain. In return, we would be able to send a large surplus of officers, who would certainly come in handy there.

The question was: would we Poles take part in the invasion of the Continent? The 'how and who' no longer depended on us.

There were discussions and reports, briefings at Corps level and at the London headquarters of the Commander-in-Chief. There were periodic briefings in Gask when the Commander-in-Chief came to visit the army in Scotland.

There was the huge, and understandable, appetite to command. Which units would the 1st Polish Corps field as its representatives in combat? It was clear that, due to the scarcity of soldiers, it wouldn't be capable of fighting as an entire Corps for a long time yet. We still had only two incomplete brigades on the coast and the 16th Armoured Brigade in reserve. In addition, another incomplete parachute brigade was training in Leven, created only thanks to the enormous energy of General Sosabowski, and it had swiped the best of our eager young parachute jumpers to fight in Poland. Several brigades made up exclusively of officers, without privates, served only as a reserve. Let us not even mention our air force and navy, which were also looking for sources of recruitment, faced with increasing numbers of positions to fill, and shrinking numbers.

Despite various ideas, it was obvious that the British could only employ for the invasion such organizational units as adhered to standard structures, and would not agree to any organizational improvisations.

We could roughly estimate that, after combining all units, we would be able to form one division. What kind of division? Infantry? Or an armoured division which still existed only in the minds of our 10th Armoured Cavalry Brigade and those who had joined it during the fighting in Poland and France?

Such was the background of the main briefing of the Commander-in-Chief with commanders and staff officers, conducted personally by General Sikorski in Gask on 14 February 14 1942. They had been summoned to decide what kind of unit the Poles would offer to the British for the invasion of the continent.

The participants were the following:

- General Marian Kukiel – Commander of the 1st Corps,
- General [Tadeusz] Klimecki – Chief of Staff of the Commander-in-Chief with officials from the staff headquarters,
- General [Tadeusz] Kossakowski – Deputy Commander of the 1st Corps and representative of the armoured arms and sappers,
- Generals: Głuchowski, Łuczyński, Paszkiewicz, Niemira,
- Colonel Sosabowski, Commander of the 1st Independent Parachute Brigade, Colonel Piestl – Commander of the 309th Air Cooperation Squadron,
- Colonel Krubski – Chief of Staff of the 1st Corps, and Lieutenant Colonels Borkowski and Spychalski.

I counted on the support of General Kukiel, of General Klimecki, with whom I had an important conference the day before, and of General Kossakowski, believing that he would opt for an armoured formation due to his own specialisation. Despite this, the supporters in favour of creating infantry formations were more numerous. Yet, this should not have decided the outcome, because the arguments that were to convince the Commander-in-Chief were more important.

Meanwhile, the main speech, delivered with great eloquence by General Kossakowski, and supported by well-prepared charts illustrating our numbers and breaking them down into specialist subunits, disappointed me utterly. Contrary to my arguments concerning the 16th Armoured Brigade and 10th Armoured Cavalry Brigade (both being unofficially trained and maturing into an armoured division), the overwhelming verdict of General Kossakowski stated that we lacked far too many specialists to create an armoured formation. But on his lists and charts, most of these missing specialists were ordinary drivers of motor vehicles – which, in our eyes, had ceased to be a specialty long ago, and was part of the recruitment training of every private in a motorized or armoured brigade.

General Kossakowski ended his speech with an ironic jibe directed at me which I still remember: 'Someone may be a great piano virtuoso, but they wouldn't be able to build a piano. I don't play the piano, but I could build one if I had anything to build it from.'

General Klimecki pointed out the weaknesses of these arguments, especially regarding the specialisation of vehicle drivers, and yet the briefing ended without a decision from the Commander-in-Chief. Closing the briefing, he ordered me, General Kossakowski and General Paszkiewicz to send written papers on the matter to London within a week.

* * *

There was an uproar in the Forfar headquarters of the 10th Armoured Cavalry Brigade. We all sat down to work on this important memorandum. If the German invasion had still been possible during this period, we would have been sitting ducks for the enemy, because for five days everyone was just writing and copying.

In the memorandum which was finally sent to the Commander-in-Chief, the main points were as follows:

- *Historical responsibility* – having the opportunity to create the first armoured division in the history of the Polish Army, how could we abandon it?
- The *combat strength* of such a division was higher compared to an infantry division, despite the smaller number of soldiers; this was crucial considering our desperate need for each and every soldier.

- The *monetary value* of materiel and combat equipment of an armoured brigade. We were not able to afford that in Poland during peacetime, whereas now it would be provided for free following the Lend-Lease Act.
- The *effective value* of such a division when we brought it back to Poland. We would be able to form infantry divisions from Poland's outstanding soldiers once back in the country, but we could neither make nor arm an armoured division on the spot.

*   *   *

We spent a good seven days waiting for the result, seven days of literally waiting for a verdict.

On the seventh day a telegram was sent to me from the Commander-in-Chief – in his own particular style:

'General, I appoint you Commander of the First Armoured Division.'

Obviously, General Sikorski and his staff did not have much trouble convincing the British that this was the correct solution, because a few weeks later, British General Sir Giffard Martel arrived for an inspection. After visiting the troops, at a modest evening reception at the Corps headquarters, he raised a toast to the success of the 1st Armoured Division.

*   *   *

From that moment on, as if by magic, everything changed.

In addition to the 10th Brigade, the 16th Armoured Brigade, the Corps' reconnaissance regiment, and later the heavy artillery regiment, were subordinated to me. We began to comb the ranks of the 1st Rifle Brigade and all Corps and non-Corps formations, reducing the ranks of all military commands and institutions to squeeze out the necessary number of privates. Outside of the formation of the armoured division, only the Parachute Brigade and the 1st Rifle Brigade were to remain separate.

From April 1942 we were transferred south into the valley of the River Tweed, famous for its numerous textile factories. Two years before, in France, we had also moved south, to the region of Avignon, but now we took it as a good omen. 'Third time's a charm,' our boys would say. It didn't work out in Poland, it didn't in France – now it was probably the turn of our soldiers' luck.

The Division spread out from Berwick-upon-Tweed through Kelso, Melrose and Galashiels to Peebles, with the headquarters at Melrose.

Organizing and training began.

The armoured division, formed according to the current British establishments, was unquestionably a huge force in terms of armour. It consisted of two armoured brigades, each with three armoured regiments or battalions and one battalion of motorized infantry. For long-range reconnaissance, it had a reconnaissance regiment with armoured vehicles. Its artillery section consisted of motorized, anti-tank and anti-aircraft artillery regiments. In addition, the divisional commander had a motorized support battalion at his disposal.

Although the ratio of 6:3 in favour of armoured units in relation to infantry, excluding reconnaissance armoured cars, seemed too generous, such an organization best suited our vision of the expansion of the Polish army for the future. Under favourable conditions, it would be easy to switch to an armoured-motorized corps or, due to the divisibility of armoured brigades, to two light armoured divisions.

Since two armoured brigades, the 10th and the 16th, already existed, this method of organization was easy for us to take on board. It shifted organizational and training difficulties to the lower levels, and we needed to meet the demand for specialists of all kinds for as many as six or seven armoured regiments.

For almost eighteen months of organizational work and training, from April 1942 to September 1943, the composition and staff of the 1st Polish Armoured Division included:

- Deputy divisional commander – Colonel K. Glabisz
- Divisional chief of staff – Lieutenant Colonel B. Noel, and then Colonel J. Levittoux; quartermaster – Colonel W. Gierulewicz
- 1st Reconnaissance Regiment – Major Z. Dudziński
- 10th Armoured Cavalry Brigade – Colonel K. Dworak, deputy brigade commander – Colonel E. Tarnasiewicz
- 14th Lancers Regiment – Major S. Starnawski
- 24th Lancers Regiment – Major R. Szumski
- 10th Mounted Rifles Regiment – Lieutenant F. Skibiński
- 10th Dragoons Battalion – Lieutenant Colonel K. Święcicki
- 16th Armoured Brigade – Colonel T. Majewski, deputy commander – Lieutenant Colonel A. Grudziński
- 1st Armoured Regiment – Lieutenant Colonel B. Sokołowski
- 2nd Armoured Regiment – Major Z. Chabowski, then Major S. Koszutski
- 3rd Armoured Regiment – Major A. Izdebski
- 16th Dragoons Battalion – Lieutenant Colonel W. Kobyliński
- Support – Colonel J. Łunkiewicz, then Colonel B. Noel
- 1st Motorized Artillery Regiment – Lieutenant Colonel J. Krautwald
- 1st Anti-tank Artillery Regiment – Lieutenant Colonel J. Deskur

- 1st Anti-aircraft Artillery Regiment – Lieutenant Colonel M. Jurecki
- 1st Rifles Battalion – Lt. Col. K. Kardaszewicz
- Engineers (the 10th and 11th Engineer Companies, the 1st Field Park Company and the Bridge Platoon) – Lieutenant Colonel W. Weryho
- Signals (four squadrons) – Lieutenant Colonel. J. Grajkowski
- Additional services: Chaplaincy – Father J. Szymała, Workshops (10th and 16th Companies) – Major Z. Bressel, Medical – Lieutenant Colonel Doctor K. Maszadro, Supplies – Lieutenant Colonel W. Bielski, Ordnance – Major E. Fryzendorf, Finances – Captain Commissar S. Nowicki.

We faced a grave and significant task.

In terms of organization, we needed to create new units and change the existing ones.

In terms of training, from the divisional commander to the last rifleman, everyone had to be trained according to their scope of duties and function.

The most pressing issue of specialists, especially those of senior ranks, was solved by the British themselves, most effectively. They opened all their training grounds, camps and schools for us, training either urgently-needed contingents or instructors, who in turn took on instructor positions at the so-called 'wings', extra courses at a given school which had been set up especially for the Poles. Among many others, this is how Polish courses at the armoured weapons centres in Bovington and Lulworth were organized – training commanders of all ranks, tank crews and specialists in armour craftsmanship – and how tactical courses for commanders of armoured squadrons were offered in Oxford.

A tank firing range in Kirkcudbright in southern Scotland and the artillery range in Otterburn, north of Newcastle, were put at our disposal.

The Polish Armoured Division set to work in a manner parallel to British formations, with the aim of producing numerous specialists.

Later, the Division went all the way to the training grounds in England to come together as a whole, and to test its worth in bilateral exercises with the Canadian Armoured Division in 1943 and with General Leclerc's 2nd French Armoured Division just before the invasion.

There were periods when the division was stationed not in our Scottish garrisons, but over almost the entire island: from the south coast of England, with its armoured training centres, through to tactical courses in Oxford, to divisional courses in the valley of the River Tweed, and even to the northernmost Polish assault training centre near North Berwick, open not only for dragoons and riflemen but also tank crews.

However, the Armoured Division was not yet a monolith. There were frictions, animosities and chauvinism between different specialisations: cavalry, the armoured personnel, infantry, etc. Some pre-war tank crew officers, entrenched in narrow professionalism, were reluctant to share their knowledge with everyone.

This led to a kind of mutiny, which reminded me in its childishness and meaninglessness of that 1920 'revolt' of cavalry non-commissioned officers when my assault battalion was being formed. Just as then, it was averted using psychology.

In one of the armoured regiments of the 16th Armoured Brigade, a dozen or so young officers submitted an application via their commander to Colonel T. Majewski, protesting against mixing them with cavalrymen.

The case was put before me.

I ordered the brigade commander to bring forward two of those young officers who had gone the furthest in their outburst, and had even expressed the view that they did not want to fight together with the 'horse-butchers'. During their report, I asked if they had ever served in a cavalry regiment and, answering in the negative, I transferred both of them – one to the 14th Lancers Regiment, and the other to the 10th Mounted Rifles Regiment, so that they would get to know these 'horse-butchers' well. After two months, they were to have the right to ask for a transfer back to their former regiments. After two months, both of these officers, in the divisional report, asked to remain in the cavalry regiments. The requests were supported fervently by their new commanders.

Thus, slowly, the ésprit de corps of the particular arms began to be replaced by the ésprit de corps of the 1st Polish Armoured Division.

*   *   *

The amount of work done by the soldiers of the Division could be illustrated by the sheer number of external and internal training courses it completed. Regarding the latter, great merit is owed to all the officers and non-commissioned officers, particularly the older ones, who were no longer fit for combat due to their age, but devoted all their knowledge, enthusiasm and hard work to the idea of creating a division.

The scale of this work could also be illustrated by the amount of combat equipment that was constantly being improved. Surely, it is enough to list the types of tanks that our tank crews used: Matildas, Valentines, and Churchills in the early days, then Covenanters and Crusaders, and finally Shermans for the armoured regiments, and the magnificent Cromwells in the reconnaissance regiment.

The case was similar with other arms.

The first test of the Division's worth as a whole was Exercise SNAFFLE, led by the Eastern Command in the Newmarket area, north of London, in the summer of 1943. The opponent was the Canadian 4th Armoured Division, our inseparable companion in later battles on the continent.

Although a snaffle is used to master a horse and to slow it down, we won the exercises owing to greater speed. Furthermore, the Polish Armoured Division chose the hussars' wings for the insignia worn on the shoulder, reaching back to the glorious tradition of cavalry and armour. The senior officers at staff headquarters began to fear that the Division would charge blindly, just as the hussars had in the past, incurring unnecessarily high losses. It was feared that this would be the case particularly for the 24th Lancers and 10th Mounted Rifles Regiments. For historical accuracy, it should be stated that the first 'charge' of the Division was in fact the attack of the 1st Armoured Regiment on Hill 111 on the third day of the Battle of Soignolles. Anyway, the concept of a 'charge' in the context of the combat of armoured regiments had a different form (justified by the conditions of the battlefield) than cavalry charges of the past.

*   *   *

While the ésprit de corps of the new Division began to manifest itself, solidarity among units and soldiers was beginning to take root, and the old chauvinism was being replaced by new loyalty to the Division and sub-units, the news of reorganization hit like a bolt from the blue.

Based on their experience in the Middle East and Africa, the British had already switched to a new structure of armoured divisions, weaker in terms of the number of armoured units, but more self-sufficient in the battlefield.

The reorganization consisted mainly of reducing the formation to one armoured brigade and adding a motorized rifle brigade.

As a condition of using us in the invasion of the continent, the transition to a new organizational form was proposed.

It was a very serious problem for the Commander-in-Chief, whose policy for the future included having a large number of armoured regiments at his disposal. Six would have made it easy to switch to an armoured corps if necessary and possible. It also became a problem for us, senior officers at all levels of command in the Division, when we faced the necessity of introducing drastic measures to units whose work, enthusiasm and achievements up to that point meant they did not deserve to be removed from the division.

As always in a crisis, unresolved grudges and ambitions surfaced. Again, cavalry, armoured weapons, infantry – in opposition.

With the new organization, there was only room for four armoured regiments; three in the armoured brigade, and one reconnaissance regiment in armoured vehicles, but not in tanks.

Two armoured regiments had to be eliminated.

However, there was room for three rifles battalions and one motorized battalion (which we called dragoons), instead of only one rifles battalion and two dragoon battalions. Both my commander and I thought hard about how to reconcile various, divergent considerations and the historical order of the units' formation, and their participation in this war in the September campaign in Poland or the French one in 1940, together with their current usefulness.

The final organizational form of the division was as follows:

- Colonel K. Dworak became my deputy, Colonel J. Levittoux the chief of staff, and Lieutenant Colonel M. Rutkowski the quartermaster
- The 10th Mounted Rifles Regiment was responsible for reconnaissance in British Cromwell tanks, under the command of Major J. Maciejowski
- The 10th Armoured Cavalry Brigade in American Sherman tanks was commanded by Colonel T. Majewski, deputy commander – Colonel F. Skibiński, chief of staff – Major M. Czarnecki; the 1st Armoured Regiment – Lieutenant Colonel A. Stefanowicz; the 2nd Armoured Regiment – Lieutenant Colonel S. Koszutski; the 24th Lancers Regiment – Lieutenant Colonel J. Kański, the 10th Dragoons Regiment – Lieutenant Colonel W. Zgorzelski
- The 3rd Infantry Brigade – Colonel M. Wieroński, deputy commander – Lieutenant Colonel W. Dec, chief of staff – Captain J. Nawara, the 1st Podhale Infantry Battalion – Lieutenant Colonel K. Complak, the 8th Infantry Battalion – Lt. Col. A. Nowaczyński, the 9th Infantry Battalion – Lieutenant Colonel Z. Szydłowski, the 1st independent heavy machine gun squadron with the 1st Reconnaissance Regiment – Major M. Kochanowski
- Divisional Artillery – commander Colonel B. Noel, chief of staff – Major A. Sulewski, the 1st Motorized Artillery Regiment – Lieutenant Colonel J. Krautwald, the 2nd Motorized Artillery Regiment – Lieutenant Colonel K. Meresch, the 1st Anti–Tank Artillery Regiment – Major R. Dowbór, the 1st Light Anti-Aircraft Artillery Regiment – Lieutenant Colonel O. Eminowicz, followed by Major W. Berendt
- Divisional Engineers – HQ Sapper Company, the 10th and 11th Field Company Engineers, 1st Field Park Company and the Bridging Platoon; commander – Lieutenant Colonel J. Dorantt
- The Signals Battalion: HQ Signals Squadron, the 1st, 2nd, 3rd and 10th Signals Squadrons, commander – Lieutenant Colonel J. Grajkowski
- The 1st Traffic Control Squadron – Captain A. Pieregorodzki

- Services: Chaplaincy – Father J. Szymała, then Father F. Tomczak; Maintenance and Repair Units – Major M. Wąsowicz, the Workshop Company of the Armoured Brigade – Major J. Kaszubowski, the Workshop Company of the Infantry Brigade – Major F. Perepeczko, the Ordnance Services – Major E. Fryzendorf, the 1st Ordnance Field Park – Major T. Lesser; Supplies – Lieutenant Colonel W. Bielski – then Major M. Żebrowski and Major H. Gwiazdecki; Medical units – Lieutenant Colonel Doctor W. Pawłowicz; Welfare Platoon – Major A. Łubkowski; the Military Court – Major Auditor N. Tomaszewski, Armoured Division Replacement Camp – Lieutenant Colonel J. Deskur; the Replacement Squadron Armoured Brigade – Cavalry Captain B. Skulicz; Head of the Military Police – Captain M. Wolnik; the 8th Military Police Squadron – Captain Z. Bojarski.

The full strength of the Division amounted to:

- 885 officers,
- 15,210 privates,
- 381 tanks,
- 473 guns (excluding those mounted on tanks),
- 4,050 motor vehicles.

On average, the armoured regiments had sufficient numbers of soldiers so that the 16th Armoured Brigade could, together with the 14th Lancers Regiment and the 3rd Armoured Regiment, be placed at the disposal of the Commander-in-Chief – as the basis for the further expansion of the army. Matters in the infantry brigade looked worse from the very beginning. The 1st Podhale Rifles Battalion was formed by reinforcing the riflemen from Podhale with those from the 16th Dragoons Battalion. The 8th Battalion grew from the one that, prior to reorganization, had been a support battalion to the Armoured Division. The 9th Battalion had to be formed from all kinds of surpluses as well as privates from reductions in ranks.

With gratitude, I took on three officers from the Parachute Brigade as commanders – they had not been assigned as they exceeded the maximum age for parachutists. Lieutenant Colonel Z. Szydłowski, Lieutenant Colonel Complak and Lieutenant Colonel Nowaczyński did wonders in a very short time, truly improving the infantry units in every possible way. It is even more worth emphasizing that they could not pick and choose personnel , and had to accept everyone who came to the unit, which still was not enough to fill 100 per cent of the positions.

My heart was very pleased as officers from the former 29th Grodno Division – *Grodnoszczaks*, as we called them – reported to me. I was especially happy with officers from the former 81st Infantry Regiment, named after King Stefan Batory, which I had commanded in the years 1929–1934. I had followed the fate of this unit and its officers in and out of the regiment during the September 1939 campaign. I was filled with joy by the fact that those of them in whom I had placed my hope did not disappoint. Major Kuferski did not fail during the fighting in the Beskid Zachodni mountains described in these memoirs, and neither did Captain Józef Jossè in the 11th Division under General Prugar-Ketling, in the heroic breakthrough at Hołosko and Zboiska, for which he was awarded the Gold Order Virtuti Militari, IV Class – and a wooden cross for his grave.

Many of them, still young during my time in Grodno, now came to me as mature soldiers; many at an age that predisposed them to functions at staff headquarters and in the services rather than combat; finally, many became specialists of various kinds, which was so necessary in any technical arms.

Thus, the following soldiers joined the Division: Lieutenant Colonel W. Dec was given a position with the staff and then became the deputy commander of the brigade, Major Władysław Bohdanowicz came to the maintenance units, and Major Stępień for a frontline position. Captain Kazimierz Chojnowski, previously mentioned, went to the supply units, Captain M. Michalczyk to the signals units. My former aide-de-camp from Grodno, Captain Borkowski, was assigned to the clerical services, together with Captain Pstrocki and others.

This did not hide the fact that the infantry battalions, being formed at the last minute and from what was at hand, did not achieve the high level of preparedness that the armoured and artillery regiments had managed to acquire over time. The quantitative and qualitative shortage forced improvisation, and it obviously had an impact primarily on the infantry and supply services units, which were formed only at the end of 1943.

Even having the privilege of a long training period, the Armoured Division up to the very end did not have sufficient numbers of soldiers to fill all the positions. There were absolutely no surpluses which could have allowed for the appropriate selection in all units and services.

*   *   *

In the autumn of 1943, under the new organizational structure, we returned from the Newmarket-Cambridge area in England back to Scotland, to our old quarters.

When we had started summer exercises a few months before, I was invited to dinner with some officers at the famous college of Corpus Christi in Cambridge. To crown the dinner, a decanter with the oldest port was going round the table in order to honour the Polish soldiers. At the end of the exercises, when we were saying goodbye, a relatively young port, from 1920, was served. The Master of the College explained why in his speech. Namely, we were bid farewell with this 'vintage' in honour of the Polish victory of 1920.

* * *

Once in Scotland, we immediately started training, incorporating the supplemented soldiers into the units, and, as usual, struggling with the inability to fully cover all the positions.

On 19 March 1944, the Division received a British order to mobilise, specifically, to mobilise the materiel. It was a real test of efficiency, both concerning the British services and the Division's supply services with Colonel E. Fryzendorf at the helm. But above all, it was a test of the flexible supply services of the 1st Corps, reliably led by Colonel Z. Łojko. It was generally known that Poles liked to be prepared for anything in advance, so not without some justification, there were fears that we would equip ourselves too well, taking many things 'just in case'. However, the British described the mobilisation as highly satisfactory and, despite some differences in views and language difficulties, even more efficient than in many British units. The very rational British approach simplified things greatly. Equipment was supplemented only where a unit had more than 50 per cent of the full establishment, and if they had less than that, it was actually taken away and replaced with a full new set.

The Division was thus combat ready, despite the camouflaged deficiencies in the numbers and the age limits being exceeded in many categories.

On behalf of the Commander-in-Chief, two commissions inspected the Division and its true state. General Zając's very insightful commission, while identifying a high level of training – especially in armoured units – drew attention to the fundamental problem: the lack of replacements to cover losses, even minimal ones. The other, General Langner's perhaps overly pessimistic commission – concerning the Division's services – emphasized the old age and poor physical condition of the men of the supply services, which posed a threat of the Division being immobilised after its initial use. Indeed, we had quite old (and even older-looking) Poles from Latin America as numerous drivers in supply companies.

All this was true, but it could not stop the use of our Division for the invasion. In the future, the greatest surprise would be precisely those old drivers from Brazil and Argentina who, during the pursuit from Normandy to Belgium, with excessively long communication lines, would work day and night without rest, never break down and add much of their toil and effort to the Division's brilliant successes.

* * *

The inspection of Allied commanders and staffs was discreet and conducted probably via reports of liaison missions. It manifested itself in only two visits of the highest British and American level of command.

The first such visit was the arrival of Field Marshal Montgomery on 13 March. The Field Marshal was preceded by his fame for his crushing of Rommel and the victory of El Alamein, as well as the popularity that he as 'Monty' enjoyed throughout the island. Such was also the view of him of any soldier of the 1st Division, whose only wish was to fight the Germans. We passed over his unique style, which did not quite agree with our notions of military order, over the pink sweater and the two badges on his beret, over his stepping out of the specially prepared Jeep as if on stage and declaring that he was 'coming with us to kill the Germans.' We passed over other ridiculous things that are supposedly characteristic for otherwise great and accomplished people.

He acquired an image of a 'hardy chap' when he came out to us one cold March day without a coat and only in Battledress, to stand in front of soldiers who were sensibly dressed in coats and gloves. The bubble burst when, before breakfast in the canteen, he began to take off as many as three sweaters from under the Battledress.

At first, I couldn't figure out if he was joking or serious when he asked which language Poles actually speak in Poland, and whether it was German or Russian.

And although all that annoyed some people, it counted for nothing when we realized that, by virtue of this visit, we had been included in Field Marshal Montgomery's 21st Army Group, ready for the invasion.

* * *

Another lucky thirteen – 13 April – brought us a new visit.

Announced as a visit by General Grouse, it caused confusion and panic for the entire British liaison mission, which, despite frantic scouring through the yearbooks of British army officers, found no such name at all.

Nevertheless, as ordered, on the morning of the named day, I was waiting for this mysterious general, about whom no one knew anything, with the Corps commander, General Boruta-Spiechowicz, and supported by an honorary squadron of the 10th Mounted Rifles Regiment. When the saloon carriage arrived at the platform, a smiling and cheerful General Eisenhower got off the train.

The mystery of the 'codename' had been revealed.

The simple and natural way in which General Eisenhower approached us, both officers and soldiers, immediately won our hearts. No speeches, no grand words. He immediately protested against all forms of prepared receptions and exercises. He toured the troops as he found them on the training field or in the quarters, during work and at meal times.

He talked freely with officers and soldiers about everything that constitutes a humble soldier's life in garrisons. He clambered into a tank, and practised shooting (very accurately) with the officers of the 24th Lancers Regiment. Perhaps the contrast with the visit from a month before made his amiable character stand out all the more.

He inspired confidence – the Supreme Commander of the Allied Forces for the impending invasion of the Continent.

The Division, from top to bottom, lived only in anticipation for this moment, for which it had been getting ready, not for months but years. We knew about the stipulation in General Sikorski's agreement with the British staff that the Polish Armoured Division would not be used to break the Atlantic Wall, but only in the second phase of the invasion, for attacks from invasion bridgeheads.

Therefore, the lack of any direct pre-invasion preparations in the Polish Division did not mean that they were not undertaken on a large scale by units participating in the first assault.

In May we were transferred back to England, to Yorkshire, for further exercises; this time with General Leclerc's 2nd French Armoured Division. However, we had not gone beyond the first preparatory stage when, during the exercises on the evening of 5 June, an order came for 'absolute radio silence'.

We took this as an infallible sign that operations had begun.

Indeed, on 6 June the invasion began.

D-Day, the immense Operation Overlord.

In the second half of June, when the use of the radio was again permitted, the Division conducted one great exercise in its entirety, at which the Commander-in-Chief, Lieutenant General Sosnkowski, was present.

In July, the 1st Polish Armoured Division moved to the southern edge of England, to the Aldershot area, waiting its turn.

Over 13,000 officers, non-commissioned officers and privates moved with 4,431 motor vehicles, including 381 tanks. We were fully aware of the strength of this combat unit which we had created together.

Before embarkation, the Division was visited by the President of the Republic of Poland-in-Exile, Władysław Raczkiewicz.

* * *

Invasion – Totalize and Tractable

The Division's first casualties were the chief of staff of the armoured division, Colonel J. Levittoux, an officer of great stature, and a British liaison officer, Captain Wills, who were killed by small-calibre aerial bombs. They had been sent in mid-July 1944 to the invasion bridgehead to establish contact with the British 11th Armoured Division, which was to be replaced by our Division. Both drivers were injured. Only the quartermaster of the division, Lieutenant Colonel Rutkowski, escaped unscathed.

I think of these events as the prelude to our invasion battles, the battles in Normandy.

Because for us, for the whole Division, it had all started out as on well-organized manoeuvres. The journey from Aldershot through London to the port of Tilbury on the Thames was executed flawlessly owing to excellent British traffic control. We were divided neatly, almost as if led on a string, each group to their ship, to their assigned places. Even the damaging of one ship by a flying bomb (V-1), with which the Germans were more and more intensely pummelling the city and the ports, did not cause confusion. Within two hours, a new ship was sent over and everything went according to the King's Regulations.

Every moment I spent on the ship I had a gnawing impression that someone would ask me for a ticket and enquire if I had booked a 'couchette', or, as it was disarmingly expressed on posters plastered all over Britain, 'Is your journey really necessary?'

The quiet, peaceful, all-night voyage took us from the mouth of the Thames, between the French and British coasts, to improvised steel 'ports' on the beaches of Normandy near Arromanches. Then followed a systematic unloading, which involved being led 'by the hand' to our assigned areas, which were simply squares of land, crushed and stripped of any greenery by the caterpillar tracks of the previous troops, surrounded by hedges and trees covered in grey limestone dust.

It was 1 August 1944.

The Chief of Staff was replaced by Major L. Stankiewicz, an old officer of the 10th Brigade, one of 'my lot', with whom, in 1940, I had covered the whole of Burgundy on foot. Since then he had remained a close and tireless co-worker and aide of mine.

It all started both at the staff headquarters and at the garrison with the studying of maps and hundreds of different orders, regulations and supplements.

Only the nights were more romantic, illuminated by flares from German aircraft and garlands of light anti-aircraft missiles, as the Germans dared to raid only at night.

The Division became part of the 2nd Canadian Corps, commanded by Lieutenant General G. G. Simonds of the 1st Canadian Army of General H. D. G. Crerar.

I reported to both commanders personally and the manner in which I was welcomed spoke to positive future cooperation. I especially liked the energetic, and very young (much younger than me) Corps commander. It seemed that the feeling was mutual, which greatly simplified our work in the difficult days ahead.

The general situation on the front in Normandy was as follows:

In July, Montgomery who, until that point, had commanded the entire invasion front, had used short-range strikes to tie down most of the German forces, most importantly the majority of the armour of Panzer Group West (six Panzer divisions) on his eastern flank in the Caen region. This facilitated the withdrawal of the American army, on the western flank, from the Saint-Lô area. In the first days of August, these forces gained freedom of action in the southern, eastern and western directions, spreading wide from their outposts. This, in turn, provoked the withdrawal of most of the German armoured forces from the Caen area in order to attack the American army moving sideways in a western direction. Only infantry divisions and static troops remained as support for this manoeuvre from the north ahead of Caen. They were in well- and widely-entrenched positions, packed with armoured guns, including the most dangerous 88mm ones, as well as heavy tanks of the Tiger and Panther type and one relatively well-manned 12th SS Panzer Division 'Hitlerjugend'.

General Montgomery, who arrived at our Division for briefing on 5 August, described this section of the front at Caen as a 'hinge' that was to be broken down by the advance of the Canadian Army moving in the general direction of Falaise, towards the flank and rear of the German 7th Army, which was attacking the Americans.

This time Montgomery made a much better impression on us than previously in Scotland. His brief, factual and very vivid presentation of his entire plan was a kind of masterpiece and remained in the memory of the commanders until the end of the Battle of Falaise. The commander of the Army Operations Group being present at a briefing for officers, including company and squadron leaders – this was something new and impressive!

General Simonds and his staff, the executors of Operation Totalize, as it was called, were aware of the strength of the expanded German defence; they perhaps underestimated the depth of this defence, which had been growing since 6 June, the day of the invasion. It was a *place d'armes* of sorts for a series of fortress formations from the Atlantic Wall: infantry divisions of various types, parachute units, and the entire Panzer Group West, before it left for the West.

The assault of the 2nd Canadian Corps in the form of three infantry divisions, supported by the armoured car brigade and two armoured divisions, had everything that tactics and technique could offer to strengthen the advance.

The strike was executed on the night of 7–8 August with huge support from British bombers and artillery. The first infantry echelons moved in columns on armoured chassis, improvised mainly from self-propelled artillery (after the guns had been dismantled). The columns, which were preceded by companies of heavy tanks, went in hard in order not to give the surprised opponent a chance to get his bearings. For the first time, we used a system to indicate directions in the dark by headlights and Bofors tracer projectiles. All this resulted in a quick seizure, with minimal losses, of the front belt of the fortified position, in particular of the towns May-sur-Orne, Roquancourt and Tilly-la-Campagne.

But it was only to the depth of about four kilometres and, even in this captured belt, there were small points of resistance where groups of German soldiers were still defending their positions.

At this point it was the turn of the two armoured divisions, Polish and Canadian, which were to be used at Falaise, and above all in the hills north of this town.

My intention was for the Division to pass through the leading 51st Scottish Division in two echelons:

- The 10th Armoured Brigade, in the lead, reinforced by the 8th Infantry Battalion and the British 22nd Dragoons, equipped with mine-removing tanks and reinforced by the 1st Motorized Artillery Regiment;
- The 3rd Infantry Brigade, sweeping the area and consolidating key positions, supported by the 2nd Motorized Artillery Regiment; the 10th Mounted Rifles Regiment was to provide reconnaissance for the eastern flank of the Division, which was otherwise not covered, while the western flank was supported by the 4th Canadian Armoured Division.

The action started at 13.45, preceded by bombings by the US Air Force. Two factors failed:

a) Aerial bombardment, which was in part too far away and in part too close, because it did not reach the targets which were holding back the tanks of the 24th Lancers Regiment and 2nd Armoured Regiment, but instead hit our rear, inflicting losses on the Polish anti-aircraft regiment and Canadian AGRA (Army Group Royal Artillery). This seriously reduced the effect of medium artillery fire, despite the brave stance of the Canadian artillery;

b) The fact that the deeper part of the German position remained intact and turned the employment of the armoured divisions into a slow and tedious job of penetrating the German defence.

From the moment the leading echelons of the 24th Lancers Regiment and the 2nd Armoured Regiment overtook the troops of the 51st Division, they came under effective fire from anti-tank guns of all calibres and mortars, but they also had to face the counterattack of German heavy tanks from the 101st SS Heavy Panzer Battalion from the 1st SS Panzer Corps and, when deploying for attack, immediately suffered serious losses. Our action was significantly hindered by the fire of German batteries on our eastern flank, which went unchallenged. Such a situation would repeat constantly in the first days of fighting. Already in the first hours of the action, even the column of the front echelon of the Division's staff, moving between the two brigades, found itself under fire of 150mm guns from this direction. One of the missiles hit right in front of a group of staff officers that I had assembled, who had been taking advantage of a break in the advance. It was a good thing it didn't explode, but ricocheted over the military equipment. It seemed that we hadn't suffered any losses. The only thing was the mysterious disappearance of a British colonel, the liaison officer of the Division's commander. It wasn't until the next day that we learned that his body had been found by the roadside in a German trench, where he had jumped during the artillery raid and had been hit by shrapnel. So far, these hard-working British officers seemed to be the unlucky ones – two killed out of a dozen or so assigned to the entire Division. The next day, assault fire of a similar kind would inflict greater losses on the front echelon of the staff, with the traffic control and military police platoon being the most affected.

In the end, during the day of 8 August (or rather half a day, because the attack began at 13.45), only the forward units of the 10th Brigade emerged from the breach carved out by the Corps' attack. After dawn on the ninth day, the Brigade became entangled in fierce, persistent and punishing battles, which resulted in it taking control of the Cavicorn area and amounted to an advance of only a few kilometres to the south, because the Germans had managed to reinforce this section, primarily with anti-tank weapons. According to Canadian sources, the section of the front where the two Allied armoured divisions fought had been reinforced by ninety 88mm guns, recently withdrawn from the air defences in Belgium and the Netherlands, and currently used as the most effective anti-tank weapons.

The threat to the eastern flank of the Division from the hills dominating the area, which were held by the Germans and not covered by any Allied units, became so serious on that day that I had to order the 3rd Rifles Brigade to pivot

90° to the east. The attack on the village of St. Sylvain and the surrounding hills executed by the Podhale Rifles Battalion and a part of the 8th Rifles Battalion, supported by artillery and aviation resulted in the capture of the set objectives by nightfall and removed the immediate threat.

Another day of unrelenting battles by the 10th and the 3rd Brigade moved the front by a further three kilometres to the line of Signallers – Estreés la Campagne, but did not give our Division or those of the Canadians a breakthrough to Falaise across the German defence.

One may recap this period of activity in the following way:

The fighting of the 1st Polish Armoured Division broke down into a series of small moments and actions, which were characteristic of battles within prepared enemy defences; laboriously, step by step, these moved us forward. All units of the Division fought persistently and with determination despite serious losses, especially in terms of tanks (sixty lost in three days of combat) and numerous wounded and killed. They achieved a number of tactical successes, such as the tank charge of the 1st Armoured Regiment on Hill 111, for which we paid dearly with the loss of the brave deputy commander of the Regiment, Major Malinowski. However, it also resulted in the recovery from German captivity of about a hundred Canadians from the British Columbia Regiment, whose tank advance had been decimated west of this hill. Another success was the Podhales' attack on St. Sylvain; not to mention the particularly vigorous attack of the 9th Battalion on Soignolles, which was a baptism of fire for this unit, the youngest one of the Division. Finally, a 24-hour-long fierce battle by the 10th Dragoons Regiment for the village and forest of Estrées la Campagne, where the Germans unsuccessfully counterattacked and defended almost every house.

I was aware of the nature of the battles in which the Division was involved – so when I received the order from the Canadian Corps to capture, with my one battalion, the square-shaped forest at Quesnay, which had been transformed by the Germans into a powerful redoubt, and which had impeded the advance of both Polish and Canadian armoured divisions, I went to the Command and managed to convince General Simonds that, to perform this task, one needed fresh forces and at least the strength of one infantry brigade. There was still a conviction among the Corps staff that the Polish and Canadian armoured divisions could not break through the German defences because they were inexperienced.

The newly-engaged Canadian brigade, despite strong artillery and air support, did not capture the Quesnay forest on the night of 10–11 August.

This may have eventually convinced the Command that, if both armoured divisions were to be thrown south and then expected to further exploit the operation, a powerful strike must be assembled once again, with all the available Corps resources.

And now a brief examination of conscience, which is not out of place, as this initial period of action had cost us too much, the success it had yielded was too minor, and it had not led us to Falaise.

Were we and the Canadian Armoured Division really so 'green', i.e. inexperienced, that we could not break through the German defences?

Indeed, it was the first battle of the 1st Polish Armoured Division, so none of us had our own experience in armoured division combat, neither the Divisional commander, nor the riflemen nor the lancers. Such experience can only be gained on the battlefield and every single soldier must earn it individually. Our personal experiences from September 1939 in Poland and June 1940 in France were obsolete to say the least, because since then much had changed in both technique and tactics. Of course, theoretically we knew about all these changes and had greedily absorbed all that we could learn about it from others, to maximise the combat training of the Armoured Division on the training grounds.

Experience does not come overnight; rather it grows over months and years.

But we could not have been so green considering that after a week, in conditions better suited for an armoured division, but isolated from the entire Allied army as we were, we fought a five-day battle, tough but victorious, against the Germans whose armoured forces and troop numbers were both superior to ours.

And here is my personal assessment: the Polish and Canadian armoured divisions did not break through the German defences on August 8–10, because it was beyond their capabilities.

The depth of the defence prepared by the Germans was much greater than the four kilometres of the initial position, which had been broken on 7–8 August by the general advance of the Canadian Corps. The best evidence was the fortifications at Soignolles and the Quesnay forest, with bunkers and shelters eight to ten kilometres from the front edge of the first position and even deeper fortifications throughout the valley of the River Laison.

The 2nd Canadian Corps' attack was launched in the most dangerous direction for the Germans, that is, leading to the shortest route to Paris; it must have been anticipated by the Germans during the phase when the attack was being painstakingly prepared. In addition to the German 89th Infantry Division which was in strong and deeply fortified positions, one of the best and most fanatical formations of the German army, the 12th SS Panzer Division 'Hitlerjugend', was focused on defending this direction as the second line of defence. Although the Germans withdrew all the armoured divisions to the general attack on the Americans at Mortain, this Division was left in the defence sector along the Falaise-Caen road. It was additionally strengthened by the 101st SS Heavy Panzer Battalion and a Panther tank battalion from the 9th SS Armoured Division. There were no exaggerations in the first report from our front units of about twenty Tigers (56-ton tanks) and painful losses suffered by our own forces even before the leading units of the Polish Armoured Division got out of the way of the advancing units of the Scottish 51st Infantry Division. As it turned out later – on this day, 8 August, on this section near St. Aignan-de-Cramesnil a well-known German armoured specialist, the commander of the 101st SS Heavy Panzer Battalion, Captain M. Wittmann, was killed.

Meanwhile, the form of the task for both Polish and Canadian armoured divisions was such that it was the easiest to define it by a paradox: they had been asked to do very little and therefore too much.

The tactical task, i.e. to force a narrow passage through breach in the defences of the 89th Infantry Division then to seize certain geographical positions as quickly as possible: Hills 206, 195, etc., as well as the hills north of Falaise – condemned both these armoured divisions to a rigid, frontal attack on a narrow front, which was the only form of action for which an armoured division was too weak.

Of course, this endeavour could have been successful had it not been for the fact that the advance of both of the divisions was opposed by the 12th SS Panzer Division, reinforced by heavy tanks. The German division fielded far fewer tanks than we did. It was operating, however, in an area prepared for defence, packed with groups of powerful 88mm guns from the 3rd Flak Corps of General Wolfgang Pickert, which were used as anti-tank guns. It acted efficiently in small combat groups, into which retreating troops from the 89th Infantry Division were also pulled, as well as the troops of the 85th Infantry Division flowing in from the Trun area. The Germans were able to impose on us and the Canadians a form of relentless step-by-step manner of fighting, in which their better armour and guns outweighed our quantitative advantage.

In addition, the open terrain with horizons spanning over two kilometres gave an advantage to their Tigers and Panthers, and their unsurpassed 88mm guns, over our Shermans and Cromwells. The 88mm missile pierced our armour from a distance of two kilometres, while a Tiger or Jagdpanther's armour would be pierced only from 400 – 500 metres. And in a generally open landscape, clusters of brick houses, small forest plots or orchards provided good protection for infantry with lighter anti-tank armour-piercing weapons.

A rather paradoxical situation. In addition to the huge amount of air support and artillery of all calibres, the Corps was able to attack with heavy Churchill tanks and carriers with mounted flamethrowers. The first infantry echelons were moved on carriers and armoured tracked chassis and, together with tanks, 'into the fire' they went, as we called it. Thus, they projected an image of an ideal armoured division of the future, which moved through the terrain on tracked and armoured equipment like a mass of iron and fire, following a perfect storm of artillery and aviation fire, breaking all resistance. The Canadian

Armoured Division and ours, with their light armoured equipment (Shermans and Cromwells) didn't have at their disposal even an approximation of such force. When faced with resistance, they had to make their infantry dismount, thus losing the element of surprise.

And as long as they could not emerge from the area of prepared defence, they could not make use of the assets that are the strength of an armoured division, i.e. speed of movement, a wide range of action of the whole formation, agility in combat and the speed of their tanks.

Therefore, although the three-day heavy fighting of the Polish and Canadian armoured divisions did not yield more than six to eight kilometres of ground, it did give the higher command accurate reconnaissance and a basis for the next general attack. And to all the troops involved it gave a sense of military duty honestly fulfilled, despite the difficult conditions.

A comparison of our own and German losses for this period on the section of the Polish Division speaks for itself.

Losses of the Division:

- privates: 656 (wounded or killed)
- equipment: 66 tanks, 5 S.P. anti-tank guns, 5 6-pounder anti-tank guns, 2 25-pounder guns.

German losses:

- Lack of records of wounded and killed; prisoners: 429 from the 85th, 89th and 272nd Infantry Divisions and the 12th SS Panzer Division
- Equipment: 13 tanks, 2 88mm guns, 7 75mm guns, 1 105mm gun, 14 15cm mortars.

Much greater losses, especially in tanks, were suffered by the neighbouring 4th Canadian Armoured Division, in which the British Columbia Regiment alone lost 47 tanks, all in the battle of 9 August near Estreés-la-Campagne – an area, as I emphasized, with heavy German defences, located more in our area of operation.

The first harbinger of a new operational plan of the Corps was the transfer of the Polish Armoured Division partly to reserve, and partly to the west of the Caen – Falaise road. The task set for 14 August, which was already a part of the new operation, was to strike on the west side of the infamous Quesnay forest, towards Potigny and Fontaine-le-Pin. At the same time, the 10th Mounted Rifles Regiment was to reconnoitre the main direction of the Corps' strike on Rouvers. It was a kind of compliment to our reconnaissance regiment, whose high value was emphasized by the Canadians throughout the entire campaign.

Despite another mistake by the British and American air forces – directed in action from London, which dropped several waves of bombs on the dispersed

Division (the Canadians, especially AGRA, were hit the most) and the supplies of the Rifles Brigade – our 3rd Rifles Brigade, after fighting through the night of 14–15 August, supported by the 24th Lancers Regiment, finally seized the ordered objectives, freeing local Polish miners in Potigny.

The main Canadian attack started on 14 August at noon from the starting bases, secured by us on 9 and 10 August on the Soignolles-Estrées la Campagne line. The attack was carried out with the same abundance of artillery and air force fire which had been used on the night of 7–8 August, the difference being that this time, considering the visibility in daytime, the surprise factor of large-scale smoke was employed, literally turning day into night. The Germans were also surprised by the technical advancement of the weapons and the use of armoured personnel carriers with mounted flamethrowers, which demoralised their defence the most. By the morning of 15 August, the entire defensive position, including the valley of Laison, was in Canadian hands, and the advance was slowly heading towards the hills north of Falaise. However, the principal point at 159 only fell into their hands at noon on 16 August.

Meanwhile, in view of the general situation on the Normandy front, i.e. the commencement of the retreat of the 7th German Army towards the east and the approach of General Patton's Army towards the town of Argentan, south of Falaise, an opportunity arose to completely cut off the retreat of the German army. The Germans could be trapped. The concept and the terms 'Falaise Gap' and 'Falaise Pocket' were born. It was a change from the original plan to cut off the German forces much further to the east – on the Seine.

The entire burden of responsibility for this new plan fell on the shoulders of both the Polish and the Canadian armoured divisions, now directed by the Corps commander to pass through the rear of the three advancing Canadian divisions, from the extremity of the Corps' western flank over to the eastern flank, to break through in the general direction of the town of Trun and to cut off the German retreat. The Corps commander, in a personal conversation with me, ordered that the two divisions, working closely together, would effect this operation along the length of Dives valley, from its confluence with the River Fraine, south of Morteaux-Couliboeuf, and leading in the direction of Trun. However, he approved my proposal to use the Polish Division to capture the dominant hills five to six kilometres east of the river, despite some risk of the separation of forces. The experience of 8–10 August taught me not to present an open flank as long as the dominant hills of the area were not covered by our own advancing forces. This correction would prove to be extremely salutary in the future, given the counterattack of the German SS Panzer Corps from the outside of the Falaise Pocket from the east, for whom the possession of the hills would have given an immediate tactical advantage over our Division.

Breakthrough At Last

The day of 15 August, the Feast of the Soldier in Poland, became one of the brightest days of the Polish Armoured Division. Everything that appeared to present the most difficulty turned out to be easy and effortless.

A soldier's luck shone over our troops, like the sun on that hot August day.

The nightmare of passing through the lines of communication of three advancing divisions turned out to be almost like a motorized unit's parade within the garrison, without a single moment of confusion or standstill. Our 'hounds', led masterfully by the 10th Mounted Rifles Regiment of Major Maciejowski, supported by a self-propelled anti-tank *dywizjon* and a squadron of dragoons, were released to capture the crossings on the River Dives near the town of Jort. They surprised the Germans, who were regrouping after their defeat during the night in the Laison valley. The result – a mass of prisoners, a six-gun battery captured, several German tanks and 88mm guns destroyed,

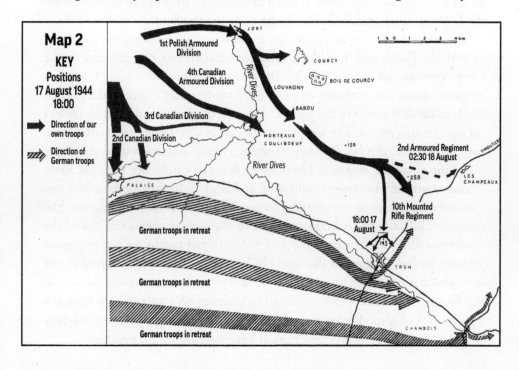

Map 2

KEY
Positions
17 August 1944
18:00

→ Direction of our own troops

↗ Direction of German troops

1st Polish Armoured Division

4th Canadian Armoured Division

3rd Canadian Division

2nd Canadian Division

JORT

COURCY

BOIS DE COURCY

LOUVAGNY

BAROU

MORTEAUX COULIBOEUF

River Dives

•159

•259

2nd Armoured Regiment 02:30 18 August

VIMOUTIERS

LES CHAMPEAUX

FALAISE

10th Mounted Rifle Regiment

16:00 17 August

German troops in retreat

German troops in retreat

German troops in retreat

145

TRUN

CHAMBOIS

and most importantly – a real treasure despite the damaged bridge – a crossing seized on the Dives in the town of Jort and fords that could be used even by tanks, some of which had already taken over the southern shore.

Following in the footsteps of the reconnaissance, the 10th Armoured Brigade built on this success and, by the evening of 15 August, the 1st Armoured Regiment had taken another river crossing in the town of Vendeuvre with the 1st Armoured Regiment and a third, south of Jort, was taken by the 2nd Armoured Regiment, reinforced with a battalion from the Rifles Brigade.

Not only did the Polish Division's artillery engage in this action, but also a section of the Canadian medium artillery.

On the night of 15–16 August, the 3rd Rifles Brigade relieved the armoured units and provided cover over the captured area, which allowed the sappers to build a bridge at Jort and to repair the minor crossings, as well as to clear the area of mines.

It seemed to me that we had achieved the objective for which we had been bleeding and toiling over eight days.

We had broken through the defences set up by the Germans and regained the freedom of action necessary to cut off the German retreat. As the only large formation of the Canadian army, we found ourselves on the south-eastern shore of the River Dives with all the opportunities such a position offered.

On the morning of 16 August, I was at the bridgehead in Jort in my tank. It was an unusual position for a divisional commander, even for a commander of an armoured formation. Normally we were rather chained to our command vehicle, with the whole apparatus of control and command having moved on from the visual observation of the battlefield with binoculars to the acoustic plane of the radio: transmitting and receiving orders and reports about the situation. I verbally ordered the entire 10th Armoured Brigade south to Louvagny and Barou. The Rifles Brigade was to advance towards Courcy and the forest, but its mission was limited to protecting our advance by seizing German observation points. It would then follow the 10th Brigade.

Colonel T. Majewski did not waste time. Already by noon, two battlegroups of the 10th Armoured Brigade had advanced on the enemy, and by evening they had taken Louvagny and Barou, crossing the Barou-Morteaux Couliboeuf road. To our right, however, Morteaux Couliboeuf held out, halting the 4th Canadian Panzer Division on the River Dives. The Germans even tried to slow down the advance of our Division by counterattacking with their tanks.

The attack of the 3rd Rifles Brigade captured the town of Courcy and the western exits from the forest.

The advances of both brigades were supported very effectively by Colonel [płka. dypl.] Br[onisław] Noel, reinforced with divisional artillery from the Jort area and Canadian medium artillery from the Sassy area.

Prisoners taken during the day added the 1053rd and 1054th Grenadier Regiments to the list of known numbers of German divisions and regiments. On the following day, 17 August, the prisoners came from the 21st Panzer Division and the 12th SS Panzer Division 'Hitlerjugend'. This suggested we were up against two German armoured divisions, although the 12th 'Hitlerjugend', according to the testimony of the prisoners, was already completely crushed.

17 August was once again the day of the 10th Mounted Rifles Regiment which, in the course of reconnaissance, successively captured:

- Hill 159 Norrey-en-Auge
- Hill 259

It had detected two German columns retreating on the road to Trun and sowed panic and confusion among these columns with fire from their tanks.

Finally, they pressed on one and a half kilometre north of Trun into the area of Hill 143, where they battled with German tanks from all sides, inflicting serious losses, but also losing several tanks of their own.

The nature of the fighting was fundamentally changing. When the dominant Hills 159 and 259 were vacated by the 10th Mounted Rifles Regiment pushing towards Trun, they were seized by the Germans retreating to the south-east, as well as new ones coming from the north-east and east from the Vimoutiers region.

Therefore, the 10th Armoured Cavalry Brigade, which was following the reconnaissance regiment, had to fight to retake these hills again until the evening. Eventually it maintained this line, holding Hills 159 and 259 firmly alongside the 3rd Rifles Brigade, which was seizing these objectives in turn.

The operational objective was the town of Trun, which constituted a major road junction where the German columns in retreat to the east and south were collecting. The town was under fire from our artillery and the tanks of the 10th Mounted Rifles Regiment, and it would become easy prey the next day.

However, it would not be the prey of the Polish armoured division, because a special order from General Montgomery, received in the evening, extended our objective by a further seven kilometres in the direction of the south-east, including the seizure of the town of Chambois. The 4th Canadian Division, which had finally crossed the tributaries of Dives near Morteaux-Couliboeuf, was to take over Trun. This order was brought by the Corps Commander with words of praise for the Division's earlier operation, which had been very rapid and purposeful. According to the description of the situation given by General Simonds, the Canadian infantry had already entered Falaise, but in the town itself there was still fighting in the streets. Furthermore, the next day, i.e. 18 August, the 4th Armoured Division was to move towards Trun from the north, which would reduce the exposure of the Polish Division, at that time driving a wedge into the German group. The action of the Polish Division had so far reduced the possibilities of a German retreat to a strip of about seven kilometres between Trun and the northern exits of the Gouffern forest complex, which was shut off by the Chambois road junction. The Americans had moved from the south, occupied the town of Argentan and should have already been in the southern part of the Gouffern forest.

The mood among the senior commanders was extremely optimistic. By quickly cutting off the remaining paths of retreat, the only thing left to do would be to round up prisoners and capture supplies. Therefore, there was pressure on us to form a detachment during the night and to send it to Chambois.

Despite the general fatigue of all troops due to fighting and advancing through uneven and difficult terrain, we formed a battlegroup tasked with manoeuvring towards Chambois, which was led by Lieutenant Colonel Koszutski and consisted of the 2nd Armoured Regiment, the 8th Rifles Battalion and an anti-tank *dywizjon*.

Meanwhile, the rest of the 10th and the 3rd Brigades were left to thrash out and untangle the very complicated supply problems.

Koszutski's detachment left after midnight. However, they fell prey to both the terrain and the dark night, as well as French pronunciation. To make sense of the routes and paths they had taken a civilian as a guide, and thus they moved east and approached 'Champeaux' instead of 'Chambois'.

Moving in the wrong direction, but still convinced that they were advancing on Chambois, they surprised the staff and some units of the 2nd Panzer Division where they had made camp for the night. Fierce fighting ensued until dawn. Once the Germans recovered from the first defeat, they forced Koszutski's troops to withdraw south.

This incident had *positive* aspects, because through the captured prisoners we found out about the presence of a new German armoured formation – the 2nd Panzer Division – on our eastern flank. In this way, we were warned of a threat that was not, however, serious at this moment due to the shock and chaos that prevailed among this division.

It also had *negative* aspects because, in the morning of 18 August, I had to acknowledge that we were not actually a single kilometre closer to fulfilling the task, i.e. closing off the German retreat to Chambois.

Nota bene: The German 2nd Panzer Division was the same division we had fought near Wysoka, Naprawa and Myślenice in the first days of September 1939. Many prisoners of war had in their service books the same names of battles as those fought by the 10th Cavalry Brigade in September in Poland.

And our 2nd Armoured Regiment was derived from the 2nd Tank Battalion, formed in Żurawica near Przemyśl for the 10th Cavalry Brigade.

Divine justice had offered us the tremendous satisfaction of a soldier's revenge.

Perhaps for these two reasons – the information about the threat from the east and the opportunity for a bloody rematch for September – I never reproached Lieutenant Colonel Koszutski for his mistake regarding the direction of the night's actions. It was easy to get lost in Normandy, forging a path with tanks, at night, among Germans, and Lieutenant Colonel Koszutski and his troops did a good job. Their input, although hard to measure, was significant for the Division's overall success.

Closing the Falaise Gap

In such nerve-wracking circumstances, on the morning of 18 August, Major Maciejowski reported to me. He described the progress of the actions of the Mounted Rifles and, despite the serious losses in the regiment and almost inhuman fatigue, did not utter a word of protest against rushing the Regiment immediately to Chambois for reconnaissance and to clear a route for the Division's troops. I had met this superb officer and commander in the first months of our stay in Scotland. I became close to him on and off duty. He would often come to me privately, asking the same question: whether Polish troops from Scotland would be used at all? His greatest concern and nightmare had always been ending the war in a peaceful garrison. When he was talking to me, he had just had an accident. Having driven a tank over a German mine, his hearing was clearly dulled. At the same time, he was so hoarse that he could only whisper. Afraid of offending him by removing him from action, I didn't tell him to take my place under the tank and sleep. On those Normandy nights, the usual lodgings would be pits dug under tanks, with deep heaps of freshly mown grass or wheat. Apart from the crew there was room there for the staff officers from various command vehicles. My 'sleeping compartment' was usually shared with the chief of staff, but in case of trouble my aide-de-camp, Lieutenant Jaś Tarnowski, and Aleksander Żyw, a painter in civilian life, found shelter there as well. Such accommodation was the easiest to arrange, provided some protection against air raids and was relatively comfortable.

I bid farewell to Major Maciejowski, promising to return to him a squadron of his regiment, which had up until now been retained in order to protect the Division's battlefield headquarters – although in our uncertain situation, it was still very much needed. We would have to make do with three tanks for the protection of the staff headquarters – the squadron from the 10th Mounted Rifles Regiment was needed far more in Chambois.

The Division's HQ on the battlefield moved to the wooded ravine of Hill 159 in the commune of Norrey-en-Auge, disturbed from time to time by Panthers approaching from the forest area near Grand-Mesnil. These German tanks did much damage to our supplies, but fortunately for us, they had neither the heart nor the will to venture into our ravine, although they approached Hill 159 several times that day and the next.

Meanwhile, Lieutenant Colonel Koszutski's detachment, after fighting through the night in Champeaux, was evidently nowhere to be found, including on the radio. The Brigade commander, Colonel T Majewski, and his chief of staff, Major Marian Czarnecki, had a great deal of trouble with the rescue operation, and then with the supplying of the detachment with ammunition and petrol.

And time was running out.

I therefore ordered a new battlegroup to be formed to follow the 10th Mounted Rifles Regiment to Chambois, while the rest of the Brigade would take control of the situation south of the Champeaux-Trun road and would be ready for further action.

The battlegroup of Lieutenant Colonel Zgorzelski, consisting of the 24th Lancers Regiment, the 10th Dragoons Regiment and the anti-tank *dywizjon*, was launched.

The fighting became more and more violent and involved all the troops of the Division; the situation on the evening of August 18 was as follows:

- The 10th Mounted Rifles Regiment with two anti-tank *dywizj*ons had already approached Chambois at 4:30pm, but had had to withdraw one kilometre to the north due to the actions of our own air force at the road junction.
- Lieutenant Colonel Zgorzelski's detachment had engaged in heavy fighting in the evening for Frenée, about one and a half kilometres north-east of Chambois, together with tanks from the 24th Lancers Regiment.
- The rest of the 10th and 3rd Brigades were five kilometres further north, in the almost mountainous region of Hordouseaux-Ecorches, and were engaged in local fights both with the Germans emerging from the direction of Trun and those returning from the east. These fights had subsided towards the evening.

From my vantage point on the southern slope of Hill 159, I could see practically with the naked eye how the Germans were retreating along the slopes of the Gouffern forest descending into the valley of Trun-Chambois. Their retreat was marked by the explosions of shells of every calibre, of both air force and artillery. The Germans, forced by the situation to retreat by day through an increasingly narrowing defile, fell prey to massive air raids by British and American air forces.

Official Canadian publications would later report that 2,179 motor vehicles and 182 tanks were destroyed on 18 and 19 August alone.

So, this conspicuous stream of retreat was to be finally cut off by the Polish Armoured Division.

The fact that prisoners were now being taken from the 2nd Panzer Division, from the 12th 'Hitlerjugend' and the 21st Panzer Division, from over a dozen infantry divisions and the 3rd Parachute Division, as well as from the German Corps and Army's rear formations – all this began gradually to make some sense; finally a captured order from the commander of the German 7th Army revealed everything. This characteristic order, describing the anaemic efforts of the Allied armoured formations on the western flank, stated that one armoured division (namely, us!) had made a fuss in the east and was seriously threatening the lines of communication of the German army. Accordingly, the Army commander ordered the 2nd Panzer Corps, which had already escaped the trap of the Vimoutiers area, to turn back and attack westwards, with the task of destroying this division and handing over the area to the 1st SS Panzer Corps, which was retreating at the head of the 7th Army.

The order therefore included an overview of the Battle of Chambois from the German side – or the 'red' side, as we called it during exercises and manoeuvres.

When, in the afternoon of 19 August, the operational map in the command vehicle was filling up with notes on the ever-changing situation, and the Division's units, operating along two axes, through heavy fighting, reached the main route of German retreat: Chambois – Vimoutiers, I worked out a concise plan to regroup. Its essence was the idea that the Polish Division should make use of all the advantages of terrain and the concentration of forces, as it had outstripped its western neighbours (the 4th Canadian Armoured Division and two Canadian infantry divisions) by seven kilometres, and was completely exposed from the east and north-east.

The plan created 2 battlegroups:

- the 10th Armoured Brigade composed of the 1st Armoured Regiment, the 24th Lancers Regiment, the 10th Dragoons Regiment, the Podhale Rifles Battalion and the anti-tank *dywizjon*, with the task of securing and holding Chambois and the southern Hill 262 about three kilometres to the north-east;
- the 3rd Rifles Brigade consisting of the 2nd Armoured Regiment and the 8th and 9th Rifles Battalions with the anti-tank *dywizjon*, with the task of garrisoning the northern Hill 262, to cover us from the east and north-east.

The Division's artillery with a Canadian medium artillery regiment was to support the battlegroups as a whole.

I wanted to keep at hand the 10th Mounted Rifles Regiment, strengthened with two anti-tank *dywizjon*s, even after the restructuring of the battlegroups was completed.

When explaining this intention to the chief of staff of the 10th Armoured Brigade, Major Czarnecki, I called the Mont Ormel ridge with these two Hills 262 [N and S] 'the Mace' (or '*Maczuga*' in Polish), due to the resemblance of the contours traced on the map. This name remained in use throughout the battle and long after it, until it entered the official history of the Canadian Army.[1]

I wanted to have two strong battlegroups, one on the Mace and one near Chambois, against which the German retreat would crash, and to have the 10th Mounted Rifles Regiment reinforced, to intervene where necessary.

However, by the night of 19 August, despite heavy fighting, the events of the day had only partially turned out as had been intended by the grouping, although most of the necessary terrain had been occupied – with the exception of the southern Hill 262. This detail entailed a number of difficulties and inconveniences, especially for the command.

On 19 August the following events took place:

The 1st Armoured Regiment, efficiently led by Lieutenant Colonel Stefanowicz, took a portion of the Podhale Rifles Battalion to Hill 262 N, after a hard fight at Coudehard, and surprised the mixed German column amassed on the road from Chambois to Vimoutiers. It destroyed it completely with tank fire and heavy machine guns. Both the road and terrain were completely blocked by this which, together with the smoke from the burning German materiel, prevented the Poles from immediately seizing and exploiting Hill 262 S. It also prevented this battlegroup from advancing south to Chambois, as planned. Therefore, the 1st Armoured Regiment gathered on 262 N with part of the Podhale Rifles Battalion, and were holding under fire a large section of the Chambois – Vimoutiers road and the area further east – where groups of Germans were trying to escape from the trap.

In the evening, units under Lieutenant Colonel Koszutski and the rest of the 3rd Rifles Brigade arrived in the 'Mace' area. This caused a huge concentration and confusion of troops, and as a result the task of capturing Hill 262S fell to Colonel Szydłowski with the 9th Rifles Battalion and the 1st Armoured Regiment. Due to difficulties related to the terrain, fatigue and supply shortages, the operation was not to commence until the morning of 20 August. However, German pressure would make that impossible on that day as well.

At the same time, later in the day on 19 August, the battlegroup of Lieutenant Colonel Zgorzelski, i.e. the 24th Lancers Regiment, the 10th Dragoons Regiment and the anti-tank *dywizjon*, supported by the action and fire of the 10th Mounted Rifles Regiment, attacked Chambois, finally capturing it around 7pm. A little while later, it established communication with the 2nd Battalion of the 395th Infantry Regiment of the 90th American Division, which was entering the Chambois area from the south. Subordinated to Lieutenant Colonel Zgorzelski, the infantry was given the task of defending the town from the south-east and south-west.

Whatever gap remained was now closed, especially for units with heavy equipment.

The concern for ammunition and petrol in Lieutenant Colonel Zgorzelski's group was partially alleviated, because the American battalion was followed by a stream of supplies for everything that was needed for the battle…except for ammunition of any calibre different to that of the Americans, including – worst of all – ammunition for the 75mm guns on our tanks. This had to be airdropped the following night.

After Second Lieutenant Karcz established tactical communication with the American battalion, closer contact was established between the supply lines, namely Lieutenant Wołodkowicz from the division's supply detachments with the quartermaster of the American 701st Tank Destroyer Battalion, Major Moore. One of the first to bring us supplies was an American of Polish descent by the name of Ułaszewski, who then made sure that we received everything we needed.

The American soldiers were as happy as Larry to see us, stuffing cigarettes and chocolate into our pockets at every occasion. One American of Polish descent was given a two-day furlough for good behaviour and came to my tank in order to see 'the Polish General'. He spoke broken Polish – as 'father and mother had taught him' – but even without his assurances, I believed he was Polish at heart.

Reports from both the Canadian and the American armies concerning the capture of Chambois reached the highest level of Allied Command; one claimed it was achieved by the Poles, the other – by the Americans.

Hopefully, neither nation's pride was hurt. The second battalion of the 395th American Infantry Regiment, which entered the town from the south at the end of the fighting, was subordinated to Lieutentant Colonel Zgorzelski, the commander of the entire 'Chambois' battlegroup. Thus, for three days between 19 and 21 August, Chambois was defended by:

- The 10th Dragoons Regiment (Polish)
- The 24th Lancers Regiment (Polish)
- The anti-tank *dywizjon* (Polish)
- A battalion from the 395th Infantry Regiment (American), and American petrol and missiles, which were supplied lavishly to the whole group.

Such a state of affairs was recorded immediately after the battle on the French plaque placed in the town centre, with a bulletin about the victory in the Battle of Normandy.

The Critical Phase of the Battle

The 20 August – the day of crisis for the battle in which the Polish Armoured Division was embroiled. Map No. 3 presents how different factors contributed to the crisis, with the main one being the fact that the Division was isolated from the units of the Canadian Corps. Admittedly, on the evening of 19 August, a detachment from the 4th Canadian Armoured Division seized Saint Lambert-sur-Dives south-east of Trun, but only the north-western part of town and only with about two hundred soldiers with tanks – who, surrounded on all sides by the Germans, found themselves trapped and had to defend themselves heroically in houses and streets, with no control over what went on beyond the battle. A gap of two and a half kilometres remained between them and the nearest Polish troops on the north-western edge of Chambois, through which roads led to the town of Bourdon, the base of the 10th Brigade's command and our artillery positions, and to Coudehard – the rear of the defences of Mont Ormel, as well as the division's supply line. Due to the gap, some German armoured vehicles broke through the base of the 10th Brigade. Some of them would ultimately reach the positions of the 2nd Artillery Regiment where they were smashed by shots fired straight ahead. At the same time, Coudehard was approached from the rear by a desperate attack of German infantry units, heavily supported by mortar fire. This attack advanced up the steep but treeless slope of Mont Ormel and ended with the complete destruction of the German troops by machine-gun fire from our riflemen and tanks. In the undulating valley between Mont Ormel and the hills of Hordouseaux and Écorchés, divided by high hedges along field roads and squares of orchards, a mass of German columns of various sizes streamed by, torn apart by the fire of our artillery and our tanks based in the 'Mace' area. Unusually, Polish and Canadian artillery observers in the 'Mace' area were directing the fire of their batteries while facing their own guns.

The situation in the east was perhaps even more difficult. The lack of any Canadian troops in the area east of us gave the German 2nd Armoured Corps complete freedom of action. It should be remembered that their task was to smash and destroy our Division, capture the Hordouseaux-Trun-Chambois area, and hand it over to the 1st SS Corps.

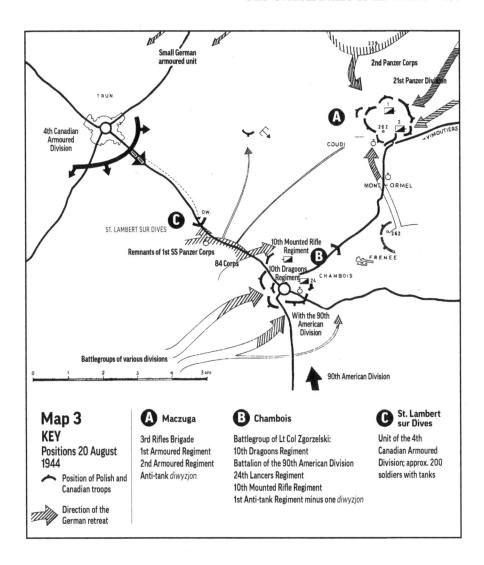

Map 3
KEY
Positions 20 August 1944

➤ Position of Polish and Canadian troops

▨ Direction of the German retreat

Ⓐ Maczuga

3rd Rifles Brigade
1st Armoured Regiment
2nd Armoured Regiment
Anti-tank *diwyzjon*

Ⓑ Chambois

Battlegroup of Lt Col Zgorzelski:
10th Dragoons Regiment
Battalion of the 90th American Division
24th Lancers Regiment
10th Mounted Rifle Regiment
1st Anti-tank Regiment minus one *diwyzjon*

Ⓒ St. Lambert sur Dives

Unit of the 4th Canadian Armoured Division; approx. 200 soldiers with tanks

On 20 August, throughout the day, the German 21st Panzer Division advanced on the 'Mace' from the east, and other units of the 2nd Panzer Corps attacked from the north, breaking through our supply lines and causing severe losses in men and materiel. In this heavy battle we lost the quartermaster of the 10th Armoured Brigade, Captain Jan Kurowski, and the quartermaster of the 1st Motorized Artillery Regiment, Captain Edward Żan-Kreysler. Both fell prey to the Panthers which presented a real threat to the area of Hill 159 and the fighting echelon of the Division headquarters, at a time when a squadron of the 10th Mounted Rifles Regiment had been covering the headquarters, and even more so from the time that all protection fell to just three tanks. Later on, we lost the quartermaster of the 8th Rifles Battalion, Cavalry Captain Józef

Lichtarowicz, and the supply officer of the 24th Lancers Regiment, Lieutenant Jan Skirmunt.

Sometimes it is just as hard and dangerous in an armoured division at the rear as it is on the front line. A pithy Austrian saying comes to mind, 'He who encircles will be encircled.'

Most of these losses among officers and privates from supply units in the battle occurred near Hill 159, as a result of German tanks foraying from the area of the Grand-Mesnil forest – probably some unit of the 2nd SS Panzer Corps.

And although nothing happened to the staff in battle, a certain psychosis arose. I remember that at one slower point of the battle, my aide-de-camp, Lieutenant J. Tarnowski arrived with a report that some real chicken broth was waiting for me at a nearby farm. Since we were all sick to the bone of the constant consumption of canned food, I took with me Colonel A. Grudziński (a representative, together with Colonel J. Krubski, of the Polish Commander-in-Chief at the 21st Army Group command), and the three of us went to the farm. However, we had not yet managed to express our appreciation for the ingenuity and culinary talent of my aide-de-camp, when the chief of staff, Major L. Stankiewicz, arrived in the vanguard of the traffic controllers, armed to the teeth, thundering against my companions: How could they jeopardize a General in such a way and drag him into an uncovered area? However, he agreed with me that, after all, the broth and the chicken must be eaten!

The crisis of the battle was influenced both by the fury of well-prepared German attacks, supported by heavy tanks, artillery and multi-barrelled mortar fire, especially noticeable in the defence of the 'Mace', and by improvised ad hoc attacks, exploding here and there, like tongues of fire jumping out every now and then from a bonfire.

Desperate attacks from the west by various units of the 7th German Army – trying to break out of the trap – crashed into two bastions, as it were.

They crashed against the brave defence of the 10th Dragoons Regiment and the American battalion supported by anti-tank artillery and the tanks of the 24th Lancers Regiment. At some point, the Germans broke through our defences in Chambois but, decimated by the fire and counter-attack of the dragoons' tanks, they surrendered en masse.

They also did not manage to win in a hard fight with the 10th Mounted Rifles Regiment, reinforced with two anti-tank *dywizjon*s, in the area of Hill 113. It was here that the German attack broke down. It had been led personally by the commander of the 84th Corps – General Otto Elfeldt – who was taken prisoner together with his staff and over a thousand soldiers. In these fights, lasting from dawn to nightfall on 20 August, the heroic Major Jan Maciejowski, commander of the 10th Mounted Rifles Regiment, was killed by a sniper bullet.

At this moment there is nothing more appropriate that I could write in honour of this brave commander than the words of his own aide-de-camp: 'He had been dead since morning – and we thought he had been in command of the battle all day.'

While these two bastions blocked the German retreat through Chambois to Vimoutiers, the north-eastern group on the 'Mace' was repelling the attacks of the 2nd Panzer Corps which had advanced from the east, trying to capture the Mont Ormel hills to open the way for the German 7th Army. The battlegroup of two armoured regiments and three riflemen's battalions, concentrated in an area of less than two kilometres, repelled not only the attack of the 21st Panzer Division from the east and units of the 2nd SS Panzer Corps from the north, but also a series of sporadic and improvised strikes by German troops who managed to penetrate the gap between Saint Lambert-sur-Dives and Chambois. Others bypassed Chambois from the southeast, due to another gap between Chambois and the American 90th Division. In critical moments, the 'Mace' was attacked from almost all directions, and we fought the encroaching Germans even at the medics' station and prisoner assembly point. The advantage for us was the Germans' difficulty in coordinating these strikes in time. In the end, the battle was won by the determination and strength of the soldiers of the Polish Armoured Division.

The commanders of the 10th Armoured Brigade had had an exhausting and nerve-wracking day, as it was forced to relocate back to Hill 259 in the face of a temporary threat from the south-west, and had to try to contain the fragmented battlefield. Therefore, the forward echelon of the Division did not move its Command HQ to that hill, as it had planned. Hill 259 was in any case already overloaded with the vehicles of two brigade commands and the divisional artillery.

As a divisional commander, I no longer had any reserves at hand which could intervene, since the potential reserve, the 10th Mounted Rifles Regiment, was in the midst of the hardest fighting and could not be moved.

All that remained for me was to provide moral support to the commanders of the various groups by radio, and to assemble help from outside the Division, by demanding action from neighbouring units, and calling for Canadian heavy artillery fire, air support and airdrops of supplies.

However, my first warnings sent to the higher command that the full thrust of the German Army in retreat had fallen on the Polish Division were met with some disbelief at the Canadian staff headquarters. The headquarters of the 2nd Corps insisted that Saint Lambert-sur-Dives, controlled by the 4th Canadian Armoured Division, sufficiently protected the Polish Division from the north-west. The misunderstanding lay in the fact that St. Lambert had been entered by only a small detachment from the 4th Canadian Armoured Division, which had captured only a small north-western part of the town. Surrounded by the Germans and cut off from their division, they had defended themselves very bravely. However, the larger south-western part of the town, blocking the view of the valley (about two and a half kilometres wide and not controlled by anyone almost up to Chambois), was in German hands all day on 20 August. There, the remnants of two German armoured divisions from the 1st SS Panzer Corps had gathered with Generals von Lüttwitz and Harmel, who little by little were pushing their troops through this gap. This was probably how the headquarters of the 7th Army managed to squeeze out, at a time when the staff of the 5th Panzer Army and the 2nd SS Panzer Corps orchestrated the relief from outside the Falaise pocket, that is, from the region of Rouen.

Only the arrival of the commander of the Canadian Corps in an armoured car at my command post changed the attitude of the Corps staff. General Simonds grasped the situation and issued a series of orders on the spot: for the 3rd Canadian Division to establish contact with us in the direction of Chambois, and for the 4th Armoured Division to attack the 2nd German Panzer Corps, to relieve the Polish Division.

I didn't hear the Canadian Armoured Division commander's reply over the radio, but from the tone and snippets of General Simonds' answer, I guessed the content. After a while, General Simonds told me that during the very same day, the 4th Armoured Division's attack on my eastern flank would alleviate the difficult situation of the Polish Armoured Division.

But on that day, 20 August, the Canadians did not advance.

Early in the morning on 21 August, the Corps commander came to me again, saying that due to a combination of various events, the attack of the Canadian division was just beginning. As he was leaving, he casually added that once I established contact with the 4th Armoured Division, it would have a new commander as of this day: the former chief of staff of the corps, Colonel T.

Somebody's head must have rolled for the attack not having started the day before.

* * *

Around noon on 21 August, the crisis in the battle ended.

The final attack of the 2nd German Panzer Corps from the north-east on the 'Mace' collapsed partly because of the stalwart Polish defence, and partly because of the attack of the 4th Canadian Armoured Division from the north to the eastern foreground of defence.

With the Canadians came supplies of everything that was running low in the Division: ammunition, petrol, food, and medicines. Lines opened for the evacuation of the wounded and prisoners as well.

The battle had been won!

Here and there, small German groups would still bite back, or some armoured vehicle would desperately and noisily try to break through, but by the time I reached the 'Mace' in the afternoon, it was all over.

Without any more fighting, the troops were clearing the area, finally assembling as ordered on 19 August, putting in order the matters of command and supplies which were the main points of concern.

One of the soldiers reporting to me on the 'Mace' was our 'Doctor', as we called Colonel Z. Szydłowski, the commander of the 9th Rifles Battalion, and for the previous two days the actual commander of the entire 'Mace' battlegroup.

He was inhumanly tired and more saddened by our losses than impressed by his own success.

But when I got to Chambois, to Lieutenant Colonel Zgorzelski, among his dragoons and the 24th Lancers Regiment, the awareness of the great victory had already overcome the fatigue and shock after the bloody struggle. Under the captured tent, whose floor was covered with a swastika banner of some SS unit like a carpet, I drank a glass of champagne, which had also been captured, in honour of the lancers, dragoons and anti-tank riflemen.

Only in the 10th Mounted Rifles Regiment the mood was serious, though not depressed. The unit, which had done so much for the Division's victory, from crossing the River Dives near Jort to breaking the attack of General Elfeldt, was bidding a soldierly goodbye to the beloved heroic commander of the regiment – Jan Maciejowski, posthumously appointed Lieutenant Colonel and awarded the Cross of the Order of Virtuti Militari, IV Class.

After all, the code name of the regiment in radio conversations was 'Maciej's children'.

*   *   *

After the battle, anecdotes from it accumulated in stories about the past and in publications in journals or books.

Our most senior prisoner, General Otto Elfeldt, had taken command of the 84th Corps on 28 July, 1944, in the defensive sector at the base of the Cherbourg peninsula, opposing the invasion of the American army. His Corps consisted of the remnants of seven divisions which had already been defeated, with the 116th Panzer Division subordinated to him. From Arromanches-les-Bains he had retreated east to the Orne River and, in the critical days of mid-August, had seized a defensive section in the hills above the town of Falaise.

From this vantage point, the general had watched the movement of British tanks on the eastern side of the River Dives (which belonged to the Polish Armoured Division, although he did not know that at the time). So when he was ordered to break through from Falaise towards the north-east, through the rear of our armoured regiments, he had considered it impossible and had obtained permission from the commander of the 7th Army, General Hausser, to join the parachute troops led by General Meindl and to push from Saint Lambert-sur-Dives towards the south-east. On 19 August, before all the roads to the east had been blocked by the Poles, some of the parachute units managed to escape.

However, following them at dawn on 20 August, he found the retreat cut off. In an attack from St. Lambert, heading across Hill 113 towards the 'Mace', he wanted to break through, but after two hours of fighting with enormous losses in equipment and men, the remains of his Corps were conquered, and he himself and his staff were taken prisoner by our 10th Mounted Rifles Regiment.

In his recap of the events, published by the famous English author B.H. Liddell Hart in the book entitled 'The Other Side of the Hill', General Elfeldt stated that the commander of the Polish Armoured Division was a fine-looking man and a gentleman. This officer had also offered him his last cigarette. Elfeldt also claimed that the Polish Division was in a desperately difficult situation where Polish and German troops were mixed up together.

I have been tempted to accept this compliment as the Division's commander.

However, what about the unfortunate cigarette? I have been a non-smoker all my life and everyone knew it, especially my companions in arms and my personal orderly, who managed my tobacco ration.

I must therefore rectify the record.

The man whom General Elfeldt took for the divisional commander was Major Michał Gutowski, the commander of the reserve squadron of the 10th Mounted Rifles Regiment and later of the 2nd Armoured Regiment. He guarded the Germans captured on that day, including General Elfeldt and his staff. Despite knowing German, Gutowski spoke French with the General and the officers, one of whom was well-known to him as a member of the equestrian team in the Berlin Olympic Games.

In the first moment after being taken prisoner, both the General and his officers behaved arrogantly and were very self-confident, claiming, in view of the fierce battle still going on, that it was not yet known who was being held captive by whom.

Their faces fell with the passage of time, in view of the number of prisoners increasing so fast that the vast clearing could no longer accommodate them. Heavily resigned, they led the procession of prisoners when we handed over the Germans to the Americans, wanting to get rid of this ballast, which was of no use in battle.

Prior to the end of the war, the Germans could not and would not recover from the huge losses in tanks and tank crews suffered by the 5th Panzer Army in the Battle of Normandy. Four months after our battle, in the German winter offensive in the Ardennes which began on 16 December, despite strenuous attempts to reconstruct and supplement the armoured divisions to their full capacity, the number of tanks in the German armoured division ranged from sixty to a maximum of a hundred tanks, which was one third, or at most a half, of their previous establishment (180). Such was the summary of the situation provided in the aforementioned book by Liddell Hart by the commander of the 5th Panzer Army, General Mantteufel, one of the most skilful tank commanders in Germany.

The official German report of 23 August provides the following numbers for those armoured divisions that managed to escape from the trap:

- the 2nd Armoured Division: one infantry battalion without tanks and artillery;
- the 21st Armoured Division: four weak battalions, ten tanks;
- the 116th Armoured Division: one infantry battalion, twelve tanks, two batteries;
- the 1st SS Armoured Division: some infantry, no tanks or artillery;
- the 2nd SS Armoured Division: 450 soldiers, fifteen tanks, six guns;
- the 9th SS Armoured Division: 460 soldiers, 20–25 tanks, twenty guns;
- the 10th SS Armoured Division: four weak battalions without tanks and artillery;
- the 12th SS Armoured Division: 300 soldiers, ten tanks, no artillery.

Two Panzer Divisions were completely and utterly destroyed, namely the Panzer-Lehr Division and the 9th Armoured Division.

The Polish Division had its honourable share in this massacre of ten German armoured divisions,

To illustrate the state of affairs even better, on D-Day the 12th SS Panzer Division (Hitlerjugend) had 20,000 soldiers and 150 tanks, half of them Panthers.

The losses among the parachute formations of the 2nd Parachute Corps, used in Normandy as infantry divisions, had such an impact on the condition of these troops that only with great effort could General Kurt Student manage to form one battalion of 1,000 paratroopers in December 1944 and use them during the Ardennes offensive.

This is not surprising, considering the desperate attempts of the paratroopers to break through at Falaise. Even the most drastic orders did not help: facing the rumours that the 3rd Parachute Division was surrounded, its commander claimed they must be false, since a German parachute division could never be surrounded, and anyone who thought otherwise was a coward and ought to be spat at in the face.

We do not know if German soldiers thought the same or differently – those whose corpses lay in their hundreds along the slopes of the 'Mace' and the frontline at Chambois long after the battle, as proof of a desperate will to break through.

Summary of the Battle –
The Highs and the Lows of the Battle of the
Polish Armoured Division at Falaise

I will start with the losses because, in the first hours after the end of the fighting, these were the most pronounced, and had the most profound influence on the mentality of commanders and soldiers.

We were a formation accumulating history.

Becoming motorized before September 1939, the battles of the 10th Cavalry Brigade in Poland in 1939 and in France in 1940, several years of hand-picking men with different temperaments, training in intensive, close collaboration, sticking together in France and Great Britain – all that created a particular atmosphere. A regiment, squadron or platoon commander lost in battle was not just a number. It was 'Maciej' or 'Władek' – a friend, colleague or a long-time subordinate. A tank driver or a rifleman was not a number either, it was 'Franek' or 'Staszek', 'the one I knew from the September campaign' or 'from France', 'the one who was brave at Wysoka or Montbard, with whom we had escaped from Hungary or France'. It was often another soldier's son or cousin, because such was the web of connections.

The Division had been under constant fire for two weeks, the last days and nights of which had been a waking nightmare. We emerged from the battle shaken hard, with numbers dwindling before my eyes. For that reason I entertained the possibility of pulling the Division back for a few months for rest, replenishment and regrouping. The commanders repeatedly asked me to do so for the sake of their troops and colleagues. The assigned British liaison officers assured me that they would obtain the approval of the Allied commanders.

After such a difficult task, I fondly envisioned myself enjoying a still-sunny September in France, with wine and the bounty of early autumn.

My misgivings were deepened by anonymous letters from Great Britain, such as the one signed 'A Polish Mother', which implored me not to envy Anders' successes and to prevent more shedding of precious Polish blood. 'Yes! Very precious,' I thought bitterly. 'As long as we shed it. It would soon go cheap, if we stopped doing so.'

However, one fundamental argument prevailed and crushed all the qualms and outweighed all considerations.

The Division had played its part in conditions and circumstances so exceptional that they could not be regarded as typical for our type of formation. And when there was finally an opportunity for the actual employment of the Armoured Division in pursuit, were we to be eliminated? And the recognition for the successful pursuit – an easy task compared to what we had done up to this point – would be enjoyed by the British, Canadian and American soldiers! Everyone but the Poles. And all this at a moment when Warsaw was bleeding out. Unable to help directly, only by fighting with Germany could we connect with those at home, albeit on a distant front! It was still so important that the name of the fighting Polish soldier remained on the lips of the world.

I wrote a brief report to the commander of the Canadian Army stating that, according to my assessment, the Division, after a week's rest and the incorporation of the reserves that were with us in France, would be understaffed but fit for use.

I prepared a longer report with fuller arguments to the Commander-in-Chief, General Sosnkowski.

And to this day I feel tremendous gratitude to the General for his immediate response, approving my 'soldierly stance', as he put it.

The fantastical theories, born a few years after the end of fighting, about some 'Sanacja-inspired conspiracy' and the pressures exerted on me to announce the Division's 'neutrality' as an act of protest are as false as they are morbidly absurd.[10] Neither in Aldershot at the end of July 1944, nor in France in August did General Paszkiewicz come to me with any warning on this matter. Nor was there any immediate reason for any ludicrous protest. We had gathered in Aldershot before the outbreak of the Uprising, so the lack of Allied help for Warsaw, which was rapidly bleeding out, could not have motivated such a step, and Yalta was several months away at that point.

*   *   *

In stark numbers, the losses of the Polish Armoured Division in the Battle of Falaise – because that is what the whole operation was called – were as follows:

- 325 killed, including 21 officers,
- 1,002 wounded, including 35 officers,
- 114 missing.

---

10. Translators' note: Maczek here dismisses the accusation that anyone from the pre-war Sanacja regime exerted any political influence over the actions of the 1st Polish Armoured Division.

Total number of losses – 1,441 soldiers, i.e. about 10 per cent of the total initial numbers, amounting in frontline units to an average of 20 per cent of losses, and in some cases coming up to over 30 per cent. Our losses were offset by many times by those on the German side. There is no record of the Germans killed and wounded in this battle, and I doubt that even an approximate number could be determined in the chaos and intermingling of the units. All in all, we named the battlefield where we fought aptly: 'Psie Pole' (lit. 'the field of dogs'), as a historical reference to the battlefield at Legnica.[11]

The German losses that we were able to record were the following:

- Prisoners of war – 5113, including 137 officers with a General and 4 Colonels, 2 Lieutenant Colonels, etc.,
- In equipment: 55 tanks, 44 guns, 38 armoured cars, 207 motor vehicles, 152 horse-drawn vehicles, not counting a significant amount of heavy machine guns and small-calibre handguns.

The amount of equipment acquired was much larger, as the above list only includes equipment with coordinates provided by the units to check the lists. It does not include equipment extracted from the bushes, orchards, forests, etc., because it wasn't the Poles who cleared the area after the battle. My deputy Colonel K. Dworak, who was in charge of the lists, was a model of conscientiousness and accuracy. He had a saying known throughout the Division: 'We Poles like to exaggerate; we did not seize 100 cannon, only 99.' These figures also do not reflect our share in that mass of prisoners and equipment, which, cut off by us in retreat, abandoned all attempts to break through from the start and voluntarily surrendered. And there were thousands of them.

Officially, the Canadians reported the following data in the area of Trun – Argentan – Chambois:

- 187 tanks, 157 armoured vehicles, 1,778 trucks, 669 passenger cars, 252 guns – a total of 3043 guns, tanks and vehicles, plus 1270 additional guns, tanks and motor vehicles abandoned further to the west.

We received praise for the actions of the Division in this decisive battle from the Corps commander General Simonds, from the commander of the Canadian

---

11. Translators' note: According to some historians, after the battle fought on 24 August 1109 near Wrocław between Bolesław III Wrymouth of Poland and his exiled half-brother Zbigniew supported by the Holy Roman Empire, the utter defeat of the latter led to the German forces withdrawing from Poland. The number of dead and dying left on the battlefield was so high that it is said to have attracted throngs of wild dogs to it, hence the name of the place.

Army General Crerar, and from General Montgomery, who would later make his historical comparison when talking about the battle of Falaise: 'The Germans were trapped as if they were in a bottle, and the Polish Armoured Division was the cork in this bottle.'

But the military professionals were most pleased by an enthusiastic article in the specialist British magazine *The Tank*. The author, stating that the Polish Armoured Division played a leading role in the victory of the Allies in Normandy by closing the gap, which was the only remaining way out for the decimated German army, wrote the following: 'No other battlefield in Normandy gives such an impression of inferno, disaster and death as that to the north-east of Chambois.'

The Division had long since shaken off the Normandy dust from its tanks' caterpillar tracks and was rushing towards the Belgian border when a tour of military attachés from London went to view the 'Mace' ridge. On the bald Hill 262, from which stretched a panoramic view of the battlefield of the 1st Polish Armoured Division, stood a tall mast with a board inscribed: 'A Polish Battlefield'. All the destroyed Panthers, Tigers, Ferdinands, Shermans and Cromwells were still there, having not yet been removed. The road from Chambois to Vimoutiers was cleared with bulldozers, as one would sweep the roads with snow ploughs after a snowstorm. And at the top, the commander of the British heavy tank brigade, which remained there to clear the battlefields, explained the positioning to the visitors. He was able to trace the caterpillar tracks of our tanks and those of the Germans and decipher exactly the course of the battle, which was the greatest tank battle of the invasion, boasting that he probably knew the story of the battle better than those who had commanded it. The Polish Division had been in the middle, fighting on two fronts with the 2nd Panzer Corps from the east and the 1st SS Panzer Corps from the west. A little further on was the 4th Canadian Armoured Division, whose tracks came up to the 'Mace' at the end of the battle. Further away, from the south and southwest, were the tracks of two armoured divisions which came to the battle after its conclusion: the 2nd French Armoured Division of General Leclerc from General Patton's army and the 11th British Armoured Division from the 2nd British Army of General Dempsey.

A few years later, searching for the reasons as to why Falaise had not become the grave of the entire German army in western Europe, such that the Allies' march eastwards to Germany would have become simply a leisurely stroll, an opinion was concocted that the Polish Armoured Division had let a part of the German Army slip out to the east. That same part of the Army would, after the defeat, regroup; its resolve stiffened, even before the onset of winter, it would be able to successfully resist and even, in mid-December, under Rundstedt's command, launch a daring counterattack in the Ardennes.

Such accusations are completely flimsy and would have had to strike far higher than the level of a divisional, or even corps, commander.

Firstly:

At the moment when 'The Polish division closed the steel gates sealing the final gap that had allowed the Germans to retreat' (an expression from the British periodical, *The Tank*), this part of the German Army had already left the 'pocket' to the east. We know for a fact that the entire German 2nd Panzer Corps got out, we have no records for other formations, but they had to be – although heavily decimated – quite numerous.

Instead of talking of 'cutting the German Army off', perhaps it would be more correct to say that it was 'cut up', with the smaller part of about 30 per cent already outside, while the majority of about 70 per cent were within the closing pocket.

Secondly:

This supposed 'sneaking out' was in fact a hard battle of all the Division's troops to the last tank, gun and rifleman, lasting from the night of 17–18 August to the evening hours of 19 August. The fighting continued, both against the troops trying to break out, and with the armoured corps on the outside of the pocket, which were tasked with the destruction of the Polish Division.

During this time, the German army, although it was being raided by the air force, was still using the retreat routes eastward through Trun and Chambois towards Vimoutiers, until the arrival of the 10th Mounted Rifles Regiment at Trun on the evening of 18 August, and then only through Chambois until the evening of August 19 – the moment it reached the American battalion. The delay in approaching Chambois, due to Lieutenant Colonel Koszutski's battlegroup's detour through Champeaux, had as many downsides as it had upsides. The lost hours in the approach to Chambois were offset by the fact that Lieutenant Colonel Koszutski's unit surprised the 2nd German Panzer Division and was therefore able to provide cover for our left flank.

Thirdly:

Already, after the final closing of the gap for the German retreat, on 20 August, when the Polish Armoured Division was in the difficult situation of being isolated in battle, certain German groups escaped, particularly through Saint Lambert-sur-Dives, for the reasons set forth above. They were only small groups, scraps really, which managed to get out of the entrapment, without heavy equipment and under constant fire from our artillery and tanks on the 'Mace'.

The reason why about 40 per cent of the 7th Army and Eberbach's Armoured Group managed to escape being entirely cut off can be traced elsewhere. It derived from a huge misunderstanding at the highest echelons of the Allied forces. As we know today, on 13 August, the American Army of General Patton was already in the area south of Argentan, so a dozen or so kilometres on the other side (south) of Falaise. As a great soldier with tactical and operational sense, the General saw clearly the importance of the southern arm of the pincers, and so his 15th Corps was marching on Argentan. However, the division of areas of responsibility between the 12th Army Group of General Bradley and General Montgomery's 21st Army Group ran about eight miles south of Argentan. Giving orders to the commander of the 15th Corps, General Wade H. Haislip, Patton ordered slow pressure until making contact with the British, not wanting to overly expose his Corps and fearing accidental American-British bloodshed. In the evening of 13 August, Patton revoked the order and ordered American troops to stop south of Argentan. This was by order of his Army Group commander.

The demarcation line drawn on the map became an insurmountable obstacle to total success, an obstacle much greater than the resistance of the German army in retreat.

The reason for the revocation of the order, apart from Bradley's fears about whether Patton would be able to oppose the swarming mass of the German army in retreat, was an exaggerated fear of a misunderstanding on the battlefield and the prospect of 'friendly fire' between American and British troops. For this reason, from 13 to 17 August, American troops were standing idly by south of Argentan, while German troops passed to the east right in front of their noses, harassed only by the air strikes until the advance of the northern arm of the pincers, the vanguard of which was the Polish Armoured Division.

Reality laid these exaggerated fears bare when, after giving up on the demarcation line and moving the American army from the south, the encounter with the supposed 'British' took the form of a courteous communication between the patrol commanded by Second Lieutenant Karcz from the Polish 10th Dragoon Regiment and the leading company of the American regiment. But this did not happen until the evening of 19 August.

Thus, in the decisive days of the battle, an extremely peculiar situation emerged. In the south:

• The army of General Patton, still in the area south of Argentan, began to move northwards on 17 August, after four days of respecting the separation between the two Groups of the Army.

In the north:

- The Canadian Army's infantry divisions finished the battle for the town of Falaise, where the last resistance was overcome only in the evening of 17 August; only then did the 4th Canadian Armoured Division seize the heavily defended crossings on the Dives river and its tributary from the town of Falaise,
- And the Polish Armoured Division, completely isolated as it was, entered the area that determined the German retreat – the area of the hills above the Trun – Chambois road. Montgomery's order to extend the area of the Polish armoured division's responsibility to Chambois only increased our isolation, as it wasn't until the evening of 19 August that a weak detached unit of the 4th Canadian Armoured Division entered the northwestern part of Saint Lambert-sur-Dives. Also about the same time one American battalion joined the Poles in Chambois itself.

To put the situation into perspective: the Polish Armoured Division, with two Allied units attached, grabbed the bull by the horns and harnessed its raging momentum, while the rest of the Canadian Army and the 2nd British Army was striking the fleeing animal on its rump and flanks, adding only to the speed of its flight.

This simile is not intended as criticism. War likes to create such paradoxical images. It only emphasizes the real situation of the 1st Polish Armoured Division, whose soldiers gave everything they had in this battle for the common cause of the Allied forces.

As the battle unfolded, increasing numbers of Canadian troops were drawn into heavy combat. German confidence, having been undermined by the troops of the 1st Polish Armoured Division, caused the mass of German troops flowing in retreat from the west to swell more and more. This, in turn, made the Germans spread sideways, outside of the lines of the intended break-through between St. Lambert and Chambois. And so mass attacks ensued on 20–21 August northwest of St. Lambert-Magny-Trun executed by the 84th Infantry Division, the commander of which, General Erwin Menny, was captured by the Canadians. Some of his troops broke through and joined the 2nd SS Panzer Corps. Meanwhile, south of Chambois, the German attack on the 90th American Division on Le Bourg-Saint-Léonard interrupted the Division's communication with its battalion in Chambois, which remained under the orders of the Polish commander of the battlegroup, Lieutenant Colonel Zgorzelski.

In an objective assessment of the whole battle in Normandy which, despite the escape of 40 per cent of the German army from the trap, was a great victory for the Allied forces, the Canadians emphasize the absolute advantage on the side of the Allies not only of the air force, but also in the size of the army. The paradox, however, was that at the decisive point for the German retreat the Polish Armoured Division fought against an absolute advantage of armoured forces and troop numbers of the part of the Germans. Only the air force was undeniably superior on the Allied side.

There was also another facet to it all. Exaggerated rumours began to spread among the Poles in London and throughout Britain about the huge losses of the Polish Division, about unnecessary bloodshed, and the insane, almost suicidal employment of the formation by its commander. The overblown news brought by the first transports of the wounded about those who had died, and those who had supposedly died and in fact enjoy good health to this day, were supplemented by overactive imaginations with random numbers and visions of hell on the battlefield.

So when I came to London for a few days, General Kukiel, who was then the Minister of National Defence, wanted to squash these rumours and brought me to a meeting of the Council of Ministers where I laid out the actual state of affairs. It became evident that the price we had paid for not merely participating in this battle, but for playing the main role in it, was lower than that of the Canadian Infantry Division and the 4th Canadian Armoured Division, and probably ten times lower than that of the German army in our area of the battle. And the German soldier was still defiant and capable, and the desperate situation had intensified the strength of his resistance.

After all, numbers are always the most convincing.

*   *   *

A week after the fighting at Chambois and the 'Mace', the Division was actually ready for further deployment.

Despite the depletion of the first reinforcements that the Division had in Normandy and the injection of specialists from Britain, we had to lower the number of platoons in armoured squadrons from four to three, and the numbers in the riflemen companies fell to about a hundred privates.

I made personnel changes to the more important positions. Current suitability for combat was the decisive factor. Following the request of Colonel Wieroński, I passed the command of the 3rd Rifles Brigade to Colonel Franciszek Skibiński, the erstwhile deputy commander of the 10th Armoured Brigade. Colonel Wieroński was a very good infantryman, decorated by me with the Virtuti Militari order for the Battle of Potigny on 15 August; however, he had not taken to the particular nature of combat at the Rifles Brigade as part of the Armoured

Division and thought that someone else would be better in this position. Cavalry Captain J. Stachowicz replaced Captain J. Nawara as the chief of staff of the 3rd Rifles Brigade. The 10th Mounted Rifles Regiment was taken over by the youngest squadron commander, Major Jerzy Wasilewski. From the first battles of the 10th Brigade at Naprawa up to Falaise, he had been getting ready to take this position and he had the greatest potential.

The command of the 24th Lancers Regiment was taken over by Major Rakowski, a seasoned officer of this regiment, and the command of the Anti-Tank Regiment was handed to Major Eastmont, who has already featured several times in this memoir.

In view of the transfer of Major M. Czarnecki to London, Major T. Wysocki became the chief of staff of the 10th Armoured Brigade.

Despite our numbers being low and despite personnel changes, or perhaps because of them, the Division was in great shape, full of fresh experiences, and with high morale.

From the Seine to the Ghent Canal, the Pursuit

Is there any word in the military lexicon which is closer to a soldier's heart? Despite hardship and toil, despite physical exhaustion, which is sometimes no less intense than that experienced by a soldier in retreat, never is the sun of success brighter, never is reality more favourable and forgiving of the errors and mistakes from which no fighting soldier's life is free.

Starting from September 1939, we had experienced all forms of fighting, from defence to offence, from counter-attack to the most exhausting retreat, from breaking through to creeping through, except for that one coveted form: the pursuit.

The pursuit was most identified in our thoughts and desires with the notion of retaliation.

We wanted our personal revenge for so many things, so many horrors. Had we not launched our battles in Normandy at the same time as the Warsaw Uprising had broken out?

The Pursuit!

Already on 31 August, without yet making contact with the Germans, the Division's wheeled vehicles swallowed up 85 km, when circumstances had allowed for them to be separated from the tracked vehicles. We had crossed the Seine via the 'Warsaw' bridge, built in a record time and manner by Lieutenant Colonel Durant's sappers, who moved ahead of us.

What an immense difference to when we had crossed this river in June 1940 with a small handful of the 10th Armoured Cavalry Brigade, harassed by the German air force, looking for a way out from the enemy closing in on us.

How radically our roles had changed!

The Division was rested, and the fighting morale among the troops was at the highest level. 'Good hunting in Europe', Montgomery had wished us at the beginning of the invasion. It was only now that these words were becoming reality.

This was despite being down by 8 per cent on the food supply, which meant at least down by 20 per cent in terms of combat-readiness.

A series of major and lesser water courses crossed our northeasterly route. I suggested to the commander of the Canadian Corps, therefore, a deviation towards the south-east, which would allow us to avoid these obstacles or to cross in places which were less wide and deep. My suggestion was adopted, but only for the Canadian formation. We were moved to the axis heading Abbeville – Ypres [Ieper].

Again, as had been the case before, we were led by the inscriptions 'Polish Forces Priority' – through the communication lines of the Canadian divisions, which were already well advanced along their routes.

But we quickly made up for lost time and moved to the front.

I sent Colonel Skibiński with Major Stankiewicz to London to attend to matters of supplementing the Division, so the Rifle Brigade was commanded by the deputy Lieutenant Colonel Dec, and my chief of staff was Cavalry Captain Kamil Czarnecki. The latter, a person full of humour and optimism, had passed the test for this position with flying colours amid all the changing circumstances. He was also pleasant company as a comrade in arms in my command tank, which was our mode of transport.

Conforming to tradition, the first day of the pursuit – on 1 September 1944, exactly five years since the beginning of the German invasion of Poland – belonged to the 10th Mounted Rifles Regiment, supported by a squadron of dragoons, an anti-tank *dywizjon* and sappers. After sixty kilometres of pursuit, the Mounted Rifles surprised the German defence on the Brezel river near Blangy, taking combat equipment and over 200 prisoners, as well as preventing the bridge from being blown up.

Instead of the most depressing sight of all – those strings of wagons, evacuees fleeing with their hastily gathered possessions, children, women, the elderly watching every retreat manoeuvre with silent reproach – instead of all this the roads, streets, villages and towns were full of joy and gaiety. Where did it all come from? So many flags of national colours, so many Polish flags, so many flowers, so much wine, champagne, aperitifs and food! And all of this in north-eastern France, which had seemingly been ravaged by Germans to the bone? And this surprising enthusiasm of the crowd that it was not the English who were liberating them, but the Poles. 'Vive la Pologne!' rolled through the streets like thunder, preceded us, accompanied us and infected everyone with enthusiasm.

On the third day, I had to issue a categorical ban on motorcyclists from Traffic Control accepting these heaps of flowers and receiving these enthusiastic greetings from the population, and God forbid, indulging in the offered refreshments. Because of all the commotion, one day our Traffic Control regulated the route of the Division so shoddily that we ended up on a circuitous route. All this to the great despair of their commander, Major A. Pieregorodzki, who was usually so resourceful, even in the most difficult of conditions, in controlling the movement of the massive machine which was the Armoured Division. The results of the reconnaissance on 2 September informed us that the Somme, a river of historic importance in the First World War, where history had repeated itself with the German incursion in 1940, as well as the equally historical city of Abbeville, had been prepared for defence by a very strong *Kampfgruppe*, i.e. a combat group with artillery and mortars. Under the cover of the tanks of the 10th Mounted Rifles Regiment, which dominated the high bank of the river and the opposite bank, the Podhale Rifles Battalion secured a part of the town on the west side of the river. At the same time, sapper and infantry reconnaissance from the 3rd Rifle Brigade explored the conditions for thrusting further north on the river in the area of the Port-le-Grand forest. The map suggested it would be easy to move troops and river crossing equipment at this location. As the commander of the operation, I appointed Second Lieutenant Dec, an officer who was well suited to this task, with whom we had 'conquered' many a crossing before the war during the manoeuvres by the River Niemen, under the leadership of General Franciszek Kleeberg.

On the night of 2 and 3 September, the 8th Rifle Battalion crossed to the other shore, partly on assault boats, and partly via a footbridge built by the sappers; then the 9th Rifle Battalion crossed, outmanoeuvring the German troops, and the Podhale Rifles Battalion approached from the front using an improvised crossing. The Germans, besieged on all sides, defended themselves poorly. At noon, Abbeville was free and celebrating. The whole brigade was on the eastern bank of the River Somme. The 10th Brigade, with their tanks and artillery, had to wait until evening to complete the construction of the bridge for heavy equipment.

The capture of Abbeville made the pursuit easier to the extent that we could finally proceed to a so-called parallel pursuit along two axes at the same time, as previously the crossings and bridges available to us had forced us into one column. The intercepted order of the 86th German Corps informed us that the Germans, unable to retreat to the east due to the pace of the Allied pursuit, had chosen to retreat to the north-east, directing three divisions – the 331st, 346th and 711th – to the beaches of Dunkirk, leaving ad hoc battlegroups stationed along water courses on our route, which were supposed to delay us.

It was all the more important to be quick and not to allow these battlegroups to get organized and to burrow into their defensive positions. But when it comes to speed, there are two kinds. One is measured by the strength of the legs of an infantryman or a horse, or the engine of a motor vehicle. The other is about arranging troops in advance into a manoeuvre to evade resistance, or to circumvent, which reduces the time needed for the preparation and orientation of the units. The latter task was made immeasurably easier by launching the pursuit in two parallel axes.

Thus, from the night of 3 and 4 September, the Division operated along two axes in order to control the crossings on the Neuf Fossé canal.

The 10th Armoured Cavalry Brigade led on both axes, with the 3rd Rifle Brigade following. The 10th Brigade was largely to bypass obstacles, especially in the towns, and push forward, while the 3rd Rifles Brigade was to finish the job by seizing territory and mopping up all remaining resistance in the town, or by methodically forcing the crossing and building a bridge, if there was no other way of pushing forward.

4 September was a day of battling against the terrain, i.e. the three rivers, Authie, Canche and Ternoise, searching for undamaged bridges and crossings, veering from the axis and returning to it when the obstacle was passed. At long last we pushed forward to the Ternoise river with a ford seized by the 24th Lancers Regiment in an elegant action near the forest of Hesdin.

The prisoners taken during the day belonged to the 245th and the 164th Infantry Divisions, and therefore, as we had anticipated, were not from the 86th Corps mentioned above, which had already turned north.

Despite the rain and gusty winds, despite the sodden roads along frequent detours, fending off the resistance of smaller German units, the Division covered over fifty kilometres on 5 September and the 24th Lancers Regiment seized an undamaged bridge on the Bléquin river near the town of Wizernes on the northern axis. But the reconnaissance, which was spread out across fifteen kilometres along the Neuf-Fossé canal, found all the bridges had been blown up, and encountered the fire of heavy machine guns and mortars from the opposite bank, and even from heavily defended outposts of the fortifications on the southern shore.

The best conditions for crossing seemed to be in the south, so the 1st Armoured Regiment cleared the southern shore and conquered the defended Belle-Croix. In an independent action, the 10th Dragoons Regiment, supported by a squadron of the 24th Lancers Regiment, seized the town of St. Omer with true bravado, thus celebrating their regimental feast. While the enemy was distracted with these developments, the 3rd Rifle Brigade seized a small bridgehead on the canal under Blaringhem, which allowed the construction of a bridge at night.

On 6 September, the bridge was put to use at 9.00 am by the Division which, passing the undefended town of Cassel and moving along two axes, crossed the Belgian border at 1.40 pm and, after breaking limited resistance in the town of Poperinghe [Poperinge], approached the historic city of Ypres.

History gazed at us not only from the walls of this medieval city, from the arch of the [Menin] gate, or from the monument of the war of 1914–18, but also from the thousands upon thousands of crosses in Allied cemeteries from the previous war, which we passed in our pursuit. Once upon a time, every metre of land seized in an offensive action was a success which had cost multitudes of fallen soldiers. And today? The triumph of the tactics of speed. The 10th Armoured Cavalry Brigade, when encountering the defences of Ypres, bypassed them quickly around both sides and came out to the north-east of the town, thus cutting off the retreat of the German units. Meanwhile, in the evening, the 3rd Rifle Brigade entered into action. First with the 9th Rifle Battalion, which captured the north and north-western part of the city in fierce fighting through the streets, and finally with the whole Brigade, which quickly cleared the city of individual groups still defending themselves in several buildings.

From the morning of 7 September, the Division continued its pursuit along two axes. After the 10th Brigade took Passendale [Passchendaele], the 2nd Armoured Regiment broke the German battalion in the city of Hoogled [Hooglede] and crossed the highway from the town of Roulers [Roeselare] to the north, while the 9th Rifle Battalion broke through the German defences two kilometres north of Roulers.

By nightfall the western edge of the city had been seized by the Brigade, which now prepared for a night-time sweep of the town. The population of the city not only demonstratively welcomed our soldiers, but also helped. Great credit in identifying the location of nests of anti-tank weapons and machine guns is due to a brave seventeen-year-old girl scout Simonne Brugghe, whom I decorated a few weeks later with the Polish Cross of Valour.

In the evening, without waiting for the battle of Roulers to end, I ordered the formation of a battlegroup, consisting of the 24th Lancers Regiment and one company, and later the whole of the 8th Rifle Battalion, and two *dywizjon*s of motor and anti-tank artillery under the new commander of the 24th Lancers, Lieutenant Colonel Dowbor. The task was to reach the town of Thielt [Tielt], so as not to give the Germans time to organize a solid defence.

This operation took the Germans entirely by surprise. The town was as yet undefended by the German troops, which were still gathering. Thus, our approach from the east was not only not halted, but even passed unnoticed, and the fighting started only in the centre of the city, with the tank platoons of the 24th Lancers Regiment competing with the rifle platoons of the 8th Battalion to seize control over the town, street by street, house by house.

Meanwhile, the leading regiment of the 10th Brigade, which on that day was the 2nd Armoured Regiment, had a lucky day as it moved out towards the northeast of the city in order to cut off the German retreat. It surprised an improvised column of tanks, motor vehicles, artillery and horse-drawn wagons in retreat, literally destroying them with fire from their tanks' guns near the town of Ruysellede [Ruiselede]. The image of destruction on this road was so reminiscent of the recent views from the Mace and Chambois that it was dubbed the 'little Chambois'.

Thus, on 9 September, the Division reached the heavily defended Ghent canal. The leading troops, buoyant with their recent success, were pinned down and sustained losses. The 10th Dragoons Regiment suffered particularly heavily, and their commander, Lieutenant Colonel Zgorzelski, was wounded in an attempt to move a part of the regiment to the northern bank.

The Division therefore proceeded to prepare for the methodical forcing of the channel, but an order from the Corps directed us to bypass this resistance through Ghent, which was already partially occupied by the 7th Armoured Division of the 2nd British Army.

The first act of the pursuit, or perhaps the pursuit as such, was over.

Over ten days, with constant, sometimes extremely heavy, fighting, and despite the hindrance of the blown-up bridges and the damp roads on detours, the Division had covered 470 kilometres!

That was like travelling from Gdynia to Kraków.

The Division had suffered the following losses from August 31 to September 9:

- 57 killed (including 2 officers),
- 170 wounded (including 13 officers)

But what a tremendous disparity between our losses and those of the Germans who, not counting the great number of killed and wounded, surrendered the following numbers of prisoners to the Division:

- 40 officers and 3,447 privates,

Combat equipment seized and recorded:

- 47 guns of various calibres,
- 2 tanks,
- 3 armoured cars,
- 2 tractors,
- 8 mortars,
- 2 anti-aircraft guns.

The extent of our revenge was apparent not only based on the above list or from the maps at the staff headquarters showing the amount of ground covered; the feeling of retaliation was palpable among every soldier of the Division. It was sometimes the cause of unnecessary losses, when caution was thrown to the wind.

The feeling was heightened by the way in which Flanders greeted us – as liberators – with the enthusiasm of the masses of the Flemish population.

The city of Ypres insisted that I reinstall the old mayor, brought out of hiding from the Germans, and at a solemn reception at the town hall, I was asked to make an entry on behalf of the Polish Armoured Division into the city's book of honour – just under the signature of Marshal Foch from 1918.

The Regent of Belgium awarded the 9th Rifle Battalion the honorary *fouragères* of the Croix de Guerre and the title of 'Flanders Riflemen', which became the official name of this brave unit, the youngest one in the Armoured Division.

From Ghent to Terneuzen

G hent, the charming capital of Flanders, known by many Polish students before the war for its university, had only been partially captured by the British troops of the 7th Armoured Division. Just outside the city centre, the enthusiasm of the liberated population faded, and suddenly there was emptiness. In the northern part of the city, the Germans were firmly entrenched, holding the port on the canal and a number of concrete structures – warehouses and factories. Several guns of extremely heavy calibre shelled the approaches and the places where the aggregation of troops was suspected, as well as the city itself.

The capture of the northern part of Ghent and pushing the Germans to the north was not the main task of the Division; it was rather a means to an end and a necessity, if a more important goal was to be achieved. It was of a preliminary and supportive nature, because the main communication lines, and not only those of our Division, would pass through Ghent. And the actual goal was to capture and clear German troops from the entire strip of land between the city and the sea, a strip more than thirty kilometres wide.

It spread between the Terneuzen Canal (connecting Ghent and the port of Terneuzen) and the River Scheldt, on the opposite bank of which lay Antwerp – the port planned for the future offensive against Germany.

Could the campaign have been concluded by the winter of 1944? The matter has been the subject of fervent discussion, starting during the war and becoming more intense as the memoirs of the main actors of the campaign on the Continent were being published: the Supreme Commander General Eisenhower, the commander of the 21st Army Group (now) Field Marshal Montgomery, the commander of the 12th Army Group – General Bradley and the posthumously published memories of General Patton, the commander of the 3rd U.S. Army.

Field Marshal Montgomery saw a missed opportunity in the rejection of his plan for a concentrated narrow strike by the entirety of both Army Groups in a northerly direction, towards Berlin. He criticized Eisenhower's decision to engage on a broad front to capture the Rhine crossings for the time being, and to postpone the final strike until the port of Antwerp was open. General

Patton, on the other hand, blamed everything on directing all support and, above all, fuel and ammunition to the 21st Group, when the 3rd Army in the south would have had every chance of crossing the Rhine and continuing its strike on Germany if the lack of fuel and ammunition had not inhibited its momentum.

Montgomery's chief of staff, General de Guingand, was leaning towards General Eisenhower, having as chief of staff a greater understanding of quartermaster matters and the fact that not having a port meant the excessive extension of the supply lines.

Leaving the future to settle who was right, this discussion clearly highlighted the great importance of the port of Antwerp for further operations, especially for the rapid and abundant supply needed for the attack on Germany.

Around 5 September, the troops of the 2nd British Army had managed to seize the city of Antwerp itself, but only up to the Albert Canal, behind which the Germans were still firmly entrenched. The use of the port, even passing over the need to repair the damaged facilities while still under German fire, was out of the question. Access to the port via a fifty-kilometre-long gulf (the Scheldt estuary) was blocked by the Germans, who held onto the Walcheren and Beveland peninsulas, as well as the south-western and eastern part of the Dutch province of Zeeland.

This fortified coastal strip was a continuation of the German defensive system stretching along the coast all the way from Dunkirk in France. It significantly impeded the advance of the 1st Canadian Army.

Under these conditions, pushing the Germans from the Albert Canal north towards the Scheldt and even up to the River Meuse became a matter of urgent necessity.

In view of the duality of the task – northern Ghent and the Dutch province of Oost Vlaanderen – the Polish Division operated initially in two different directions: a localized attack by Colonel Skibiński directly north of the centre of Ghent to capture the northern part of the city and to remove the threat from the north, and an operation by Colonel Majewski towards the east to control the future starting base in the Lokeren and Sint-Niklaas area, and to survey the terrain to the north of these towns for a future operation.

In the first days, the emphasis was on the former direction of action in Ghent. In a two-day assault, the 3rd Rifle Brigade, consisting of the 8th and the 9th Rifle Battalions, and the 24th Lancers Regiment, supported by the 1st Motorized Artillery Regiment and by Typhoon air strikes (used occasionally to soften the German resistance in the concrete facilities), expelled the Germans from the northern part of the city, but only up to the River Lieve.

Meanwhile, until 14 September, the 10th Armoured Brigade, without the 24th Lancers Regiment, but with a battalion of the Podhale Rifles, seized and cleared the area north of Sint-Niklaas, which included the towns of Stekene, La Trompe, and Sint-Gillis-Waas.

In the face of these achievements, I regrouped the Division, leaving a detachment north of Ghent composed of the 24th Lancers Regiment, the 8th Rifles Battalion and two motorized artillery and anti-tank *dywizjon*s under the command of Colonel Dec. It was given the task of protecting Ghent from the north. I focused the rest of the Division on the captured area north-west of Sint-Niklaas.

The detachment left in Ghent fulfilled its duty to the hospitable city in a chivalrous manner, when the 24th Lancers Regiment attempted a daring raid on 16 September and seized the German heavy artillery whose 210mm guns that had been plaguing the city for some time.

Noblesse oblige!

* * *

Ahead of the Division's detachment which, as part of the 3rd Brigade, was striking northwards, towards the shores of the sea, there lay a new country: the Netherlands. In fact, it was its exposed protruding part, the province of Zeeland to the west of the mouth of the Scheldt river (which still belonged to Belgium). As a border province, Zeeland had defensive remnants from the old days in the form of forts, whose defensive power consisted not so much in the strength of shelters and fortifications, although they were strong enough against the Armoured Division's smaller-calibre guns, as in their well-chosen locations, dominating the flat terrain and floodplains. The names of the saints guard these fortresses at the Belgian-Dutch border: Fort St. Ferdinand, Fort St. Niklaas, Fort St. Livinins, Fort St. Jacob, Fort St. Joseph, Fort St. Jean. They also shielded the first serious stumbling block, the access to the Axel-Hulst Canal.

Despite the terrain bristling with forts, the troops of the 3rd Brigade coped with them easily and, taking numerous prisoners from the 712th Infantry Division, they crossed the Belgian-Dutch border on the evening of 16 September, approaching the Axel-Hulst Canal. The 9th Rifle Battalion approached the town of Axel from the south, but were held up at a wide lagoon, defended from the edge of the city. We did not have any so-called 'ducks' or assault boats. The 10th Dragoon Regiment was led very ambitiously, but too hastily, by a young officer who was the deputy commander in the absence of Lieutenant Colonel Zgorzelski, who had been wounded at Aalter; it forced the canal near Kijkuit, five kilometres east of Axel. Without a bridge, without heavy weapons, and, most importantly, without anti-tank guns, they pushed too far beyond the canal. This was exploited by the Germans, who instigated a counterstrike, supported by armoured cars and self-propelled guns, and pushed the dragoons back, inflicting severe losses (two officers and seventy-eight dragoons) despite the effective intervention of our artillery from the south bank. Our tanks were powerless because the high embankment on the other side blocked a direct shot.

Colonel Skibiński's ambitious attempt to rapidly overcome this obstacle had failed. One needed to rein in the temperaments of the unit commanders and proceed to more methodical action.

Leaving the 10th Armoured Cavalry Brigade, reduced to only the 2nd Armoured Regiment and the 10th Dragoon Regiment, with the task of surveillance and simulating an attack towards the town of Hulst, I reinforced the 3rd Rifle Brigade with the 1st Armoured Regiment and the 10th Mounted Rifles and gave them the task of forcing the channel east of Axel, with the support of the entire divisional artillery.

This well-organized and skilfully implemented action, with particularly outstanding input from the divisional sappers, led to the capture of the city of Axel on 19 September. Taking advantage of this success, the Division's units spread out and, after fierce fighting, reached the shore, cutting off the German retreat towards the sea.

The port of Terneuzen fell. The fire of our artillery and of the tank squadron of the 10th Mounted Rifles Regiment completely destroyed five large evacuation barges, full of troops, which were stranded in the shallows due to the low tide. The commander of the 712th Infantry Division, General Neumann was said to have been killed on one of these barges, as the prisoners later testified, when the remnants of this Division found themselves on the route of our Division's advance.[12]

Our losses from the period of battles for Ghent and the province of Zeeland amounted to:

- 75 killed – including 6 officers,
- 191 wounded – including 12 officers,
- 63 missing.

The Division took 19 officers and 1,154 privates prisoner and seized the following equipment:

---

12. Translators' note: Despite what the prisoners said, General Friedrich-Wilhelm Neumann survived, continued to command other German units (Kampfgruppe Von Tettau and the XXXIII Army Corps), became a PoW and lived until 1975.

- four 210mm railway guns,
- two 88mm guns,
- twelve 75mm guns,
- sixteen 50mm anti-tank guns,
- six 20mm anti-tank guns,
- six 81mm mortars,
- twelve heavy machine guns,
- two invasion barges,
- forty-two motor vehicles,
- a propellant depot.

The soldiers of the Division particularly valued the expressions of enthusiasm from the population, especially in Axel, where one could appreciate the friendliness and hospitality of the Dutch; all those moments of light that dispel the inevitable shadows of war. In spite of such differences in disposition, customs and the language barrier, the Polish soldier was greeted with joy and enthusiasm, surpassing everything that we had encountered not only in France, but also in hospitable Flanders. The soldiers felt at home and reciprocated with real affection and the readiness for sacrifice when required.

In Axel, the 9th Rifle Battalion was the first one to enter the city from the south and to fight on its streets. The soldiers and their commander, Lieutenant Colonel Z. Szydłowski, conquered the hearts of the locals eternally, which would be demonstrated long after the end of the war in perpetual commemorations.

The rapid completion of the clean-up operation of the area leading up to the sea between the Terneuzen canal and the River Scheldt gave the Division's troops time for a well-deserved and much-needed rest. The five days also allowed for the incorporation of replenishments that had reached the Division, the supplementation of equipment, and necessary repairs and maintenance.

With a retrospective glance at the executed operations, what emerges from the shadows is the fact that the Division's movements and its pace of action was never held back by the lack of supplies. Notably, our sources of supply remained in Normandy, so the supply lines grew longer every day. When the Division reached the area of Antwerp, it was 350 km away from sources of ammunition, and 250 km from sources of fuel and food.

I would like to emphasize at this point the great merits of the precise functioning of our quartermaster's office, run by Major Jan Marowski and his tireless subordinate officers and non-commissioned officers.

The older 'vintage' of volunteers from Brazil, Argentina, France and the United States, about whom the inspecting officers had been so pessimistic before the Division transferred to the Continent, also did not disappoint. Day and night at the wheel, they turned out to be top-class soldiers, both in pursuit, as well as before at Falaise, when they often had had to abandon their vehicles and fight in order to break through with supplies to the troops.

The workshop companies repaired 196 tanks and 291 motor vehicles in September.

The only limitation that the troops had to endure was the reduction of the quotas for artillery ammunition, which, due to the departure of the Canadian medium artillery regiment during this period, was reflected in the reduced firepower of the artillery support.

The only radical remedy for this would be the opening of the port of Antwerp. But to make that happen, it was necessary first to fulfil the second condition which I have mentioned – to push the Germans north up to the River Meuse or even beyond.

And on the way to the Meuse estuary lay Breda.

Advancing on Breda

Breda awaited its liberation.

Breda – the capital of the province of North Brabant and of the Catholic part of the Netherlands.

Breda was becoming impatient.

Quite rightly, because the news, the distant roar of guns and the nervous movement of German troops all indicated that the Allies were close; meanwhile, members of the Dutch Resistance were dying before everybody's eyes, and the Dutch feared even to imagine the possible horrors of combat.

The Germans were already well-known to them. The mask of culture and civilization they had put on for the West had long since fallen off the faces of the Teutonic barbarians.

And the British were slow in coming.

The malicious rumour was that they were busy with more important things, namely football games between units.

Thus, before I move onto the operation on Breda itself and the liberation of the city by the Polish 1st Armoured Division, I want to outline what those 'football games' looked like on the British side, with the Polish division recently transferred from the Canadian Corps to the 1st British Corps. Indeed, these 'games' were an important prelude to the attack on Breda.

Immediately after the completion of the Axel-Hulst-Terneuzen operations, the 1st Polish Armoured Division was redeployed east of the Scheldt and became part of the 1st British Corps of General Crocker, which was to be found on the right flank of the Canadian Army. And while the rest of this Army was entangled in further arduous clearing of the area west of the river, and the 2nd British Army was striking in a divergent direction to the north-east through Nijmegen, the weakened Corps, composed of 2 divisions (the 1st Polish Armoured Division and the 49th British Infantry Division) was given the task of striking from the Turnhout Canal northwards to Tilburg. It was all part of a larger-scale operation aiming to open the port of Antwerp. This port had already become a *sine qua non* condition for further attacks on Germany.

The task was performed by the British Corps with a wedged strike at the German battlegroup, with the spearhead being the 1st Polish Armoured Division.

The 49th British Armoured Division took over the area and secured the sides of the wedge, extending to the rear.

The German Units Facing the Corps:

Three weakened infantry divisions of very low morale due to their defeats, namely:

- the 711th Infantry Division
- the 719th Infantry Division
- the 346th Infantry Division

All reinforced with additional anti-tank weapons, heavy machine guns and self-propelled guns.

Two of these divisions, the 711th and 346th, were our acquaintances from Normandy that had evaded our pursuit by moving northwards to Dunkirk and from there had been evacuated to the Netherlands.

Would they be able to dodge our movements now?

With the development of operations, these divisions would be reinforced with a number of battlegroups, sometimes as strong as, for example, Battlegroup No. 743 with about:

- 1,280 men,
- 105 light machine guns,
- 23 heavy machine guns,
- 30 mortars
- The additional reinforcement of anti-tank guns

Besides this were the aviation troops such as Flieger Rgt. 51, used as infantry, and parachute troops such as Fallschirmjäger-Regiment 6 from the 2nd Fallschirmjäger Division.

When the Polish Division threatened Breda, new units from the German 245th Armoured Division and the 256th Armoured Division appeared.

Against these German forces stood the 1st Polish Armoured Division, also with reduced personnel, reinforced by the 53rd Canadian Medium Artillery Regiment, and also, temporarily, two light and one heavy artillery regiments, not counting the additional artillery reinforcement provided at Moerdijk.

The tactics of the Division were flexible: both Brigades did not act as organic formations, but as combat groups composed of regiments from either brigade, depending on the task. Although we were organized according to British establishments, we were becoming increasingly similar to an American armoured division, while employing methods of fighting which the Germans had been using for a long time. Hence, sometimes a Polish combat group under the banner of the 10th Cavalry Brigade had most of the organic units of the Rifles Brigade; and vice versa, the combat group of the 3rd Rifle Brigade would field most of the organic units of the Armoured Brigade. Parallel to this tactic, which had grown from the experience of bloody battles, the armoured regiments were gaining experience in using 'fire terror'. It consisted in firing the high-calibre guns and the tanks' heavy machine guns at all suspicious objects in the field that might have potentially obscured German anti-tank guns, before the troops surged forwards. This tactic was made possible by the enormous abundance of equipment, and was justified by the need to avoid unnecessary tank losses to well-hidden and camouflaged anti-tank guns.

The terrain was very difficult for the operation of armoured weapons.

Flat heaths with shrubs, forests on marshy grounds, and a large number of factory facilities, all created favourable conditions for defence. The terrain became more and more difficult as we approached the line of the Wilhelmina and Mark canals and in the terrain north of the canals as far as the Hollands Diep river.

In these field conditions, combat was difficult and unrelenting for our spearhead, which was best illustrated by the course of its operations.

On 29 September, the Division crossed the Turnhout Canal, capturing four officers and 161 privates, mostly from the 719th Infantry Division.

On 30 September, the battlegroup of the 3rd Rifle Brigade captured Merksplas after fierce fighting, capturing seventeen officers and 227 privates, six 75mm guns and five 20mm guns.

On 1 October, the entire Division, in a hard battle for Zondereigen and Noordbos on the Belgian-Dutch border, captured four officers and 218 privates, together with six 155mm guns.

On 2 October, again after heavy fighting, the 10th Armoured Cavalry Brigade seized Noordbos, capturing one officer, 262 privates from the 719th Infantry Division and the 346th Infantry Division, as well as:

- three 75mm guns,
- two 88mm guns,
- and three 20mm guns.

On 3 October, fighting for Baarle-Nassau throughout the day ended with the capture of the city at night by the 3rd Rifle Brigade. One officer and 172 privates from the 719th Infantry Division were taken prisoner.

On 4 October, the Division expanded the captured area around Baarle-Nassau, in the face of fierce German defensive resistance and even a counterattack supported by tanks. Another three officers and 221 privates from the 719th Infantry Division were taken prisoner, and one German tank was destroyed.

Troops of the 49th British Infantry Division relieved some of the Polish Armoured Division's units on the sides of the wedge, enabling regrouping for a further Polish attack.

5 October was marked by the following attacks:

- The 10th Armoured Cavalry Brigade attacked Alphen,
- The 3rd Riflemen Brigade – the forests to the west,
- The 24th Lancers Regiment and dragoons – Terover.

The Division thus took the following towns:

- Alphen,
- Terover,
- Baarle Bosschoven,
- Alphen Bosschoven,
- Oordeel Heikant.

They captured 2 officers and 192 privates from the 719th Infantry Division, destroying two 155mm guns and a single 88mm one.

By order of the Corps command, on 6 October the Division went on the defence with the task of holding the ground, i.e. remaining in the wedge until the arrival of larger Allied forces.

This short summary of the course of the 8-day-long battle, which took the Division from the Turnhout Canal to the area directly south-east of Breda, best illustrates the tedious and difficult process of driving the wedge into an area well prepared for defence and supplied by the Germans with more and more reserves from adjacent sections.

In addition to the conquered territory, the Division's success was best illustrated by the total of 34 officers and 1,502 privates taken prisoner, and the capture of:

- eight 155mm guns,
- eleven 75mm guns,
- five 88mm guns,
- eight 20mm guns.

Our own losses amounted to about fifty soldiers per day, with thirty-four officers and 351 privates killed or wounded. Certainly a lot for an alleged game of 'football'.

At that point the Division stood on the threshold of the route leading to Tilburg and Breda and, further on, to Hollands Diep.

The Breda Offensive – Reaching the Meuse –
Occupying Moerdijk

Although the period of defensive action from 6 to 26 October, with constant rain and exhausting front-line duties, cannot be regarded as a time of rest, we had the opportunity to repair and overhaul the equipment, while also replenishing the troops somewhat. The shortage of tank crews resulted in the decrease in numbers to two-thirds of establishments in the armoured regiments, and to only 60 per cent in the rifle companies.

Meanwhile, on 22 October, the long-planned Allied action began to unfurl on a larger scale.

- To the south-west, the main attack of the 49th British, the 104th American, and the 3rd and 4th Canadian Armoured Divisions was launched. They advanced in the direction of Roosendaal – Hollands Diep.
- To the east, the 4th British (Independent) Armoured Brigade struck from the south at Tilburg while the 7th British Armoured Division and the 51st (Highland) Infantry Division struck from the east.

Between 22 and 26 October, the defensive actions of the Polish Armoured Division took on the role of a 'hinge' of sorts in this action, but a hinge protruding far ahead of both of these grand attacks.

The Germans were mainly focused on the threats to Breda from the west and south-west. Their field fortifications, especially the powerful anti-tank ditch armed with mines and well-hidden heavy weapon emplacements, closed off two main directions:

- from Bergen through Roosendaal to Breda,
- from Antwerp – straight north to Breda.

Civilians had been forced to dig this anti-tank ditch, which stretched in a wide arc from the north, from the River Mark in the area of Den Emer, stretching to the houses of the town of Beck, and extending from there to the south, covering the exits of the western neighbourhood of Breda – Princenhage and

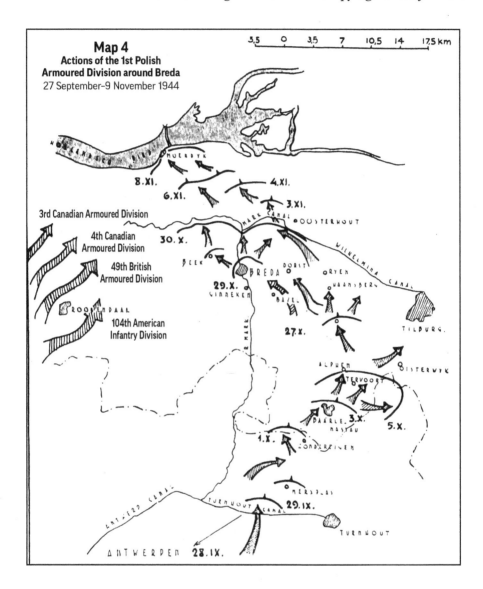

the western edge of the Mastbos forest. It formed a huge, sixteen-kilometre-long bridgehead of the city of Breda, the defence of which reached deep down to the perimeter canal of the city.

It looked like the Germans would put up a long, hard and relentless fight, which could have meant the complete destruction of the city, considering the strength of the Allied air force and artillery.

On 26 October, the Polish Division received the order to pin down the Germans in the direction of Oosterhout to prevent them from regrouping in the direction of the main strike, i.e. Roosendaal-Breda-Hollands Diep.

The forests stretching from Breda to Alphen were easy to defend effectively. Thus, it seemed to me that the only way to accomplish the task would be to concentrate the Division's troops on its right (eastern) flank and to strike hard through the gap in the forests, from the area of Alphen-Terover towards Oisterwijk-Gilze. By doing this, we could draw the Germans to us and give them no opportunity to regroup towards the west.

With that in mind, on 27 October, the attack of the 10th Armoured Cavalry Brigade began in the Vijfhuizen-Alphen-Oisterwijk direction, and the 3rd Rifle Brigade entered the woods north of Alphen, to cover the Division's main strike. Both of these attacks quickly achieved the ordered objectives, and thus the Division's reconnaissance regiment, i.e. the 10th Mounted Rifles Regiment, taking advantage of the success of the attack, had already seized Gilze at noon, and at 2.00 pm crossed the main Breda-Tilburg road near Haansberg.

This roaring success of the Polish Division, in view of the slow advance of the main attack of the four Allied divisions on Roosendaal, put it at the forefront of operations. The role of the Division expanded from auxiliary to principal.

By capturing the Gilze-Haansberg area, the Division now had a number of possibilities:

- to continue the attack northwards, seizing the crossings on the Wilhelmina Canal, for which it had been preparing, in line with the original orders. (A detachment from the 24th Lancers Regiment and the 10th Dragoon Regiment was already fighting in the southern part of the town of Rijen.)
- to turn east to Tilburg, to facilitate the task of the advancing 2nd Army
- to cut off the German retreat by attacking Hollands Diep.

This third possibility was of the greatest operational importance on the whole, and so Field Marshal Montgomery changed the Division's assignment to advance to Hollands Diep. However, in order to reach it and take over the area of the bridges near Moerdijk, we first had to capture the main junction of roads leading in this direction, that is, the city of Breda.

Thus, Breda became the primary target of the 1st Polish Armoured Division. The prisoners taken throughout 27 October – from the 256th and the 719th Divisions, as well as Flieger Regiment 51 – would state that the Germans were completely taken by surprise by the Poles' success in this direction. In order not to give them time to regain control of the situation, I regrouped only the rifles battalions to the left flank and changed our direction by 90 degrees: from north to west. From the morning of 28 October, it was divided into two arms, north and south.

- In the north: the 10th Armoured Cavalry Brigade was moving along the Tilburg-Breda road, with the tasks of capturing the north-eastern outskirts of the town and protecting the Division from possible German countermeasures from the north, as well as capturing the crossings at the Wilhelmina Canal south of Oosterhout.
- In the south: the 3rd Rifle Brigade was moving along the northern edge of the forests stretching to Ginneken, with the task of capturing the southern and central parts of the town and quickly proceeding towards the Mark Canal.

Their action led to the seizure and mopping up of the German troops from the entire Gilze-Haansberg-Rijen-Molenschot-Dorst-Bavel region on 28 October. Along the entire section, starting points for the attack on Breda were secured.

The Germans defended themselves fiercely and, even during the morning of 29 October, they tried to change the course of events by attacking Dorst from the north with two infantry regiments. There was even a critical moment on the right flank of the Division, when the 1st Motorized Artillery Regiment and the Anti-Tank Regiment had to repulse the German attack. The latter was firing directly ahead at the enemy which was only a few dozen metres away! But the situation was quickly brought under control.

On the other hand, our 9th Rifle Battalion took over the eastern part of Ginneken after a truly hard fight through the night.

Throughout the day and night of 28 October, until the dawn of the next day, 5 officers and 276 privates were taken prisoner, and two tanks, three 75mm guns, two 55mm guns, three 37mm guns and many more armaments were seized.

On the morning of 29 October, the entire Division attacked Breda.

- The battlegroup of the 3rd Rifle Brigade moved through Ginneken towards Princenhage. It took over the south-eastern part of the town and the bridge in the Oranjeboomstraat area, and in the afternoon it cleared the centre.
- The battlegroup of the 10th Armoured Cavalry Brigade captured the north-eastern outskirts of the city and, in heavy fighting, expelled the Germans from the area between the Tilburg-Breda road and the Wilhelmina Canal.

On 30 October, the fighting around and partly within Breda lasted all day. The 9th Rifle Battalion cleared the northern part of the city, the 8th Rifle Battalion took over Princenhage, and the 2nd Armoured Regiment seized the forest to the west and made contact with the American 104th Infantry Division. Both the 24th Lancers Regiment and the 10th Dragoons Regiment ultimately drove the Germans north beyond the Wilhelmina Canal.

The Division's reconnaissance (the 10th Mounted Rifles Regiment) moved along the northern edge of Breda towards the town of Beck and, scouting carefully, reached the Mark Canal. Earlier during the night, the 8th Rifles Battalion, brought over from Princenhage, seized a small bridgehead on the canal.

When the Germans were finally driven away to the northern bank of the Wilhelmina and Mark canals, the town of Breda was free, but free only in a narrow sense, as it was still within range of heavy German artillery. German shells were still falling on the city and the blood of the liberated often flowed together with the blood of the liberators. With the same energy with which it had captured the town, the Division tried to remove the threat and quickly reach Hollands Diep.

After the fierce battle of Falaise, the four-day-long Breda operation was another significant success for the Division.

It fulfilled not only the secondary task of blocking the enemy's advance, but also the main one: the capturing of the town of Breda on which the main force of a potential Allied attack was aimed. This attack, which would have been so much stronger in terms of the numbers of divisions, the power of artillery fire and air support. Undoubtedly, the Division saved the city from serious destruction.

From Alphen to the Mark Canal, this action yielded 30 kilometres of conquered territory within four days.

In that time, seven officers and 7,569 privates were taken captive, and the following equipment was captured or destroyed: three Mk. IV tanks, one 88mm gun, four 75mm guns, one 55mm gun, and three 37mm guns, not counting the spoils of war of the Canadian 2nd Armoured Brigade. The Canadians, assigned to the Polish Division, had advanced on Breda from the south, taking over and mopping up the wooded area. Similarly, the 18th Armoured Car Regiment captured equipment while covering the Division's north-eastern flank in the final phase of the fight.

As the Division's troops, one by one, were preparing for action towards the north, Breda experienced its first moments of indescribable delight at its freedom. A true carnival! Streets were crowded with cheering civilians, flowers and garlands, and shop windows plastered with signs in Polish, 'Dziękujemy Wam, Polacy!' ('Thank you, Poles.') Their enthusiasm reached its peak when I triumphantly led the former mayor, van Slobbe, into the Town Hall; he had been in hiding for several months.

The ambitious intentions of the Polish Armoured Division, to fly as far as Hollands Diep in a single breath, were thwarted by the terrain, which was extremely favourable for the defenders.

The area was flat, partially flooded, muddy, limiting traffic to roads situated along high embankments. It had been carefully prepared for defence a couple of years before, with concrete shelters and pillboxes at important points. The Germans defended it with troops drawn from all directions in order to defend the threatened routes. So when the attempt to leave the narrow bridgehead along the main road straight to Moerdijk was paid for with painful losses and failed, the Division reorganized to force the Mark Canal on a wide front between the abandoned crossing point and Oosterhout.

On the morning of 3 November, the crossing of the canal began in two areas: at Ter Aalst and south of Vraggelen, while we also pretended to want to cross elsewhere as a distraction tactic to deceive the Germans.

The crossing in Ter Aalst was successful due to the fact that the Podhale Rifles Battalion took the Germans completely by surprise.

At Vraggelen, the Germans held firm, and only the intervention of Typhoons dampened the murderous fire of German artillery and mortars, enabling the construction of a bridge and the transfer of tanks to the northern bank. By the dusk of that day – owing to the taking of Vraggelen-Den Hout and the forest complex to the west – two small bridgeheads merged into one, large enough for the Division to lead its troops across two bridges built by the sappers.

The cooperation of the British 7th Armoured Division turned out to be very helpful, as its tank fire from the flank made it easier to escape from the bridgehead.

On 4 November, fighting throughout the day, the Division was already spreading wide north of the Mark Canal, seizing a number of towns and villages: Made, Oudekerk, Helkant, Hoogerheide, Stuivezand, and Wagenberg.

The most visible effect of this action is the fact that, on that day, the German heavy artillery finally fell silent, retreating beyond Hollands Diep.

Breda was now truly free.

We were now left with completing the operation, which meant pushing the remaining German troops back across the Hollands Diep. On 5, 7 and 10 November, the mouth of the Meuse was reached, but the Germans still held on to their bridgehead in Moerdijk; the terrain has been turned into a veritable fortress with its flooded area and concrete fortifications.

The Polish Division prepared a decisive attack on this bridgehead for 8 November. Due to bad weather conditions, only the artillery under the command of Colonel Bronisław Noel could provide support. There were nine artillery regiments, namely:

- 2 regiments from our Division,
- 6 Canadian AGRA regiments

- 1 regiment of heavy artillery, plus Canadian multi-barrelled rocket launchers (so-called Land Mattresses).

This 1st Rocket Battery was an experimental unit of Canadian design, used for the first time on 1 November 1944 in the fight for Flushing. It had twelve launchers with thirty-two barrels each. Launched electrically, 384 rounds of medium calibre projectiles were fired simultaneously.

The bridgehead was captured in three phases:

- 1st phase: The destruction of reinforced concrete barricades by the tanks of the 10th Mounted Rifles Regiment. Their Cromwells approached to a distance of several dozen metres to literally carve their way through concrete barriers, firing directly ahead.
- 2nd phase: The entire artillery went into action to silence the German heavy artillery on the northern bank of the Hollands Diep.
- 3rd phase: The 24th Lancers Regiment attacked through the breaches, along roads on the embankments. The 8th and 9th Rifles Battalion attacked, wading up to their waists in water and mud. All this under the fire of the defences.

In this extremely arduous operation, the bridgehead was eliminated by the evening, although fighting continued practically all night for each and every house, or rather the ruins of every house, in Moerdijk.

* * *

This was the end of the operation which had started by the canal at Turnhout on 27 September and ended at Hollands Diep on 9 November. In Polish records it has been called 'Operation Breda'.

The tally of both sides' losses alone speaks for itself.

Not counting the killed and wounded, during those six weeks the Germans lost 53 officers and 2,892 privates, who were taken prisoner by the Poles. There was also plenty of equipment. I would like to list only the most important pieces: eight 155mm guns, fifteen 75mm ones, six 88mm ones and three 50mm ones, plus four tanks and eight self-propelled guns.

Polish losses, minimal in equipment, amounted to 69 officers and 876 privates killed or wounded.

That was immeasurably less than the German losses, but so much more painful, because the Polish Armoured Division had great difficulties with replenishing its ranks. It did not have its own supply of reinforcements and had needed to adapt to include Poles that had been forced to enlist in the German army – and who were now surrendering to the Allies at every opportunity.

*   *   *

Simultaneously with the 1st Armoured Division reaching Hollands Diep and the Meuse, the remaining units of the Canadian Army were seizing the area immediately to the west and, after fierce fighting, clearing the entire western part of Zeeland province west of the Terneuzen Canal.

When the Walcheren and Beveland peninsulas were captured in an action almost resembling an invasion, it was finally possible to open the port of Antwerp.

On 28 November, the first Allied convoy passed through the cleared Scheldt estuary and entered the port, and on 1 December the first 10,000 tons of war materiel were unloaded.

The port of Antwerp was still the target of German flying bombs during the winter and early spring of 1945. The Polish anti-aircraft artillery regiment from our Division took an active part in defending the air over Antwerp for two weeks, shooting down nine flying bombs.

Winter in Breda

Breda became the winter quarters of the 1st Polish Armoured Division. It is the capital of North Brabant, a province that has much more in common with smiling Flanders than with North Holland, which was stern-faced and harsh.

It is also a medieval city of wealthy merchants and brave soldiers.

The duality of its character is emphasized to this day by its commercial and industrial prosperity and the fact that the headquarters of the Dutch military academy is based there.

Breda, with a rich historical past, a fortress surrounded by a canal, had been besieged so many times in the past; in 1577, 1581, 1590, 1625, 1637, 1793, 1813...

The future king of Poland – then Prince Władysław – participated in one of these sieges on the Spanish side, learning the art and craft of besieging and conquering cities. This historical fact was mentioned in a speech by the city's mayor, van Slobbe, at a ceremonial banquet in honour of the Division.

He spoke more or less thus:

'Your Polish prince – and then king – learned the art of war from the Spaniards, capturing and besieging cities for many months. His training clearly left a strong legacy, visible when, three hundred years later, a Polish armoured division liberated our city with one attack, protecting it from the horrors of destruction and ravage.'

The source of the deepest gratitude – evident from the very beginning up until this day, and still bursting with the same flame of enthusiasm for the Polish soldier on each anniversary of the liberation of the city – was the fact that Breda suffered almost no losses among its residents and buildings during the battle. From the very first day, the inhabitants realized what their city would look like if it had not been the Polish Division but the main force of the Allies with their great firepower which had fought the battle of Breda. There was too much rubble and ashes around, what remained of previously flourishing towns and villages of the Netherlands. The gratitude of the people of Breda was not a flash in the pan. Many of the Division's men found best friends here, and many would soon find homes and families.

For the time being, this gratitude manifested itself in a frenzy of joy in the streets of the city, 'Thank you, Poles' signs in every shop window, and truly Dutch hospitality, which went above and beyond what we call the proverbial old Polish hospitality. Polish soldiers would be given the best accommodation possible.

Despite the comings and goings of Canadian and British units, headquarters and offices over the winter, and despite the fact that during Rundstedt's Ardennes Offensive in December the Division's headquarters moved partly from Breda to the east, the city remained faithful to us. Neither the quartermaster of the British Corps command, nor the one of the Canadian Army (which settled in the town for good) even attempted to remove us from the better lodgings.

Bearing in mind the frequent misunderstandings and incidents – often bordering on open war – occurring when troops of two separate Polish units were quartered in one city, I must emphasize the far-reaching politeness and positive attitude of both British and Canadian troops towards us Poles. Surely, people here and there are people – and sometimes, especially in the hot atmosphere of some cafe, there were brawls – but neither nationality nor membership of a different formation played a role here; there was no incident of such magnitude as to reach my level of command or above.

When we solemnly celebrated Polish Independence Day on 11 November – in which honorary guests from the Netherlands and from the Canadian Army participated – I received honorary citizenship of the city of Breda, offered to me individually, and to the entire Polish Division. A visible symbol of that was a medal-plaque with the town's coat of arms and an appropriate inscription. Made of bronze, promises were made to replace it with a silver one in the future, which occurred a year later – on the first anniversary of the city's liberation.

*   *   *

The divisional headquarters, divisional artillery staff, the command of the supply services and the divisional reserves were quartered in the city, and the troops stood guard over the Meuse on a section of the front up to eighteen kilometres wide, later extending to fifty kilometres. The width of the river, and the passive behaviour of the Germans – apart from a few difficult moments and periods of tension – made it possible to complete the task of defending the Meuse (or rather surveilling it) with only a part of the Division's forces.

This enabled us to gradually reinforce the troops and to train intensively.

The Division had reached Breda and the River Meuse in a state of almost complete exhaustion, both in terms of manpower and machinery.

Instead of the five platoons stipulated by the standard establishment, armoured units struggled to field three; in the infantry and dragoons the numbers fell to

c. 50 per cent. The reason was not only losses in combat in the recent period, but a large number of soldiers falling sick when climatic and weather conditions deteriorated. The combat equipment required partly supplementing, partly essential repairs.

The infantry and dragoons units experienced the greatest shortages. Although partly supplemented 'on the go', with volunteers being directed straight to the battlefield – Poles from France and Belgium, and PoWs (Poles conscripted into the German Army), our troops required constant replenishment of various specialists.

We weren't the only ones to suffer from an acute lack of infantry units. The Allied invasion army was experiencing this at the same time, the Canadians the most severely perhaps. Only the reasons for this crisis were different. In the case of the Allies, it resulted from a false calculation that in a modern, mobile and rapid war, armoured units would suffer the greatest losses. They did suffer when it came to the number of destroyed or seriously damaged tanks, armoured cars or self-propelled anti-tank guns. But it turned out that for every five lost tanks, a single tank crew was also lost, about five soldiers. With the shortage of troops in the infantry units and a surplus of trained tank crewmen, the Allies were sometimes forced to transfer these (expensively trained!) soldiers to the infantry. Such decisions were very unhealthy for soldiers' morale, which occurs when a tank crewman, paratrooper or any kind of high-value specialist is shifted to be a 'mere' infantryman.

When it came to us, we could not act in such a way due to the lack of trained tank crews. Although the 16th Armoured Brigade was training more soldiers for us in Scotland, it was not enough.

Shortages in the infantry had to be covered with whomever could be found in Scotland – mainly from among Polish PoWs from the German Army. Deficiencies in the armoured and anti-tank regiments were covered by soldiers trained in the 16th Brigade, and when that was not enough – from soldiers in the reserves who would likely have become specialists.

This state of affairs dictated the need to create training institutions for armoured and motorized troops in Breda and the surrounding area, as well as training camps of all specialisms for the infantry.

The winter months were quiet, which even allowed us to delegate the Anti-Aircraft Regiment as an infantry unit to supervise the Meuse. Thanks to that, and the great energy and enthusiasm of the officers involved, the task of training armoured and infantry units was accomplished in its entirety during the winter.

Between mid-November 1944 and the first days of April 1945, our work was interrupted only by two events: Rundstedt's winter offensive and the activity of German paratroopers used as infantry over the Meuse on the Kapelsche Veer section.

The Polish Armoured Division did not participate directly in countering the Rundstedt offensive. Our section of defence on the Meuse gained more importance in view of the massing of the parachute army of Generaloberst Kurt Student over the lower Meuse. It was the emerging northern arm of the German pincers, which were to close on this area by striking at Antwerp across the Meuse in the north and through Liège-Namur in the south. The Division was to face the direction of the most likely strike, between Breda and Tilburg. As a consequence, it forced my staff to change the command post in order to be closer to the troops and important directions. On a wet and blisteringly cold December night, we made our way to the tiny village of Heuneind, north of Tilburg, returning to field conditions. I spent the first night sleepless, trying in vain to warm myself over an old kerosene lamp which filled the whole room with black smoke. We had been extremely pampered after three weeks of luxury accommodation in Breda.

Constant alarms about the drops of German paratroopers would always turn out to be false but nevertheless they kept us alert in this generally tense situation. However, they did not prevent us from organizing a traditional Christmas Eve in the units and headquarters. I finished my Christmas tour of the units at the staff headquarters of the divisional artillery, renowned for the hospitality of the host, Colonel Bronek Noel. It was a Christmas Eve party like no other – organized with the officers of the Canadian Medium Artillery Regiment who had been assigned to us: officers from the province of Quebec, and therefore of French origin. They had similar temperaments to us and were prone to laugh loudly as well. We really let our hair down, walking with full glasses among tables laden with food and singing Canadian and French songs as well as our Polish Christmas carols.

Outside, the frosty night sparkled with a thousand stars and rockets fired from both sides. But apart from the rockets, there were no gunshots. The Christmas mood reigned over both banks of the Meuse and one could for a fleeting moment believe that there were such things as good Germans.

As certain units were withdrawn to take part in the counterattack in the Ardennes, the width of our front changed. There was a period when our section stretched from Raamsdonk to Lithoijen, exceeding fifty kilometres. The British 1315 Wing RAF Regiment and the Canadian 19th Army Field Regiment RCA were placed under my command, together with the Canadian 8th Light Anti-Aircraft Regiment and the British No. 47 (Royal Marine) Commando, which enabled me to draw the entire 10th Armoured Cavalry Brigade to my reserve. The 24th Lancers Regiment was left as a Corps reserve, while the Brigade was preparing for a counterattack in several major directions. With the final collapse of Rundstedt's winter offensive, we returned to normal conditions, warm quarters and our interrupted training.

But the German parachute units sent as 'Christmas gifts' remained for good on the other side of the Meuse. No longer used as paratroopers, they became elite infantry, often showing us signs of their activity. In order to give them combat training and experience, General Student exploited the specific area on the Meuse with large pools of water and high coastal embankments, and created a small bridgehead at the former crossing of the Kapelsche Veer river. The bridgehead garrison sat silently and passively until they bit into the ground and dug into the high bulwarks; then, with the strong support of highly-accurate artillery and mortars, turned taunting and irritating. Their reconnaissance patrols increased, which was easily achieved since the Division's troops had been dispersed over fifty kilometres. The Germans had turned the bridgehead into a de facto training ground, changing the crew every three days and thus retraining their ranks in this ingenious manner.

It was an unpleasant thorn in the side of the front.

I had already tried to eliminate this bridgehead with the Division's own units at the end of December, and then with an action on 7 January, but to no avail. It was difficult to manoeuvre the tanks in the flat, boggy terrain, which lay under a thin layer of ice and snow. If they were to advance at all, they had to drive in small groups. On the verge of finishing their training, the newly arrived infantry was not yet well-coordinated and far from being in 'assault' mode.

My arguments were recognized by the commander of the 1st British Corps, General Crocker who, for 13 and 14 January, assigned to me the troops of the 47th Royal Marine Commando.

Although specially trained for such tasks, even these soldiers failed to drive the stubborn paratroopers out of their holes, cleverly built into the high embankments. It was only at the end of January that the entire combat group from the 4th Division was engaged. This Canadian formation consisting of two infantry battalions and two armoured regiments, with the powerful support of artillery of all calibres, benefitted from the already slightly harder ground and after a five-day battle eliminated this German bridgehead, suffering numerous losses.

Such serious casualties could have ruined the entire personnel policy of putting the Division back on its feet for Spring operations, and hence it was ultimately beneficial that we were spared from this fighting.

The Corps commander showed an even greater understanding of our position. At the beginning of February, our section along the Meuse was narrowed to eighteen kilometres, giving us the maximum opportunity to train replacements. In these favourable conditions, February and March were not wasted. The armoured and artillery regiments reached their peak, and fresh infantry reinforcements were rallied and improved, though we were far from the form we had been at Falaise.

The period of peace also produced positive results in another field: both engineering companies did a lot of work, repairing 270 tanks and 1,496 motorized vehicles.

So both men and machines were in good form.

*   *   *

The stagnation of larger military operations often leads to military parades, decorations and inspections by senior commanders.

When I was temporarily in London, summoned to the headquarters of the Commander-in-Chief immediately after the capture of Moerdijk and the battle for access to the sea and the Meuse, I was urgently summoned back to Breda by an order from the Commander-in-Chief of the 21st Army Group. Only this seniority of rank made it possible for me to return on time, because after two days of waiting in vain for the weather to allow a flight, a destroyer was put at my disposal; I sailed to Ostend, and from there reached Breda by car.

I arrived just in time to be decorated with crosses and British 'Orders' on 25 November by Field Marshal Montgomery, along with a dozen senior officers of the Division. The medal ceremony was arranged with great pomp – in Breda's largest hall, filled with delegations of troops, and in the presence of the commander of the Canadian Army, General Crerar, and two more of our Corps commanders: General Simonds from the 2nd Canadian Corps and General Crocker from the 1st British Corps. In a long speech, the Field Marshal emphasized the bravery and toughness of the Polish soldier. It was then, speaking of the battle of Falaise, when he quipped about the 'bottle' in which the Germans found themselves and the Polish 'cork' cutting off their retreat.

In response, on behalf of the Commander-in-Chief, I decorated Field Marshal Montgomery with the Order of the Virtuti Militari, V Class.

Four days later, General Eisenhower toured the units in an unassuming manner, talking to tank crews and taking interest in various trivialities in our soldiers' lives. One of the extraordinarily pleasant visits that lasted a few days was that of the Chief of the General Staff, General Stanisław Kopański, renowned for the siege of Tobruk and his Polish Independent Carpathian Rifle Brigade. Apart from my personal friendship with him, General Kopański was associated with the Division due to the fact that he had once commanded the 1st Motorized Artillery Regiment in Poland. He had a lot of former subordinates in the Armoured Division, including many young officers.

The Poles in Breda began to settle in almost as before, in our Scottish 'little Poland'. True, there were no Polish families, but the 'Lwów Wave' theatre company arrived, delivering its performances all the way to the front line, to the bunkers on the Meuse.

The 'ubiquitous' war correspondents by the names of Kiersnowski, Feldhuzen, Walentynowicz and Wołkowicki perpetuated their reputation among the soldiers, mainly perhaps because they stubbornly pushed themselves to the front line. Not to mention the fact that two of them, Ksawery Pruszyński and Aleksander Janta-Połczyński, had been richly rewarded for such boldness by being hit and escorted to hospital. When the stagnation in military activities limited their chances for sensational reporting, they fought a fierce fight on the territory of the Canadian Army – when it was necessary to correct them, that it was not Canadians but Poles who had captured this or that town, taking care that no achievement by a Polish soldier was credited to anybody else.

During the winter respite in the area of Breda and operations on the Meuse, there were changes among the most senior positions in the Division.

At the beginning of January 1945, the Brigade commander, Colonel Tadeusz Majewski, left for London. He had been associated with the Division since 1940 and Montbard, when he had been the commander of the 16th Armoured Brigade; then, during the heaviest fighting, he had commanded the 10th Armoured Cavalry Brigade. It was due in great part to his military knowledge, moderation and personal tact that the merging of the Armoured Division, despite the antagonisms of individual specialisms, had gone quickly and smoothly.

The command of the 10th Cavalry Brigade was taken over by Colonel Franciszek Skibiński, talented both in the management of the staff and as a commander. He had been successively chief of staff of the 10th Armoured Brigade from its formation in Poland until France, then commander of the 10th Mounted Rifles Regiment in Scotland, deputy commander of the 10th Armoured Cavalry Brigade in the Battle of Falaise, and later the commander of the 3rd Rifle Brigade. Through such different positions within the Armoured Division, he had gained enormous military experience.

The post he vacated, commander of the 3rd Rifle Brigade, was in turn taken by Colonel Władysław Dec. I had known this seasoned infantryman since peacetime, through the 29th Infantry Division and various exercises led by General Franciszek Kleeberg. As a subsequent commander of the Podhale Rifle Brigade and deputy commander of the Rifle Brigade, he made a name for himself in the Division as a specialist in crossing rivers and fighting for towns.

Colonel Antoni Grudziński remained the deputy commander of the Armoured Brigade. He had taken up this position in October 1944, in the final period of operations on Breda.

Colonel Zdzisław Szydłowski, with a PhD in Natural Sciences, was the former commander of the 9th Rifle Battalion and was now appointed the deputy commander of the 3rd Rifle Brigade. The battles at the Mace and for the town of Axel had ranked him as one of the most remarkable commanders of motorized units within the Rifle Brigade.

Colonel [Józef] Krautwald, an officer with great knowledge of artillery, left to become a lecturer at the Higher Military Academy in Scotland.

These changes resulted in shifts at a lower level. The command of the 1st Motorized Artillery Regiment was taken over by Lieutenant Colonel [Marian] Borzysławski, and Major Stępień took over the 9th Rifle Battalion.

The Yalta Conference – Arc de Triomphe

While we wintered in Breda, the Yalta Conference took place. It appeared first in whispers, fragments of conversations, and rumours, only to finally fully reveal its grim and tragic face.

The feeling among the army was one of depression. What next?

How uncertain our advance through defeated Germany had become. Our advance, which, as we had believed passionately, was to return us to Poland. Our advance, which had begun in Normandy. Our advance to our homes, many of which were located beyond the Curzon Line.

And yet!

I did not need to conduct a survey among my soldiers to seek their opinion on what to do next!

Wasn't I one of them? Of course we would keep fighting.

Germany was still Enemy No.1.

Just because a new enemy – an Allied one for a change – had reared its head from the East, were we to forget about September 1939, about Warsaw lying in ruins, about Auschwitz and Dachau?

No! We would fight again in the heart of Germany. This most sublime of a soldier's hopes could not be denied to us.

We were never ones to misuse big words, words written with capital letters.

We did not misuse the name of God and His saints.

We did not take in vain the name of Poland – Freedom – Independence; we had a soldier's disgust for any sort of declamation.

And as long as we would be able to, we wished to proclaim it – our Polish, soldierly truth – not with words, but with the roaring of motorcycles, the clatter of caterpillar tracks, the rumble of guns, the sounds of honest soldierly work.

Nevertheless, the depression settled in.

Again, as in the first days of the Warsaw Uprising, the radio vehicles were swarming with clusters of soldiers, listening in with worried and focused faces.

This did not escape the attention of British and Canadian liaison officers, who tried to understand the depth of our disappointment and our tragedy.

Many understood and many showed up for us as true friends would. On the other hand, there were also those to whom we didn't even bother explaining our thoughts.

The reaction of the Allied military command was gentlemanly. Moods and opinions were not probed purely through liaison officers, but I was directly addressed as a commander with a request for my interpretation of how the Polish Armoured Division would behave going forwards, in the face of Yalta, which had visibly touched the hearts and minds of Poles.

Would we fight the Germans?

And the form in which I was addressed was also typically British.

General Crocker, the commander of the 1st British Corps, invited me for lunch under the pretence that he had some important matters to discuss with me.

And over black coffee, Yalta came up.

He said that politics was not a matter for military men, but that he was trying to understand the degree of our disappointment and heartbreak. I could sense in the words of General Crocker his great concern for us, compassion and a desire to understand these matters which seemed so complicated for the English.

A few days later, I was invited to have lunch with the commander of the Canadian Army, General Crerar, who announced in advance that he had talked to General Crocker, and there was nothing left for him to offer but words of sincere sympathy that high-level politics could have put the Poles ('gallant Poles', as he put it) in such an exceptionally difficult situation.

Although it would seem that the Polish and Canadian-British sides had spoken enough about the subject, after about two weeks I was invited to see Field Marshal Montgomery.

As was always the case with Monty, things had to be done differently.

The outdoors setting: lunch was served in his caravan and I was greeted by two small dogs, one of which was called Stalin and the other Hitler. Inside, the table was set for three, because a colonel, who was a political advisor for the 21st Army Group, was also present. The conversation at lunch was casual, about this and that, up to the point when the black coffee arrived at the table, and with it – the third time for me – Yalta.

I was so prepared by the previous conversations that it seemed to me that what I said on my part was in fairly comprehensible English. I clearly emphasized the essence of the problem, which was that most of the soldiers of the Armoured Division were from the eastern borderlands of Poland. I myself was born in Lwów, which had never been, even in post-partition times, under the rule of Russia, and it was now being handed over so arbitrarily.

Montgomery interrupted me with a smile and said that in that case all was well, because I would now be a Soviet general.

That took me aback. I retorted that although it was difficult even to compare these two relationships, namely what the Polish Army was to the Soviet Army and what the British Army was to the American Army, but what would the

Field Marshal say if I offered him the rank of a general in the American army. It was already widely known at that time that Montgomery felt some antagonism towards the Americans and, to some extent, had a sense of the British Army's superiority.

Montgomery flushed. The political advisor did not know what to do with his cup of coffee. Finally the Field Marshal laughed and turned everything into a joke. Maybe it had indeed been intended as a joke from the start, but given the hopelessness of the Polish situation after Yalta – even over black coffee – we did not find such jokes digestible.

I have always had great respect for Field Marshal Montgomery as a commander, for his indisputable military talent, and so has our Division. We had long since got over his pink sweater and his penchant for theatre in public speeches. They were a part of his personality. I wanted to interpret his habit of sometimes speaking out of turn as a tactic to catch out the expected response of the listener. But it was difficult for me to accept three of his statements, especially since I did not want to see them as a sign of his complete ignorance regarding these matters:

- His question back in Scotland, during his first visit to the Polish Division, about which language Poles actually speak at home: German or Russian;
- His jokey remark that I would become a Soviet general;
- His statement on television in 1959, before leaving for Moscow. While envisioning an international thaw, he proposed leaving one or two Allied corps in Western Europe, and permanently maintaining the Russian Corps in Poland.

Giving everyone their due – operational and strategic geniuses included – I wonder why some generals so willingly enter into politics unprepared, in which field they can only count on being beginners and amateurs.

I did not get to lunch with the American Supreme Commander.

Apparently, the problem with the Polish Armoured Division was judged to be a fleeting and a strictly internal matter regarding a British dominion .

* * *

At the end of February 1945 I was invited to Paris with the Division's squadron of honour for a ceremony to decorate a dozen or so of our soldiers with French medals. The rest of the French decorations awarded to officers and privates of the Division were brought to Breda at the end of March by the deputy chief of staff General Charière.

The decoration ceremony in Paris was quite unusual, in particular because of the location.

The Place des Invalides, traditionally used for such occasions, had been abandoned in favour of the Arc de Triomphe on the Place de l'Etoile. The decoration was performed by the Chief of Staff of the National Defence, General Alphonse Juin, in front of the honorary battalion of the Garde Nationale and in the presence of crowds of civilians.

It was more than a gesture in honour of the Armoured Division – it was undoubtedly a gesture in honour of Poland. I wonder whether it did not emphasize even further the tragedy of our situation after Yalta. It represented a chivalrous gesture by the French towards their betrayed allies.

For all of us who went through September 1939 in Poland and then, after leaving Poland, took up the fight for our own weapons and our own army in France, who would never forget being patronized and looked down on, being treated as poor relatives who had seemingly let themselves be beaten so easily and quickly – it felt like revenge on a grand scale.

The pale early spring sun was shining upon the figures of my beloved boys, standing at attention as the members of the squadron of honour representing the whole Division. The sun was glinting off our banner, the helmets, the Sten guns, the white of the leather glove cuffs; it jumped off the myriad of colours on the uniforms of the Garde Nationale, off the shimmering musical instruments of the orchestra, and on to the audience, already dressed colourfully for the spring.

And history once again looked at us from the Arc de Triomphe – from the names of the Polish battles engraved upon it.

*   *   *

After the ceremony, I was received by General de Gaulle. Speaking concisely, he thanked me, as the General of the Polish Division, for everything it had achieved on French soil, for its decisive role in the Battle of Falaise, for Abbeville, Saint-Omer and a number of other French towns. And then he went on to discuss the general subject of our geopolitical situation and our difficult situation post-Yalta.

He had recently returned from Moscow.

He was extremely concerned and what he said was infused with extraordinary affection for Poland, and warmth for us, its soldiers.

It was clear that he already knew more than he could say. Finally, he made it abundantly clear that if I or any of my soldiers ever found ourselves in a difficult situation, we should not hesitate to turn to him and, if possible, he would certainly help.

Did de Gaulle already know back then that we would not return to Poland, at least not all of us?

I have not yet made use of the offer of assistance made by the General –
today the President of France. My optimism makes me always assume that the
present situation is not the worst that could be, and my pessimism – that even
more difficult moments might fall upon us.

* * *

I did pay a visit, however, to the Colonel of the French Foreign Legion, Prince
André John Willard Poniatowski. How strange are the tangles of history!
Receiving the Legion of Honour under the Arc de Triomphe, where history was
palpable in the air – with Prince Józef Poniatowski and the Virtuti Militari – a
medal which I, in turn, had brought for this visit.[13]

It was back in 1940, in Coëtquidan, Brittany, that the son of the prince,
Marie-André Poniatowski came to me one day – a young, lean boy. Speaking
in French, he apologized that he did not know Polish, but assured me he had a
Polish heart, and asked to be admitted to the Polish Army. Once admitted, he
was incorporated into the 14th Lancers Regiment, and after completing the
Polish cadet school in Scotland, as a second lieutenant he started his service
with the 1st Armoured Regiment. He went through the whole campaign as a
platoon commander, all the way to Holland. There, he fell on the island of Tholen,
commanding his platoon and very bravely blocking the path of a German raid.

I was welcomed in Paris by his father in the ceremonial dress uniform of the
Foreign Legion and by his mother, an American, née Harriman. They apologized,
as their son once did, that they did not speak Polish, but their son's service in
the Polish Armoured Division proved his Polishness most emphatically.

I presented to them the Silver Cross of the Virtuti Militari, awarded
posthumously to their son, a second lieutenant of the 1st Armoured Regiment
of the Polish Armoured Division, Marie-André Poniatowski.

Ten years after the war, at a reception of the Polish Legion of American
Veterans in Buffalo, William Averell Harriman, who was then a candidate for
the position of governor of New York, emphasized in his speech his relationship
with the Polish Armoured Division through the late Marie-André Poniatowski.

* * *

There was another mock-foreigner in our division – an American of Polish
origin, who had graduated from a Polish cadet school. This one spoke superb

---

13. One of the ancestors of Prince A.J.W. Poniatowski was Prince Józef Poniatowski (1763–1813),
    one of the first, most distinguished and famous recipients of the Virtuti Militari order.

Polish and a soldier's luck had proved kinder to him. Although wounded in the bloody battle at the Mark Canal, he recovered and later did a lot of good for both Poland's name abroad and that of soldiers in general. Immediately after the war he released the first three-language book about the armoured division entitled *Caen to Wilhelmshaven with the Polish First Armoured Division*.

Leopold Lorentz, second lieutenant of the 8th Rifles Battalion. I can still see his disappointed face when I refused to call his battalion 'the Bloody Shirts', as it had been dubbed after the battle of the 'Mace', when their lightly wounded commander, Lieutenant Colonel Nowaczyński, was indeed plentifully covered with his own blood. The name, however, was not officially approved.

Another foreigner in our midst, Second Lieutenant Auberon Herbert, had no blood relation or Polish origin to speak of. He was an Englishman with a genuine sympathy for the Polish predicament that made him report to us to serve in our ranks. The long months of common plight taught him not only the Polish language, but created in his mentality a certain passion for our Polish issues, which did not peter out with the end of the war, but rather was directed to a broader track.

There was also one volunteer, an Englishwoman, Diana Tauber. She was later promoted to the rank of second lieutenant, and even later still she became Mrs. Wołkowicka, when she married Lieutenant Wołkowicki, a soldier of the Armoured Division and an artist painter.

Our detachments included these beloved 'canteen girls', deeply devoted to the units which they served. They were nicknamed 'aunties', for reasons unknown to me.

I have two enduring memories associated with the final days in Breda. One of these was the arrival of General Anders, at a time when he was already the acting Commander-in-Chief. And the second one happened to be related to his stay at the Division.

General Anders had already visited us in Scotland in 1943; if I recall correctly, it had been for the exercises organized by the 1st Polish Corps. He was interested in our tanks and, as a cavalryman himself, he wanted to know how the cavalry in our Division was trained. But to Breda he came radiant with the glory of Monte Cassino, and as our Polish superior. The whole division was honoured by his arrival and tried to show their best side. We were happy that the form we had achieved over the winter in Breda reflected both our recent combat experiences and our continued battle-readiness.

The presence of Anders among us, a commander of the Battle of Monte Cassino, linked our Division to the operations of the 2nd Corps in Italy; all part of one military effort. On a broader scale, his presence as the Polish Acting Commander-in-Chief united us under the banner of Polish achievement, with the successes of the Polish Air Force and the Navy. It raised our hopes that we would unite into one Polish Army in the West, under one Polish command.

After all, the Canadians did not have many more combat units (three infantry divisions and one armoured division); in Normandy they had already fought under the banner of the 1st Canadian Army.

I accompanied General Anders when he paid a visit to the Canadian Corps and Army commanders. Due to the considerable distance to where the latter was based, we flew from the Gilze airfield near Breda in two small two-person surveillance aircrafts of a type we called 'Kubuś', which were piloted by Polish pilots Major B. and Captain K.

When we flew over 's-Hertogenbosch, which was already on the front line, my pilot, Captain K. – a good friend of mine back from 1940 from Bollène in France – remarked that we were over Tilburg. I corrected him that it was 's-Hertogenbosch. The mistake was caused by a similar outline of canals and silhouettes of the two cities when looked on from above. The difference was that Tilburg was twenty miles within our territory. It was most likely that it was this similarity which led to the unfortunate mistake of the pilots. They returned to Gilze airfield after the warm welcome prepared for Anders by the Polish No. 131 Fighter Wing RAF under Wing Commander Aleksander Gabszewicz, who had been in constant operational cooperation with our Division. At nightfall both Polish pilots set off to return to the army. I do not know for what reason they decided to land, but again they mistook 's-Hertogenbosch for Tilburg, and thus landed in territory occupied by the Germans. They paid for this mistake by being taken prisoner, though fortunately for a very short time, because the end of the war freed them after a month. Later they told us about a rather interesting course of investigation conducted by the Germans. They tried to find out the reason why the Polish Armoured Division, which enjoyed the reputation of being a very good unit, had been left on an inactive section of the frontline and not used in the fighting beyond the Rhine.

We too had been racking our brains about it a few weeks before, but not at the time when these questions were being put to our pilots. On 7 April, when Anders and I flew east to the Canadian Army, we observed from our aircraft the movement of the first units of the Polish Division to the east, towards the Rhine.

'Zum Rhein – zum Rhein', the words of the patriotic German song proclaimed, but the 'Watch along the Rhine' was already broken – the Allies were advancing into Germany.

On the day before we had studied the orders of the Canadian Army; our future objective led us into an area hopelessly criss-crossed with canals. The map was blue with these lines, big and small, crowding along the border of the

Netherlands and German Friesland. Someone aptly commented that boats would be more suitable for the task than tanks.

* * *

On the threshold of action on German soil, the face of the Division in terms of the personnel in senior positions was gradually changing. This was required by the Commander-in-Chief's personnel policy. On one hand, we were to make use of the experience of previous commanders; on the other, to open the way for new officers to gain experience and to prove one's worth, who had so far been used in another theatre of war or at higher staff headquarters.

This was why we had to say goodbye to one of the oldest officers in the Division – General Kazimierz Dworak. He had been with us from Zaolzie, through the 1939–1940 campaign until the end. He had been successively the commander of the 24th Lancers Regiment, the 10th Armoured Cavalry Brigade, and the deputy commander of the Division. A tried-and-tested soldier – dedicated heart and soul to the service and the Division – the best of friends. In his place arrived General Klemens Rudnicki, with rich combat experience at the 2nd Corps, who would later take over the command of the Division after the end of hostilities, when I left to take command of the 1st Corps in Scotland. This period would mark a new chapter in the Armoured Division's history of neither war nor peace, i.e. the occupation in Germany.

After the cessation of hostilities Colonel Skibiński would leave for Italy to become the deputy commander of the 2nd Armoured Division of General Rakowski. The command of the 10th Armoured Cavalry Brigade would be taken over by the former deputy Colonel A. Grudziński, with Lieutenant Colonel W. Zgorzelski as his deputy. The latter had been the vigorous commander of the 10th Dragoons Regiment throughout the campaign, except for the period of his hospital stay after being wounded at Aeltre while crossing the Ghent Canal. Major M. Gutowski took over the command of the 2nd Armoured Regiment from Lieutenant Colonel S. Koszutski, well known from the earlier pages of this memoir.

In September 1945, Lieutenant Colonel L. Stankiewicz ceased to be the chief of staff and took command of the 10th Dragoons Regiment. He was replaced in the staff by Lieutenant Colonel Z. Dudziński, the last commander of the reconnaissance unit of the 1st Corps from the time in Scotland, and later commander of the 4th Armoured Regiment in the 2nd Corps.

On German Soil. The End Of The War

On 8 February, a huge Allied offensive began, in which the 1st Canadian Army struck from the Nijmegen area on the Dutch-German border, between the Meuse and the Rhine. The advance targeted Reichwald-Hochwald. The goal was to break the Siegfried Line, which extended in this direction to the west bank of the Rhine.

Operation Veritable had massive fire support:

- artillery: more than 1,000 guns of various calibres and twelve 32-barrel rocket launchers, which had first passed the test when used by our Division the previous November at Moerdijk.
- aviation: 1,000 fighters and light Canadian bombers, over 1,000 medium and heavy RAF bombers, and a large portion of the 8th and 9th U.S. Army Air Force.

By 20 February, two branches of the Siegfried Line had been breached, but it was not until 26 February that a new phase of the operation, including a strike by the American army, resulted in the elimination of German resistance on the west bank of the Rhine and allowed the Allies to seize the river along the entire section from Nijmegen to Düsseldorf by 10 March.

The 2nd British Army and the American Armies finally pushed through the Rhine at the end of March, and on 1 April, the 1st Canadian Army crossed the Rhine with a twofold task: to seize the northern part of the Netherlands, previously held by the Germans, and to mop up the entire strip of the German waterfront between the Ems and Weser rivers.

This second task fell to the 2nd Canadian Corps, which included the Polish Armoured Division, reinforced by a battalion of Belgian SAS paratroopers and the Canadian 4th Medium Artillery Regiment.

The Polish Division was supposed to strike the Dutch-German border, and its distant operational target was the port of Emden. The 4th Canadian Armoured Division was to operate to the right and the 3rd Canadian Infantry Division to the left.

The simple task was complicated by the terrain, riddled all over with channels of all sizes, with the Ems flowing on the German side parallel to the border. During the operations, once on the eastern side of the Ems, the operational target was broadened from Emden to Wilhelmshaven.

The distance from Breda to the new divisional assembly area on the Dutch and German border was 250 kilometres. It was covered by the Division in eighteen hours of strenuous march, heading for the bridge over the River Meuse near the town of Gennep, then through German territory through the almost completely demolished towns of Goch and Calcar, and over the bridge on the Rhine near Rees, from where we continued northward back to Dutch soil in the area of Borculo.

We were preceded by two detachments, one of which took over the Coevorden junction from the Belgian paratroopers, the other captured the canal crossing in Goor.

One did not need a map or knowledge of the area not to confuse German and Dutch settlements when going back and forth over the border. The contrast was stark: Dutch towns and villages, largely spared from the bombings, were decorated with flags of national colours and a mass of flowers, while the German ones were mostly gloomy, grey ruins, the only decoration on the spared houses being a white flag. We were struck on the one hand by the sight of joy and cheer among the Dutch population lining the streets, and by the blank closed shutters, clamped gates and pale faces of the skulking Germans on the other. Later on, we would encounter masses of people from various European countries who had been deported to labour camps. They were swarming the streets, greeting us with tears and laughter, expressing their joy. And then our path led us among people liberated from concentration camps, with all the horrors of those places visible upon those who had survived them.

In order to meet the task of straddling the border, as well as with our own safety in mind once the division crossed the Ems River into German territory, it seemed necessary to me to first clear the Dutch territory up to the Dollart bay, on the northern side of which lay the port of Emden, by striking north along the border.

Actions towards that goal had already been initiated by the detachments of both Lieutenant Colonel Zgorzelski and Lieutenant Colonel Koszutski. I subordinated these units to the new commander of the 3rd Rifle Brigade, Colonel Dec. Thus strengthened, I charged the Brigade with this operation, which was of a preliminary nature for the whole Division.

The target was Winschoten, the town and the road junction, which lay only a few kilometres from the bay.

On 10 April, part of the 10th Mounted Rifles Regiment with a squadron of dragoons reached a battalion of French paratroopers, dropped two days prior, with orders to capture the crossings on the Oranje Canal.

On 11 April, the detached units and the Brigade seized the area of Emmen and Ter Apel, leading the Division into a relatively drier and more tank-friendly area.

The Germans did not seem to have envisaged any broader defences of the areas, but local units from mostly naval battalions fought fiercely and ferociously, defending access to the German border and soil, no doubt motivated by the ubiquitous propaganda. In the battles that ensued, the Mounted Rifles, the Dragoons, and the Podhale Rifles fought exceptionally well. On 14 April the detachment of Lieutenant Colonel Koszutski with the 2nd Armoured Regiment and the 8th Rifles Battalion would engage in a heavy battle with a battalion of the 366th Regiment, the complete destruction of which allowed us to seize the towns of Bourtange and Neurhede. The eight 88mm and 75mm guns, eight 20mm guns and two German tanks standing demolished on the battlefield spoke for themselves.

15 April was the culminating day of the battles of the 3rd Rifles Brigade, when the Brigade, after breaking the resistance on the Vereenigd Canal, in Weener and Rhede and on the Veele Canal, took over the town of Winschoten with a concentric attack with the Podhale Rifles Battalion and the Belgian paratroopers battalion. I myself was at the staff headquarters of the 3rd Brigade when Colonel Dec reported to me in the evening of that day that the Brigade's patrol had reached the bay at Dollart, four kilometres west of the German border.

However, it was only on 17 April that the conquest of the town of Rhede and the defeat of further naval infantry battalions from the 363rd and 366th Regiments completed the operation of cutting off German troops in the Netherlands from German territory, and allowed us to turn our attention completely to the principal task on the German side of the Ems river.

At that time, as the race to the sea continued, an event took place on the western side of the Ems river that affected the entire Division deeply.

There was no battle for this place.

There was no air or artillery support.

Supposedly it required as little as a single burst from a Bren gun taking down a single German guard in a guard tower that did the job. Maybe even that was unnecessary.

And yet it was a great achievement for the Armoured Division.

I am thinking of the liberation of Oberlangen and Niederlangen, where there was a camp holding 1,700 female Polish soldiers of the Home Army from the Warsaw Uprising.

If flowers were due to the Polish Armoured Division for our hardships and losses, then fate threw us these flowers in the form of the opportunity to liberate this camp, as a direct result of the actions of the Division.

And it happened quite unexpectedly!

On hearing the report of the reconnaissance unit about a camp with female Home Army prisoners from the Warsaw Uprising, the commander of the 2nd Armoured Regiment, Lieutenant Colonel Koszutski took several tanks and Universal Carriers and simply entered the camp, bulldozing through barbed wire fences with tanks and releasing the prisoners. And from that moment, for the soldiers of the 1st Polish Armoured Division, the camp in Oberlangen became a part of liberated Poland.

Rows upon rows of cars, Universal Carriers, lorries and tanks crowded in from all sides, from the front and from the staff headquarters, from the rear and from the Division's supply lines. They were all full of soldiers looking for their families or hoping to get some news about them. Some simply wanted to lay their eyes on the heroic Polish women of the Warsaw Uprising.

Then followed wagons loaded with everything that could be needed or useful. Everyone wanted to do something, to be helpful. At the request of the camp commandant, Lieutenant Maria Irena Milewska, I had to issue a ban on bringing provisions, because the warehouses were overflowing. But the front was moving north, and the Division had to say goodbye to its brave sisters-in-arms.

Several of the women commemorated these moments of liberation in the pages of their memoirs. Vibrant with emotion, they have not lost any of the strength of their expression to this day.

Already during the operations of the 3rd Brigade in the direction of Winschoten, the Division's staff developed a new plan, and collected divisional forces not currently engaged in combat to cross the Ems into German territory and begin operations along the eastern bank of the river towards Emden.

The projected task looked hellishly difficult on the map. The terrain was positively crawling with channels, swamps and peatlands, with two serious obstacles: the Küsten Canal and the River Leda, which form miles-long floodplains. A variation of the order, towards Wilhelmshaven, added on 16 April presented us with two more obstacles: the Jümme and the Jade Canals.

These difficulties, visible on the map, would turn out to be even more serious in practice, due to well-thought-out demolitions by the Germans and the wet Spring.

Crossing the River Ems itself was easy. Minor units of our Division took advantage of the 4th Canadian Division's clearing of the area south of the town of Haren, approached it from the east, and occupied it almost without fighting. The divisional sappers built a bridge in record time, finishing it on the night of

14 April – so that on 15 April, the weakened 10th Armoured Cavalry Brigade moved into German territory, approached the Küsten Canal and conducted reconnaissance activity and preliminary operations.

Meanwhile, the completed action of the 3rd Brigade allowed for regrouping and the considerable resupply of the 10th Brigade.

I left a minimum of troops with the 3rd Brigade on the west bank of the Ems, mainly to cover the bridge near Haren and our lines of communication on the Dutch side. I reinforced the 10th Armoured Cavalry Brigade to include the following units:

- the 1st Armoured Regiment,
- the 24th Lancers Regiment,
- the Podhale Rifles Battalion,
- the 9th Rifle Battalion,
- an assigned squadron of Crocodiles, i.e. Churchill tanks with mounted flamethrowers,
- 1½ companies of engineers,
- an anti-tank *dywizjon*.

The assault of the 10th Armoured Cavalry Brigade, aiming to cross the Küsten Canal, was supported on 19 April by Typhoons, the whole divisional artillery and medium artillery in the form of the Canadian 4th Artillery Regiment which had been assigned to us, as well as flanking fire from the west bank of the River Ems provided by a special group of artillery called 'Kurpiel', cleverly composed of the 2nd *dywizjon* of the 2nd Motorized Regiment and a squadron of the 2nd Armoured Regiment.

Colonel Skibiński – recently appointed as the commander of the 10th Armoured Cavalry Brigade after Colonel Majewski was transferred to the London staff – was not wanting for clamour, fire and smoke to accompany his crossing of the canal.

From my vantage point I saw the flat region in front of the Küsten Canal. I could observe the action of Typhoons falling from the sky like hawks on their prey and faultlessly hitting their targets. The power of the projectiles was enormous. I once saw a German heavy Tiger tank being hit by a rocket, flying high up and falling on its turret with its tracks in the air.

After the capture of the Mark Canal in the Netherlands, thanks mainly to the Typhoons, the commanding officer of the German *Kampfgruppe*, who had been taken prisoner by us, described his fresh impressions as follows:

'Your artillery is extremely unpleasant – especially the heavy type – your bombers are even worse, but the most terrible are your aircraft with missiles. My commander, Major W., a fearless soldier, who had been awarded the Iron Cross 1st Class, fled along the ditch like a frightened hare when the aircraft came.'

The undeniable fact was that, with the presence of several Typhoons in the air at the moment of forcing the crossing, not a single mortar or gun stirred, although on the day before they had inflicted considerable losses on the units, both in men and crossing equipment.

The crossing, well-assembled and prepared, went smoothly. I had postponed the date of the commencement of the action twice, not wanting the first large-scale operation on German soil to be a fiasco.

The 9th Rifle Battalion quickly crossed the Küsten Canal on boats and footbridges; due to the Germans being terrorized by fire, only a few of these were lost. The sapper company built a bridge sufficient for the transfer of tanks in a few hours.

Until evening, the Brigade sat firmly on the northern bank and on the captured edge of the forest, which would become the basis for the attack on the town of Aschendorf the next day.

The main role in the capture of the town was played by the tanks of the 1st Armoured Regiment, which outmanoeuvred the German defence from the east, leaving the infantry to clean up the town itself, or rather the ruins of this once charming German town. In the evening, the Brigade conquered Tunxdorf and approached the edge of Papenburg, a larger city perched on a relatively dry scrap of land.

Meanwhile, the 3rd Rifle Brigade, or rather a fraction of it left on the west bank of the River Ems, eliminated a rather anaemic counterattack from the west, from the occupied part of the Netherlands, where the German Army of General Blaskowitz was lurking.

As they entered the area, Canadian troops began to relieve our units, allowing for the assembly of troops of the 3rd Brigade in the area of the Haren bridge, with the intention of extending the effort of the 10th Brigade to the north.

On 21 April, the battlegroup of Colonel Grudziński conquered the city of Papenburg by a coordinated action of the Podhale Rifles Battalion with the tanks of the 24th Lancers Regiment. Fighting in the streets was still in progress when I drove my Jeep into the city. There was a strange contrast between the fanatical resistance of the fighting German troops and the resignation and passivity of the civilians, who eagerly displayed white flags as a sign of surrender where it was necessary, and even where it was not.

I came across a group of our looters who could not resist the temptation to snoop a little in the ruins and abandoned homes. My presence alone flushed them out – I didn't have to use force of any kind.

Please note! I did not care about the Germans, nor their property or their lives. I cared about my soldiers. We must not allow the beast to awaken in the man. Our wrongs could not be set right through vengeance and retaliation. Because otherwise we would cease to be an army.

My experience of so many years at war had taught me that not even the smallest theft could be permitted. A soldier who robs and becomes rich through robbing also becomes a coward. His life, which he risks every day, suddenly becomes exaggeratedly precious to him, or at least, as precious as the comfort or pleasure that can be provided by the looted property.

Such is the psychology of war.

On 22 April, the 10th Brigade took over the town of Collinghorst, the central point of a relatively dry area amid mud and peat bogs, in front of the River Leda. This dry area was called Oberledingerland. There were two main roads leading from this area: through Leer to the port of Emden and through Posthausen-Stickhausen in the general direction of Wilhelmshaven. Both directions were surrounded by the marshes and peatbogs of the Leda and Jümme rivers.

Leaving the 10th Armoured Cavalry Brigade with the auxiliary task of clearing the triangle of the Ems-Leda rivers, I took the battlegroup of the 3rd Rifle Brigade in the direction of Posthausen-Stickhausen. Later on I reinforced them to include:

- the 24th Lancers Regiment,
- the Podhale Rifles Battalion,
- the 8th Rifle Battalion,
- the 10th Dragoons Regiment,
- a mounted heavy machine gun squadron,
- the 10th Engineer Company,
- the 1st Motorized Artillery Regiment.

Thus, I initiated the operation of the 1st Polish Armoured Division on Wilhelmshaven.

* * *

Our battles with the Germans increasingly turned into even more arduous battles with the terrain.

It would not be an exaggeration to say that we were drowning in mud, especially the tanks and self-propelled guns, ripping off the thin layer of peat with caterpillar tracks and plunging into the dark mud. The Leda turned out to be more marshy than any in Polesie back home, and the area leading to and beyond the river was so wet and riddled with channels that not only bridges but roads and access roads had to be built to move forward. The proximity of the mouths of the Leda and Jümme rivers to the sea meant that each coming tide not only raised the water level, but also soaked this already waterlogged strip of Frisian land. German technicians masterfully used these advantages of the terrain for defence. Each intersection, or section of the road running along the embankments between the swamps, had been transformed into a huge crater, 50 feet in diameter, which could often only be crossed by the construction of a Bailey bridge. These craters had been created by the explosions of high-calibre aerial bombs.

The pace of tearing through such an area was dictated by the pace of the tireless work of both of our engineering companies, with Lieutenant Colonel Dorantt and Captain Neklaws in charge. The Division owed a considerable part of its successes in this period to the Division's ever-reliable 'ants'. However, the ingenuity of the troops in crossing these craters was also enormous. Material from demolished houses was used to fill holes and to create footbridges for the infantry. German transport barges were pulled across canals to act as improvised pontoon bridges. In one case, the 10th Mounted Rifles Regiment, with all of its vehicles, crossed one of the craters by levelling it with blocks of pressed straw.

Where the canals, passages and craters were defended, the most effective means of combat were flamethrowers, mounted on Universal Carriers, especially in the dragoon units. The Division was assigned squadrons of Crocodiles for the more serious crossings, as they were equipped with longer-range flame throwers.

As the Division approached Wilhelmshaven, the German defence, composed of ad hoc units including naval detachments, parachute formations, and the SS, was becoming tougher.

On 25 April, after heavy combat, the 3rd Brigade conquered the town of Posthausen, and crossed the Leda on the following day, creating a bridgehead on the northern bank against which the Germans launched unsuccessful counterstrikes. But the road to crossing the strips of swamps to Stockhausen, the Jümme river and further canals was still very long. Without interrupting the action of the Division, I turned to the Corps command with a proposal to force a crossing of the Leda at Leer, on the axis of Emden, and to lead the whole division through Leer towards a drier region, or to divert even a part of the Division through there, which would then operate on the northern bank of the Jümme and thus extract the 3rd Brigade from the mud, or at least make it easier for it to get out.

I received approval for this plan only on 29 April, when the Canadian Division seized a bridgehead by Leer.

On 30 April, a battlegroup of the 10th Armoured Brigade passed through this bridgehead and, finding itself on the northern side of the Jumma, advanced in an easterly direction. They shook hands with the 3rd Rifle Brigade, which on 1 May occupied the town of Stickhausen from the south. The Division continued to operate eastward on two axes: the 10th Brigade – Reels, Moorburg, Halsbek; the 3rd Brigade – Filsum, Apen, Westerstede.

On 3 May, when the battlegroup of Colonel Grudzinski (the 2nd Anti-Tank and the 10th Dragoons regiments) seized Moorburg, Westerstede and Halsbek, they entered a dry area, but with forests, to the north of Bad Zwischenahn. From there I intended to turn north to Wittmund, Jever, and Wilhelmshaven for the final act: the seizure of the port and the town of Wilhelmshaven.

On the evening of 4 May, we were ordered to cease operations as of 5 May, 08.00.

Germany had surrendered.

The final assault fire of our artillery had hardly ceased – though it already sounded differently to our ears, like a salute of honour to mark the end of the war – when I was summoned to report in the afternoon of that day, i.e. 5 May, to the headquarters of the 2nd Canadian Corps in Bad Zwischenahn. I was to take part in the act of dictating the peace terms within the 2nd Canadian Corps' sector. At the same moment, General Foulkes would receive at Wageningen, on Dutch soil, along with the other commanders of units within the Canadian Army, the surrender of General Blaskowitz's 25th Army.

But at our end…

In a large hall behind a long table, the commander of the Corps, General Simonds took his seat along with the chief of staff and the commanders of divisions subordinated to the corps. There were no other chairs in the room, which clearly meant that there would not be even a pretence of courtesy towards the German officers.

I was sitting next to the Corps commander.

Six German officers entered the room. General Erich Straube, the commander of the military units between the Ems and the Weser (a formation which had only been created a few days before), accompanied by the local naval commander, the chief of staff and three commanders of sectors in eastern Frisia.

They went in, lined up in a row in front of the table, saluted, and stood at attention.

They seemed different people to those I had seen taken captive in the heat and the dust of the battle, with the emotions of combat not yet extinguished on their faces.

Their faces were drawn and grave; they were masks that could have been hiding everything, or nothing.

General Straube began to say something.

A gesture of impatience from General Simonds stopped him short: 'You did not come here to negotiate with us – you are only to listen to the conditions of the unconditional surrender.'

Point by point, in a hard, emphatic voice, he began to read these conditions.

I quickly lost the thread of what he was saying, because my thoughts had wandered to a time a few years back. I could not shake the insistent memory of General Kutrzeba and Colonel Pragłowski at the surrender of Warsaw in 1939.

Was not this payback for that tragic moment?

Meanwhile, General Simonds had proceeded to the orders relating to the occupation of territory for the formations of the Corps:

'The 2nd Canadian Infantry Division – the area along the River Weser; the 4th Canadian Armoured Division – to the west; the 1st Polish Armoured Division *(did I imagine it or did General Simonds pronounce every word particularly slowly and clearly and deliberately?)*

- – – Wilhelmshaven.'

But no.

For the first time, something like a spasm passed across the faces of the German officers still standing at attention. The eyes of the Germans, which had previously avoided me, glanced for an instant at me, at my Polish uniform.

After all, there was no need to remind them that they had first unleashed this terrible war upon the Poles, and now they were laying down their weapons before a representative of one of the Polish formations which had never laid down its arms.

A Polish Division would occupy a piece of land in western Germany.

This was probably the first time in the history of our numerous struggles with this nation.

I have always liked General Simonds.

I liked him in Falaise, when we were in pursuit, and in Germany.

I liked it when he dictated the conditions to the Germans and the style with which he did it.

What I especially appreciated is the fact that he did not choose the easy route and direct a Canadian formation to Wilhelmshaven, which was a port and a naval base. It might have been tempting, from the point of view of Canadian prestige. Instead he handed it to the Polish Division. 'Troops will occupy the territory which, according to the Corps' final combat order, they were to have acquired by fighting.'

* * *

A small anecdote, which I heard much later. It came from Brigadier Roberts, the commander of the 8th Canadian Infantry Brigade, whom I knew from the briefings at the Corps. He was the one who had escorted General Straube from the point where he had made contact with our Division, and had led him to Bad Zwischenahn.

The General was very talkative on the way, asking questions about everything and everyone. But as a German officer bred on Prussian militarism, he experienced two deep shocks on his way to the briefing.

The first one, when he learned that the commander of the Canadian Corps, General Simonds, was only forty-one years old.

And the second when Brigadier Roberts told him that he was not himself a professional officer, but had a civilian job as a small manufacturer.

Prussian hubris, even before the briefing in Bad Zwischenahn, had indeed been exposed to huge blows!

* * *

I returned late to headquarters and found the staff officers working feverishly on the details of the detachments' march to take over the area covering Wilhelmshaven, Jever and all the way to the North Sea, including the two islands of Wangerooge and Spiekeroog. I appointed the 2nd Armoured Regiment with the 8th Rifle Battalion to cover Wilhelmshaven. The whole thing was to be commanded by Colonel A. Grudzinski, deputy commander of the 10th Armoured Cavalry Brigade. He was then also given the command of a battalion of the British Royal Marines.

On the morning of 6 May, German officers waited in designated places with white armbands on their shoulders to guide our columns safely through minefields and dismantled barricades. The columns of Polish tanks and motorized units passed German troops gathering in grave silence. Along the road lay abandoned guns, among them a number of 88mm ones; they would fire no more at Polish tanks from the belt of heavy fortifications around Wilhelmshaven.

At the entrance to the town, Colonel Grudzinski was awaited by the commander of the fortified area, Captain zur See Mulsov, the municipal commander, the mayor and the commander of the police force.

The port facilities were taken over by a Briton, Captain Conder.

The port already housed the cruiser Köln, the Niassa command ship, and a number of destroyers and submarines. And there were still further units of the surrendering German fleet arriving, including the *Nürnberg* cruiser and the newest heavy cruiser, *Prinz Eugen*.

In total, the following units surrendered to us in Wilhelmshaven:

- Command of: forts and naval bases, the Ostfriesland fleet, ten infantry divisions and eight infantry and artillery regiments.
- In numbers: two admirals (Weiher and Zieb), one general (Gericke, divisional commander), 1,900 officers and 32,000 privates.

The seized equipment included:

- 3 cruisers,
- 18 submarines,
- 205 minor warships and auxiliary ships,
- 94 fortress guns,
- 159 field guns,
- 560 heavy machine guns,
- 370 light machine guns,
- 40,000 rifles,
- 280,000 artillery missiles.
- 64 million rounds of ammunition for small arms,
- 23,000 hand grenades,
- Numerous mine and torpedo depots
- Food supplies for 50,000 soldiers for three months.

The formal act of surrender of the German fleet took place aboard the British ship HMS *Royal Rupert*, to the British Rear-Admiral Muirhead-Gould, accompanied by Colonel Grudzinski and Captain Conder. It had a similar emotional tenor for us Poles as the briefing in Bad Zwischenahn. And the presence of a representative of the Polish Armed Forces at the proceedings had a similar significance.

In 1941 we had been posted on a section of the Scottish coast, in anticipation of a German invasion. The Barry Links beach was manned by the 14th Lancers Regiment which, back then, belonged to the 10th Brigade. It was there that a lifebuoy from the *Piłsudski*, which had been torpedoed a year earlier off the Norwegian coast, washed up on the sand. We thought it was a good omen for the future.

When we entered Wilhelmshaven, we had been greeted by the Polish eagle displayed on the arch of the harbour gate. The emblem had been removed in 1939 from the Fleet Command building in Gdynia. It had been taken as booty by the Germans to Wilhelmshaven, the cradle of the German navy. We handed over the recovered Polish eagle to a representative of the Polish Navy, along with the German eagle which had been removed, as an eternal reminder. ORP *Conrad* then transported the Polish eagle to England, where it is now kept at the Sikorski Institute in London.

Shortly after the occupation of the entire area, a note arrived about the arrival of the Commander-in-Chief, General Anders.

There was only one place where the Polish Armoured Division wanted to host him and greet him, and it was Wilhelmshaven. Colonel Grudzinski had one night to arrange appropriate decorations in the town, or rather in its ruins. He used that time to the full. The disciplined German population received the order to sew white and red flags and decorations with Polish eagles, as if they had been sewing German flags with swastikas for Hitler's arrival.

And when, on 19 May, General Anders received the report of the Polish Armoured Division troops in Wilhelmshaven, the long stretch of the town's main avenue shimmered with the white and the red of the Polish flags, hoisted on eight-metre high posts.

This note marks the end of the epic of the 1st Polish Armoured Division, '1st' not only by name, but also by precedent in the history of the Polish Army.

Before it was officially established, it had lived in the desires and aspirations of a number of soldiers, officers and privates, both in its initial forms of the 10th Cavalry Brigade in Poland and the 10th Armoured Cavalry Brigade in France. It would be difficult for me to mention the names of the soldiers of all arms, who by their efforts created the Division, and fuelled its momentum in its journey from Normandy to Wilhelmshaven. For I would omit many of those whose names have faded from my memory, though their merit would always endure.

Perhaps the title of these scribblings of mine should be 'Three Times The Charm'. However, if I were to change it, I would rather use the words Father Starowolski addressed to the king of Sweden: 'Fortuna Variabilis – Deus Mirabilis'.

Scotland, 5 July 1960, 15 years after the end of the war.

List of Abbreviations

Polish Rank in Full	English Equivalent in Full	English Abbreviation
aspirant	Aspirant	Asp.
bombardier	Bombardier	Bomb.
bombardier podchorąży	Cadet Bombardier	Cdt. Bomb.
chorąży	Warrant Officer	W.O.
dragon	Dragoon	Drag.
generał dywizji	Lieutenant General	Lt. Gen.
generał brygady	Brigadier General	Brig. Gen.
kanonier	Gunner	G.
kapral	Lance Corporal	L. Cpl.
kapral artylerii	Artillery Lance Corporal	A. L. Cpl.
kapral piechoty	Infantry Lance Corporal	I. L. Cpl.
kapral podchorąży	Cadet Lance Corporal	Cdt. L.Cpl.
kapitan	Captain	Cpt.
kapitan dyplomowany	Captain*	Cpt.*
kapitan intendent	Captain Commissary	Cpt. Comm.
kapitan lekarz	Captain Army Doctor	Cpt. A. D.
ksiądz kapelan	Chaplain	Chap.
major	Major	Mjr.
major dyplomowany	Major*	Mjr.*
major lekarz	Major Army Doctor	Mjr. A. D.
ogniomistrz	Artillery Sergeant	A. Sgt.
ogniomistrz podchorąży	Cadet Artillery Sergeant	Cdt. A. Sgt.
plutonowy	Corporal	Corp.
plutonowy podchorąży	Cadet Corporal	Cdt. Corp.
pułkownik	Colonel	Col.
pułkownik dyplomowany	Colonel*	Col.*
porucznik	Lieutenant	Lt.
porucznik dyplomowany	Lieutenant*	Lt.*
porucznik lekarz	Lieutenant Army Doctor	Lt. A. D.
podpułkownik	Lieutenant Colonel	Lt. Col.
podpułkownik dyplomowany	Lieutenant Colonel*	Lt. Col.*
podpułkownik lekarz	Lieutenant Colonel Army Doctor	Lt. Col. A. D.

Polish Rank in Full	English Equivalent in Full	English Abbreviation
podporucznik	Second Lieutenant	2nd Lt.
podporucznik lekarz	Second Lieutenant Army Doctor	2nd Lt. A. D.
rotmistrz	Cavalry Captain	Cav. Cpt.
rotmistrz dyplomowany	Cavalry Captain*	Cav. Cpt.*
saper	Sapper	Sap.
sierżant	Sergeant	Sgt.
sierżant podchorąży	Cadet Sergeant	Cdt. Sgt.
starszy dragon	Dragoon	Drag.
starszy ogniomistrz	Artillery Sergeant	A. Sgt.
starszy saper	Sapper	Sap.
starszy saper podchorąży	Cadet Sapper	Cdt.Sap.
starszy sierżant	Sergeant	Sgt.
starszy strzelec	Rifleman	Rif.
starszy strzelec podchorąży	Cadet Rifleman	Cdt. Rif.
starszy szeregowy	private	priv.
starszy szeregowy podchorąży	Cadet	Cdt.
starszy ułan	Lancer	Lan.
starszy wachmistrz	Sergeant	Sgt.
strzelec	Rifleman	Rif.
szeregowy	private	priv.
ułan	Lancer	Lan.
ułan podchorąży	Cadet Lancer	Cdt. Lan.
wachmistrz	Sergeant	Sgt.
wachmistrz podchorąży	Cadet Sergeant	Cdt. Sgt.

Translators' notes:
* An asterisk indicates that the given soldier has graduated from a military academy (in the Second Polish Republic, the Warsaw War College [Wyższa Szkoła Wojenna]) and has obtained the title 'dyplomowany'.